ORGANISING IN THE INFORMATION AGE

*For her commitment to truth and courage in a world of distributed care,
this book is dedicated to Mary Hossack, mother, friend
and intellectual companion*

Organising in the Information Age
Distributed technology, distributed leadership,
distributed identity, distributed discourse

Edited by

LEN HOLMES
University of North London

DIAN MARIE HOSKING
Tilburg University

MARGARET GRIECO
Napier University

ASHGATE

Published by
Ashgate Publishing Limited
Gower House
Croft Road
Aldershot
Hampshire GU11 3HR
England

Ashgate Publishing Company
131 Main Street
Burlington, VT 05401-5600 USA

Ashgate website: http://www.ashgate.com

British Library Cataloguing in Publication Data
Organising in the information age : distributed technology,
   distributed leadership, distributed identity, distributed
   discourse. - (Voices in development management)
   1.Organizational behavior 2.Technological innovations
   3.Organizational change 4.Computers and civilization
   I.Holmes, Len II.Hosking, Dian Marie III.Grieco, Margaret
   303.3'5

Library of Congress Cataloging-in-Publication Data
Organising in the information age : distributed technology, distributed leadership,
distributed identity, distributed discourse / editors, Len Holmes, Dian Marie Hosking,
Margaret Grieco.
      p. cm. -- (Voices in development management)
   Includes bibliographical references and index.
   ISBN 0-7546-3067-6
      1.Information technology. 2.Information society. I.Holmes, Len. II. Hosking, Dian
Marie, 1949- III.Grieco, Margaret, 1950- IV.University of North London voices in
development management.

HC79.I55 O743 2002
303.48'33--dc21   2002024919

ISBN 0 7546 3067 6

Contents

List of Figures and Tables

List of Contributors

Stewart Clegg   Professor of Management,
University of Technology, Sydney

David Crowther   Reader in Marketing,
University of North London

Peter Daale   Cancer Support Association of
Western Australia Inc.

Miriam Green   Senior Lecturer, Business School,
University of North London

Anne Marie Greene   Industrial Relations Research Unit,
University of Warwick

Margaret Grieco   Professor of Transport and Society,
Napier University

Paul Griffin   Postgraduate Researcher,
Napier University

Julian Hine   Professor-elect of Transport,
University of Ulster

John Hogan   Royal Holloway College and Bath Spa
University College

Len Holmes   Director (Acting), Management Centre,
University of North London

Dian Marie Hosking   Professor of Development and Change,
Tilburg University

Earon Kavanagh   Relational Consultant, Canada

Stephen Little   Senior Lecturer in Knowledge Management,
                        Open University Business School

Perry Morrison   Community Technology Special,
                        Northern Territory

Jeff Turner   Research Fellow, Department of Planning,
                        Manchester University

Alfons van Marrewijk   Vrije University, Amsterdam

Marcus Wigan   Professor of Transport Systems,
                        Napier University

Chapter One

Introduction

Margaret Grieco

This volume has as its goal the opening of discussions around the consequences of the advent and emergence of distributed technology for organisational life. Both in the workplace and in the pattern of governance, the new distributed forms of technology have far reaching consequences. In the work place, the development of computer supported collaborative work and teleworking have come upon us without substantial organisational theory reflections on the consequences of these forms: in the field of governance, the advent of distributed technology has been used primarily as a mechanism for reducing the costs of delivering services, for example, on line medical diagnostic services.

By distributed technology, we are drawing attention to the widespread access to information technologies in the home and in journey. Through modems, home computers, lap tops and WAP telephones the individual can be in interaction with information systems: it is no longer the case that the individual simply receives messages broadcast by much larger institutional actors but rather the individual is now able to send out globalised messages through the web from the home or from the bus or walking down the street. This access to information and this access to the power to develop and transmit information has major consequences for leadership structures: traditional bottlenecks on information can be broken. Through distributed technology, individuals and groups can gather information to track the performance or actions of their 'opponents' whether the opponent wishes this or not. For example, low income communities in Newcastle are now tracking the performance of their public transport system (http://www.goneat.org.uk): the information which was previously solely in the hands of the operator and, occasionally, regulators can now be generated by the community itself as it reports into a central community data base on failures of the system. Real time information on performance can be relayed back to the community via the web. Conventional leadership existed in a context where information could be highly segregated and barriers placed to the access of all to relevant information: the new distributed technology permits a more distributed form of leadership as our community transport monitoring example indicates.

The distributed character of the technology, the distributed access to that technology and the distributed leadership structures which emerge in this context have consequences for the distribution of identity. In a globalised information context, specific e-relationships will still develop as a consequence of a pattern of communication exchange between specific parties but such exchanges can now be viewed by the many and the number of domains in which e-conversations can take place has radically overtaken the matching capabilities of any specific place. Finding a discourse partner to develop a particular identity or aspects of identity in a given location in physical space and place is subject to many mobility and scheduling constraints. The e-form in its asynchronous but highly interactive capabilities can support the individual in the exploration of many pairings or discourse groupings and interaction spaces. The balance of identity which continues in local or physical space and place may be reduced as a consequence of the development of virtual identity. Importantly, identity may become increasingly computer supported: memory tasks that the individual previously performed for self or through interaction with others may now be performed in interaction with technology. The development of e-calendars, personal organisers and correspondence recall technologies all have consequences for the distribution of identity at the level of the individual and the group. E-tools can be harnessed by others in assisting in the social 'grooming' process whether this be in the workplace or elsewhere.

Distributed technology, distributed leadership, distributed identity take us along the path to distributed discourse. The new e-forms allow for many voices in a way that conventional bureaucracy, work organisation and governance could not. The technology allows for discourse from every direction: protocols can be used to develop filters in one location but the nature of the world wide web permits any person or any group from any location to raise a globalised message which can reduce the power of individual organisational filters. If suppressed in one location, discourse pops up as powerfully and as visibly elsewhere. The World Bank, a leader in generating feedback options through new technology, has experienced the power of distributed discourse: discourse critical of the Bank's operation which has not been taken up or filtered out of its feedback channels has simply emerged elsewhere to block even closed meetings.

Organising in the information age is different to any other time in history: the globalisation of communication at the level of image, text and talk; the distribution of technology for receiving and for sending globalised messages; the reduction in the transaction costs through the new information technologies of monitoring opponents' behaviour and intentions; the distribution of discourse in which the voices of the many are gaining volume in relation to previous elite strongholds and bottlenecks on information – all of these phenomenon suggest that it is a time to reflect on the changing shape of organisational, social and political life.

If we need any further reminder or prod to reflect on the processes of globalisation and their consequences, the attack on Manhattan on 11 September 2001 indicated the tight coupling which now exists in terms of global connectivity and global reach. The structures which provide for the enhanced reach of capitalism – and most particularly US capitalism – now provide for the enhanced global reach of terrorism. The few set out to demonstrate the power that can be achieved by harnessing the 'globalised organisation' of the most powerful: the weapons of wealth creation were converted into weapons which were designed to decompose American ascendancy. The time to rethink the need for buffers or looser couplings between the various parts of the globalising world has arrived most unexpectedly: the paradox is that the technology can provide the high levels of connectivity which ensure efficiency in normal times but exactly the high level of connectivity and routine interdependence are problematic at the point of crisis. The issue becomes one of whether we will see a decoupling by globalisation's front runners (until now clear winners from activity in those regions which help generate the primacy that captures profit) with the opening up of more channels of communication between those possessing different world views or will we see the development of better back up systems and tighter surveillance systems? What future globalisation is the question which comes out of Manhattan and out of our identification of distributed technology, distributed leadership, distributed identity and distributed discourse as key elements of organising in the information age.

Chapter Two

Why Distributed Discourse Matters

Stewart Clegg

In this chapter the epistemological, ontological and ethical foundations for distributed discourse are outlined. They rely not on a model of social science premised on physics envy, and moral philosophies appropriate to this envy, but on a more discursive, phronetic model of science as wisdom rather than either episteme or techne. Central to this outline is a realist grasp of power as the central concept of the social sciences, which stands in a particular relation to what passes for rationality.

Rationality

Rationality is always situational. And because it is always contextually situational it is always implicated with power. No context stands outside power. If it were the case, then it would exist nowhere, outside of understanding, outside of possibility, outside of sense. As Foucault (1977: 27-28) says 'power produces knowledge ... power and knowledge directly imply one another ... there is no power relation without the creative constitution of a field of knowledge, nor any knowledge that does not presuppose and constitute at the same time power relations'. In such a view rationalities and powers are fused. Different power actors will operate in and through different rationalities. The different rationalities will have their different rules for producing sense – at the more formal outer limits – for producing truth. In fact, sense and truth cannot be separated from the ensemble of rules that constitute them – and their obverse – as such.

To adopt a discursive analysis of rationality is to see what people say as the means whereby rationality and power become interwoven. People may be in a position to say anything, given the infinity of discourse, but they rarely surprise the well-grounded analyst with their discursive moves. Which is not to say that language games are predictable – although sometimes they are – but to suggest that they are explicable. We can understand and constitute the senses that are being made as well as the conditions of existence and underlying tacit assumptions that make such sense possible. And in this way we can begin to understand the different forms of agency that find expression in organisational contexts, where the players make sense of rules that they actively construct and deconstruct in the context of their action.

Rather than being law-like phenomena, rules are always constituted locally, in context, by the actors themselves, rather than being the objective instantiation of a general principle or law. Contextualism implies that whatever regularities occur empirically will always be situational. Researchers need to understand that these are not likely to be the result of either remote laws operating behind the backs of the actors concerned nor are they likely to be the result of an idiosyncratic researchers interpretation of the scene in question. To the extent that the researcher has researched the situational ethics of the context at hand then they will have a sound grasp of the socially and historically conditioned context within which sense is made. With these understandings researchers can avoid the relativism that they are sometimes charged with: their understandings will be framed within deeply embedded foundations that the actors find normal and acceptable to use. In matters of interpretation there is always room for disagreement and it is no different for the organisation researcher. One interpretation is rarely as good as another. Some will always be more plausible in terms of the contexts within which they are produced and received.

Unlike phenomena in an object realm, where the matter at hand has no understanding of itself, organisations are always populated by actors who possess understanding both of each other and those artefacts that they constitute (and which sometimes constitute them – for instance, a machine operator) and with which they interact. Thus, organisations are always more subject-realms than merely object realms, albeit that as objects of reflection, they can be subjected to object-like treatment and routines. But this does not inescapably secure their nature as something ontologically just so. Of course, there is no shortage of theories in organisation studies that presume to offer abstract context independent concepts. Contingency theories, institutional theories, population ecologies, transaction cost analysis, and so on. But on close examination, these theories always betray the origins of their context dependent assumptions. It could not be otherwise. These assumptions may be more or less tacit or more or less reflexive but their context cannot be excluded because such context always defines the relevancy of the phenomena that any theory addresses.

What Shall We Do and How Shall We Live?

All inquiry is fundamentally narrative – it tells a story about states of affairs that are more or less plausible within the conventions of particular narrative communities. Or as Wittgenstein (1972) puts it, science is a language game – like any other. Or in Rorty's (1991) similar terms, experience ordered though our sense data may cause us to hold certain views of the matter in question but it cannot tell us which views we should be considering in the first place. The insight is old, however. Weber (1948: 143) quoted Tolstoy in a speech to students at Munich University in 1918 to this effect:

> Science is meaningless because it gives no answer to our question, the only question important for us: 'What shall we do and how shall we live? That science does not give an answer to this is indisputable. The only question that remains is the sense in which science gives 'no' answer, and whether or not science might yet be of some use to the one who puts the question correctly'.

As Wicks and Freeman (1998: 127) note, the consequence of positivism in organisation studies has been to obscure this most basic question. It has created an epistemic context in which such a question cannot even be considered. (As an aside, if all those who accuse Weber of being a positivist, hung up on the fact/value distinction, were to take more cognisance of this remarkable essay, they would be hard put to maintain that belief.) Instead, ethics are something else outside the questions one asks of reality as a scholar: that certain causal regularities may be empirically observed of a phenomena does not enable one to ask why these regularities and not some others? How, for instance, is authority achieved as a set of patterned preferences whose prevalence demonstrates its facticity?

Pfeffer (1995) calls for moral rearmament around functionalism, which would be one sure way of ensuring that these questions remain mute, because functionalism suppresses internal conflict concerning methods and epistemologies. Such conflicts he regards as dangerous, corrosive of moral authority, and destructive of professional reputation and discipline. Order is what is required. I would argue to the contrary: I would argue that intellectual communities – just as political communities – that suppress conflict do so at considerable risk to their vitality. As Flyvbjerg (2001: 108) suggests 'suppressing conflict is suppressing freedom, because the privilege to engage in conflict and power struggle is part of freedom. He goes on to suggest that 'perhaps social and political theories that ignore or marginalize conflicts are potentially oppressive, too'. I think he is right.

Organisation theory, in as much as it would only allow for debate on its own terms – the Pfeffer option – would be repressive, oppressive and antithetical to the spirit of an intellectually open society. It is not the kind of club that I would want to be a member of. I am utterly committed to the proposition that it is conflict that sustains openness and that without such conflict the genuine democracy that is essential to the articulation of reason is lacking. Reason resides not so much in what is said, as Habermas (1971) argues, as in the formal conditions that constitute the conditions within which what is said can be expressed. The more democratic a discourse the more legitimate will be the inevitable conflicts of interest that arise and the less their will be barriers to their expression. And there is every reason for democratic discourse as the basis of science: if there are barriers to expression, if certain styles of work are demonised or disdained, then there is no open society. Just a certain exclusively cultivated clubbishness, a cultish commitment to things being seen the way that people like us (and not people who are not people like us) see them. Sterility, banality, orthodoxy – this is what ensues when debate is stifled in the name of order. In political science it is called totalitarianism. It is what happens when power overwhelms imagination – especially the imagination of those out with of power, whose imagination could rewrite history.

Power

One of the advantages of Foucault's approach to power is that it 'integrates rationality and power, knowledge and power, reason and power, truth and power' (Flyvbjerg, 2001:124). Power frees imagination and power writes history. Without power poverty, disease, and despair is what faces the human condition. Only power – the capacity to make a difference to existing conditions of existence in ways that are significant for the actors concerned – can free imagination. Otherwise it rots in the gutters of history. For it is power that writes history. That the histories we inherit have overwhelmingly been those of the dominant actors strutting their stuff in the various stages of the human comedy – the men, the whites, the colonialists, the rich, the powerful, the educated – is hardly surprising. Life on the margins, in service, bondage or slavery of one kind or another, rarely affords room, time, or tools for intense reflection. As Foucault (1977: 27) suggests, 'we should abandon a whole tradition that allows us to imagine that knowledge can exist only where the power relations are suspended and that knowledge can develop only outside its injunctions, its demands and its interests'. On the contrary, as he goes on to suggest, power produces knowledge, they are directly implicated in each other. Reflexivity is essential to understanding this relation, suggests Foucault. We need to be able to see how power actually functions in context. Elsewhere, in the context of a discussion of the significance of reflexivity, I have elaborated a general and guiding theoretical point:

> Those theoretical positions able to account, reflexively, for their own theorizing, as well as whatever it is that they are theorizing about, will be clearest about their own identity, and the extent to which it is partial or formed in dialogue with other positions. The recognition of the 'other' is crucial: self-regarding behaviour in the absence of the recognition of the and by others is of no value in itself. On these criteria it is not the alleged 'disinterestedness' of a position that makes it worthwhile, but the degree of reflexivity that it exhibits in relation to the conditions of its own existence. Severing the conversational elements that nurtured the theory in the first place and which link it to practice makes it harder to attain this reflexivity. Thus we argue for the grounding of theoretical claims in local and specific circumstances rather than their radical and rapid translation out of them. In an organizational world that is part of the social, which is inscribed with the materiality of words, and the indeterminacy of meaning, such conversational stretch is essential. Otherwise the paradigm closes, conversational practice becomes monologue, and reflexivity declines accordingly (Clegg and Hardy, 1996: 701).

Reflexive analysis is never innocent of context – that is its beauty and strength. It situates itself on the boundaries between the seemingly possible and the impossible with the desire to shift these boundaries. Such a position is the ideal place from which to think differently in order to act differently, as Flyvbjerg (2001: 127) puts it. It is from such a position that one is best able to use power in the service of imagination and the making of history.

Discursive Plurality

Organisation theory and analysis is best cultivated not in an ideal world of paradigm consensus or domination but in a world of discursive plurality, where obstinate differences in domain assumptions are explicit and explicitly tolerated. A good conversation assumes engagement with alternate points of view, argued against vigorously, but ultimately, where these positions pass the criteria of reason rather than prejudice, tolerated as legitimate points of view.

It seems barely reasonable to hold to a standard for analysis that Flyvbjerg (2001: 1) and Sennett (1995: 43) refer to as 'physics envy'. Conventionally, it is proposed that organisation studies should 'model reality and search for essentialist underlying structures via scientific study' (Wicks and Freeman, 1998: 130). Essentially, in philosophical terms, this is the propositional strategy that was outlined by Wittgenstein (1922) in the *Tractatus Logico-Philosophicus*. And in the *Philosophical Investigations* (1972) the same author decisively repudiated such a position. The earlier philosophy suggests that one should seek to make ideal representations, in an eternal, unchanging way, through absolutely lucid and unequivocal propositional statements, concerning the essential qualities of the social world of organisations – as if they were as simple to read as iron filings around magnetic poles. The later Wittgenstein (1972) suggested that one should explore a phenomena first hand instead: he used a very clear representational, cartographic metaphor to make his point.

> Imagine this case: I tell someone that I walked a certain route, going by a map which I had prepared beforehand. Thereupon I show him the map, and it consist of lines on a piece of paper; but I cannot explain how these lines are the map of my movements, I cannot tell him anything rule for interpreting the map. Yet I did follow the drawing with all the characteristic tokens of reading a map (Wittgenstein, 1972: 653).

I recall Wittgenstein writing about maps on another occasion (Gasking and Jackson, 1967). Here he said that, rather than establishing the unequivocal mapping of a reality in a precise representation, one should instead seek to know a phenomenon, such as the City of London, by walking its streets, both highways and byways, side streets and main streets. In parlance more contemporary than that which Wittgenstein had available to him, one who aspires to explore the underbelly and side streets of a city would probably be considered a 'rough guide'.

Wittgenstein's metaphor of the city can be extended further. Organisations are somewhat like the city: organic, constantly recreating themselves, tearing out the present heart and soul, routing new freeways through the existing geography, creating new aesthetics that overwhelm but never entirely eradicate the old, leaving traces of lost realities, past triumphs, and buried beliefs. Having no static essence the city can never truly be represented cartographically any more than organisations can ever be truly represented propositionally. The city is its conflicts, its power struggles over real estate, its aesthetic imagining of its possibilities, as well as its history. It is alive, organic, contested, peopled, a space for human possibilities, impossible dramas, overweening ambitions, and great tragedy. Just like organisations. Or at least organisations as I see them.

Towards a Reasonable Conclusion

What does this tell us about reason? It is not the voice of an omniscient narrator, doing Science, and cudgelling all those whom are not true believers or defenders of the faith, into abandoning their heresies and joining the one true church. As my metaphor are meant to suggest, I would think religion a better way of describing such 'defences' (Donaldson, 1985). In achieving reason in the pragmatic mode of phronesis one demurs:

> the role of omniscient narrator and summarizer in favour of gradually allowing the case narrative to unfold from the diverse, complex and sometimes conflicting stories that people, documents and other evidence tell them. This approach leaves ample scope for readers to make different interpretations and to draw diverse conclusions (Flyvbjerg, 2001: 86).

Hence, the possibility of multiple interpretations is admitted and structured into the accounting that one does. 'There are multiple interpretations of events and different concepts and classificatory schemes could be used to describe phenomena' (Wicks and Freeman, 1998: 134). However, this is not an embrace of nihilism, an abrogation of perspective to the relativism that all views are equal. One does not simply celebrate difference for the sake of difference. Not all accounts are as good as others. Some are more useful for the purpose at hand than are others. Which of various accounts will be most useful will depend, precisely, on the purpose at hand. The criteria of reasonableness must include some notion of fitness for purpose: some accounts will better serve the task at hand and thus better enable people to accomplish relevant goals than will others. And that is a compelling reason why organisation studies should not be rigidly scientist in its forms of method and writing: these may not be the most appropriate forms of communication for the particular audience one is seeking to address. And as Stablein (1996) has taught us, in writing organisation studies (as anything else), the intended audience should not be ignored.

Not being positivistic, not suffering from physics envy, is not the same as an abandonment of scientific rigour. A persuasive narrative must provide reasons – it must be reasonable – and recognise that reasons, reason and positivistic science are not the same thing. A compelling narrative will be one that persuades rigorously, aesthetically, and through the conventions of its chosen mode of discourse. It can never be paradigm-independent, in the jargon. Hence, it does not mean that 'social scientists should stop using control groups, double-blind studies, regression analyses, and other techniques that are associated with social scientific research' (Wicks and Freeman, 1998: 137). However, it is how and for what purposes one uses these which matters. Flyvbjerg (2001: 166) stresses that 'we must drop the fruitless efforts to emulate natural science's success in producing cumulative and predictive theory; this approach simply does not work in social science'. Hence, the use of such methods should be oriented towards understanding and explaining contextual particulars rather than be seen as elements for a law-like grand theory of predictive power. Such a colossal immodesty in the face of the many standing conditions that cannot be controlled is, at worst, sheer stupidity or at best, the worst kind of cultural cringe. Case studies, documentary analysis or other forms of narrative are not, a priori, second rate. Narratives make sense not simply because they fetishise certain narrative techniques but because they address existential dilemmas in meaningful ways. They speak to our human and organisational conditions of existence in ways that we find useful and desirable. They propose ways of extending our powers and freeing our imagination, perhaps – or sometimes they represent ways of enslaving the imagination of others or limiting their powers.

Whichever direction one goes is an ethical issue for which one's own conscience, constituted in tension with the public realm, is the best, but never unequivocal, guide. There is an ethical dimension to this contextual, pragmatic conception of organisation studies. Being a part of the social scenes that s/he investigates, the organisation analyst has a responsibility towards the subjects of that science. When we investigate organisations we are messing with people. We are not just observing rats in a laboratory or iron filings round a magnet. We address the impact of major structures of society on the lives of ordinary people. We have a responsibility to these people – as human communities – just as much as to the professional communities of methods and theories that sustain us. Indeed, if we cannot effect a conversation, a dialogue, between the two, then it is not clear what we are doing that is useful – although it may be very clear what privileges we are abusing by doing so. Hence, it matters not only how we study what we study but also how we choose to study such phenomena in the first place. We can address ourselves to issues that are arcane and inconsequential for all but an elite community of scholars – perhaps no more than two or three people. Or we can engage in the human comedy and address things that matter to people in their everyday lives. Flyvbjerg (2001: 166) suggests 'we must take up problems that matter to the local, national and global communities in which we live, and we must do it in ways that matter ... [and] ... we must effectively communicate the results of our research to fellow citizens'. To which I would add we must do so in conversations that engage as many as possible: through distributed discourse this is no longer a utopian ideal but a distinct possibility.

Bibliography

Clegg, S.R. and Hardy, C. (1996), 'Representations', in S.R. Clegg, C. Hardy and W.F. Nord (eds), *Handbook of Organization Studies*, London: Sage, pp. 676–708.

Donaldson, L. (1985), *In Defence of Organization Theory: A Response to the Critics*, Cambridge: Cambridge University Press.

Flyvbjerg, B. (2000), *Making Social Sciences Matter: Why social inquiry fails and how it can succeed again*, Cambridge: Cambridge University Press.

Foucault, M. (1977), *Discipline and Punish*, Harmondsworth: Penguin.

Gasking, D.A.T. and Jackson, A.C. (1967) 'Wittgenstein as a Teacher', in L. Fann (ed.), *Ludwig Wittgenstein: the Man and His Philosophy*, Sussex: Harvester.

Habermas, J. (1971) *Knowledge and Human Interests*, London: Heinemann.

Pfeffer, J. (1995) 'Mortality, Reproducibility and the Persistence of Styles of Theory', *Organization Science*, Vol. 6, No. 6, pp. 681–6.

Rorty, R. (1991), *Objectivity, Relativism, and Truth*, Cambridge: Cambridge University Press,

Sennett, R. (1995), '"Sex, Lies and Social Science": An Exchange', *The New York Review of Books*, 20 April, 28.

Stablein, R. (1996), 'Data in Organization Studies', in S.R. Clegg, C. Hardy and W.F. Nord (eds), *Handbook of Organization Studies*, London: Sage, pp. 509–25.

Weber, M. (1948) 'Science as a Vocation', in H.H. Gert and C.W. Mills (eds), *From Max Weber: Essays in sociology*, London: Routledge and Kegan Paul, pp. 129–158.

Wicks, A.C. and Freeman R.E. (1998), 'Organization Studies and the New Pragmatism: Positivism, anti-positivism, and the search for ethics', *Organization Science*, Vol. 9, No. 2, pp. 123–40.

Wittgenstein, L. (1922) *Tractatus Logico-Philosophicus*, London: Routledge and Kegan Paul, 1922.

Wittgenstein, L. (1972) *Philosophical Investigations*, Oxford: Blackwell.

Chapter Three

Relational Identity and Relational Technology: Implications for Everyday Life

Len Holmes and Margaret Grieco

Introduction

This chapter argues that the new technology opens up a new relational terrain with consequences for organisational identity, i.e. both identities within organisations and identity of organisations. The chapter uses the term *'relational technology'* to draw attention to the essentially interactive and participative characteristics of the new information technology. For example, turning directly to local government and administration, there have been major developments in the areas of distributed action, distributed responsibility and distributed decision making. Local government is now equipped to consult with its citizenry in a continuous and inexpensive manner which has a high level of transparency; this will, in time, have consequences for perceptions of accountability. Similarly, citizens can now organise, through the new technologies, for lobbying of special interests. More importantly perhaps, there are new prospects for community organisation and for its interactions with local government and local commerce through the new technology which now exists. The new information technologies enable individuals to interact more extensively with a greater range of persons and issues; they also enable individuals to be proactive at low transaction costs in the intensification of existing aspects of identity through interaction with others. The relational opportunities afforded by the new information communication technology raise the issue of *'relational identity'* or identity as realised practices of association, membership and participation. Using case study materials derived from recent policy developments in the UK transport sector, this chapter provides an overview of the emergence of new forms of action and decision making in organisational and administrative life.

Relational Identity and Relational Technology – Framing and Reframing Action

New communications technology opens up a new relational terrain with consequences for organisational identity, i.e. both identities within organisations (Holmes, 2000a; Holmes, 2000b) and identity of organisations. The boundaries on social action and identity historically presented by distance and time constraints are much transformed by the new communications technology: in-home access to information technology which connects with the workplace or formal organisation enables the individual to remain in continuous contact with organisational actions and events from a distant location. Accessing information on events from home is in essence no different to accessing information between locations in the physical infrastructure of 'head office' within the new Information Communication Technology (Little, 2000).

In the same way that the boundary between the individual workers' place of residence and the organisational workplace has been adjusted so too have the boundaries between organisations and the outside world. The new communication technologies create the possibility of shared working spaces between those formally inside and those formally outside of the organisation: the 'networked organisation' links customers, sourcing operations, sub contractors, local and national government and administration though its continuous communication paths and patterns (Jackson and Harris, 2000). Daily routine interaction between these different functional groupings and domains becomes manageable through the 'task bundling' capabilities of the new technology (Denning and Grieco, 2000). Agencies external to the organisation can interact within the main communication space of the organisation with major impact upon the setting of the organisational discourse and, therefore, of organisational identity.

When viewed from this perspective of the expansion of organisational discourse to accommodate the expansion of organisation-linked voices made possible through the technology: it becomes clear that the new Information Communication Technologies are *'relational technologies'*. By use of the term 'relational technology', we are drawing attention to the highly participative character of the new information technology and the radical alteration it has made in the ability to interact with others both in terms of number of relationships that can be maintained at lowered transaction costs and in terms of the potential for shaping and maintaining new relationships with those at a distance. These relational technologies are paralleled by the emergence of new dynamics of *'relational identity'* – firstly, the number of relationships individuals can form and maintain with either other individuals or institutions (for example, contributions to a web site) are substantially increased in the context of the new information technology and this provides new domains in which identity can be formed in conjunction with others. Secondly, the new information technology provides the equipment for self-grooming as others views of self are globalised through the web and can be retrieved easily by the individual involved in self grooming. Perhaps, one of the most interesting aspects of relational identity in the context of the new information technology is the growth of single issue politics on the World Wide Web – the individual can now readily locate others with same interest and move to intensify that interest on very low transaction costs. Identity can be re-inforced by the new relational patterns of interchange that are available.

Social movements around the relational character of the new information technology are many: in the world of work, the large corporations such as IBM and Boeing have become involved in funding conferences on Computer Supported Collective Work. The technologies enable very high levels of interaction and iteration between participants and increasingly the design focus within the technologies is upon enabling group working and expanding participation. Even at the level of individuals organising their own web sites the development of bulletin board technology and the insertion of bulletin boards on individual web sites creates an important form of relational space.

The essentially distributed character of these technologies (messages can be raised and broadcast from any point to any other point within a frame which can be simultaneously accessed globally en masse) coupled with their asynchronous options (messages can be accessed at any time convenient to the collector and from any location) enable new patterns of organisational interaction (Stanford-Smith and Kidd, 2000).

Similarly, the new communication technologies enable those external to an organisation but not in common step with an organisation's purpose to 'shadow' and globally describe that organisation from the outside. The identity of the organisation is no longer shaped simply by corporate intent; rather the performance of organisations can be monitored from the outside with consequences for organisational identity (see Travelproblems.com at http://www.travelproblems.com/; http://www.bilderberg.org/railways.htm; Turner, Holmes and Hodgson, 2000; see also Holmes, 2000b for discussion on 'emergent identity' as arising through the dialectical interplay of self-presentation and ascription by others). A classic example of this emergent shift in the locus of '*knowledge building*' (Green, Holmes and Grieco, this volume) and social framing is to be found in the British transport sector. The reshaping of the 'national' rail network into a structure which depends upon the efficient 'networking' of a number of separate corporate bodies or organisations coupled with the advent of a number of 'rail disasters' has generated a new (though not yet highly effective) information environment. The separate organisations are necessarily involved in a potentially public exchange of information to perform the range of tasks which were previously performed within one organisation with relatively strong boundaries on information leakage. The recent discussions about the deficiencies in Britain's rail track infrastructure have been pursued between the numerous rail operators and rail agencies in a very public forum. The complexity of these structures and, some would argue, the resulting poor performance of the British transport sector has resulted in passenger information and action groups which make use of the new technologies to reintegrate information on the performance of the railway structure.

The argument here is that technology enabled the dismantling of rail's old national organisational structure as coordination between many separate and competing agencies was accomplishable within the modern information communication technology (ICT) environment: this new network structure generates a public exchange of information which can heighten transparency of performance. In the event, the quality of 'networking' between the different agencies in the rail structure has not been adequate with the consequence that disasters have happened and that the processes leading to these disasters have been rendered transparent. Groups such as the Safety on Trains Action Group (http://www.staguk.org.uk/) have emerged to place transport safety issues on the policy agenda: institutions concerned with personnel issues have begun to discuss the relationship between organisational change in the rail sector and rail disasters on line. Similarly, the transparency of the rail transport environment has been enhanced sufficiently for schools to be able to build on line tool kits which enable young students of economics to explore the complex policy and financial arguments (see Wood Green School economics kit on rail disasters and rail privatisation).

The collecting together of customer criticism and customer comment on the performance of the rail industry might not at first sight seem a scenario that rail operators and government policy agencies would welcome. However, in a context where passenger levels are down by 40–50 per cent after Britain's disastrous rail month in terms of infrastructural inadequacies, transport disasters and major environmental challenges, gaining rapid on-line customer feedback may be precisely the tool required in assisting rail to recover. Presently, a major complaint from the client environment is that the transport services are not responsive to customer needs and customer views. The use of new information communication technologies can do much to keep passengers informed (see UK Government document on national public transport information system at http://www.local-transport.detr.gov.uk/pti/capf9800/), ease their travel and keep transport management informed of deficiencies in the service provision by the use of customer feedback technologies. In order to explore the prospect of such a future, it is worth noting that the Scottish education service which was viewed as having failed badly in terms of examination administration this summer has expressly indicated that it wants to make use of pupil and parent alert systems in the future administration of the service.

Transport is an area in which we would expect to see the new communications technology enabling new relational practices both at the level of individuals and small groups and at the level of large organisations precisely because transport is essentially a network activity in which coordination over distance is critical and user-feedback can provide cost-effective knowledge building over large geographical areas (Turner, Holmes and Hodgson, 2000). There is, however, another aspect of transport which has to be brought into the equation: intelligent auditing technologies are already well developed in transport. Buses and trams have steps which electronically count the passengers boarding and can relay the information for storage and review at later dates: vehicle routes and timings can be recorded by intelligent technologies which permit performance measurement from within and without the transport organisation itself. Violations of authorised air routes out of Manchester airport are automatically recorded and enable the ready identification and disciplining of offenders: pilots receive notification of their offence as they land at their destination. The transparency of action has consequences for the portfolio of action options and therefore for identity.

The transparency of performance achieved through new technology is not simply the transparency of self's action to others, whether self be an individual, group or organisation but it is also the transparency of self to self. The capability of using information collected by others to review the action of self and of recollecting aspects of 'identity' from various locations, and thus perspectives, to form this view at a very low transaction cost is a new phenomenon. The distributed character of the new technology and its quasi-infinite information processing capabilities permits the use of small windows of time to organise complex materials into sensemaking tools on own performance. Effectively, the individual, group or organisation is assisted in its self grooming by the availability of information tools.

In essence, the new information technologies enables self better facilities for self social grooming through its ability to retrieve information, to infinitely reproduce detail and supplement the power of memory. Indeed, much of the focus of self social grooming in the present has been focused at the organisational level: the concern has been with knowledge crystallisation within the organisation and the development of technologies and protocols for enabling that process (see Cobos and Alaman, 2000, for information on the KnowCat knowledge crystallisation application). The application of computer technology to the concept of the 'learning organisation' has resulted in the development of people centred models which turn individual knowledge into corporate knowledge For example, Meta 4 have developed a knowledge management platform entitled KnowNet.

> KnowNet is a tool that creates the right virtual infrastructure for a creative business environment. It enables knowledge storing, sharing and searching in an organised way. It measures the activities and outcome. It includes functionality to build Yellow Pages that connect individual profiles with the knowledge flow (Pastor, 2000).

> Access to anyone, anywhere: The technological platform that supports KnowNet ensures unlimited scalability to the system. This means that knowledge can be deployed throughout large organisations up to thousands of users allowing anybody in the company (if permissions are given) to participate in the process of knowledge regeneration and reuse. The platform provides remote access through Windows clients or web browsers, ensuring access to knowledge regardless of the physical location. Security is guaranteed by the role based security model, which protects the confidentiality of the corporate knowledge repository (ibid.).

> Cooperations with third parties: Most companies lack the means to track and learn from the experience of third parties they work with, such as partners, providers, customers and even competitors. A reoccurring situation within organisations that outsource experience is the loss of new knowledge created during these cooperations. Often this knowledge stays outside the company and has to be purchased to be used again. A typical case is that of external consultants. Outside resources, such as business partners, consultants, suppliers and even customers can be connected to KnowNet as guests with restricted access. This will capture knowledge generated through these collaborations bringing knowledge management beyond the limits of the internal organisation (ibid.).

Viewing these new knowledge sharing experiments and applications (in which the simultaneity of interaction across an enlarged set of actors is now possible) as expanded social grooming (the social grooming capabilities of the individual minus technology are limited at approximately 150 persons: see Robin Dunbar on social grooming at http://www.liv.ac.uk/www/evolpsyc/rimd.htm) provides us with a clear relationship between the relational character of the new technology and the prospect of new relational organisational identities. The time-space constraints which forced closure on individual, group and organisational definitions of membership and thus identity have been greatly transformed and are likely to be subject to further transformation. Electronic adjacency permits new identity patternings.

New Communication Structures: the Enhanced Ability to Distribute and to Recollect Task

The development of knowledge crystallisation and knowledge capturing technologies such as KnowCat and KnowNet as organisational tools for knowledge management have consequences for the distribution and recollection of tasks. Through knowledge management systems tasks can be distributed which were previously preserved for expert performance. The new distribution of tasks accomplishable within the context of the development of knowledge management technologies clearly has consequences for leadership structures, however, this dimension of the new technologies remains relatively unexamined.

Whereas historically the decomposition of tasks into component parts and the distribution of those parts largely represented an act of deskilling with the component task performers rarely having an overview of how the various parts related to one another and the reintegration of the component parts largely being the province of management, the new information technologies enable each task performer to gain both an overview of process and detailed relevant information through the knowledge management platform. The decomposition of tasks into component parts need no longer be an experience of reduced autonomy or task isolation. The key issue in the new communication structures – knowledge platforms – is a political one: technical access is possible from any location in the knowledge platform/management system but who has access to which parts of the system is a political decision.

Historically, the access of all to information was not a technical possibility and consequently the ability to widely distribute tasks and to recollect or reintegrate these tasks was severely time/space constrained. At the simplest level, service users who make use of electronic reservation systems are an example of the distribution of task – the task of booking that was previously the responsibility of the travel agent, theatre booking office, hospital clerk, air line counter staff is now performed through the separately performed but aggregate action of a large number of actors. The manner in which the task is performed – electronically – generates an immediate record which can be stored and reviewed. Opening up the stored and retrievable data for universal examination is a technical capability – the decision as to whether this occurs is a political one.

The pressure for 'open government' and for the transparency of performance data in respect of public services, not least of which are transport (where public policy documents are increasingly placed on line – DVLA rationale at http://www.dvla.gov.uk/) and education, must necessarily engage with the implications of the availability of knowledge platforms for public participation in local government and administration. The contribution of the electorate and of service users are not constrained simply to the provision of feedback and the use of on-line services but within a knowledge platform strategy, the greater community can play a role in direct involvement in the governance and operation of public services. The regulatory function can be shared beyond the office of a particular nominated official (Rail user groups UK at http://www.rail-reg.gov.uk/docs/48new/contents.htm).

Currently, there are major European and other international developments concerned with distributed action, distributed responsibility and distributed decision making within the 'domain' of government and administration. The Regional Government of Valencia in Spain has invested in the large-scale implementation of a Smart Community model of governance (Muro, 2000). Muro discussing Infoville – the Smart Community Model used in Valencia – tells us that it was launched 'with the aim of modernising the Public Administration in the region of Valencia' (Muro, 2000). The project was supported by the 4th Framework Program of the European Commission and the city of Villena was chosen as the pilot site.

> By the end of 1997 Villena was the most advanced city in Spain in terms of its citizens' involvement in the Information Society. People living in Villena could make a restaurant reservation, ask for a certificate from the town hall, send a mail to a relative, update personal data with the bank, participate in a discussion about a school's performance, receive local news, create personal web pages or even select a time slot on a doctor's agenda. It was also a huge change for local

organisations. With no major costs, they became content providers: banks, hospitals, clinics, the local police, shops, private associations, the football team and most of the existing businesses were connected ...

Since its launch in 1996 Infoville has been implemented in nine sites in the region ...

Using Oracle technology to offer inherent flexibility and scalability, Infoville is rolled out via each local authority incorporating specific local information and data, simply, quickly and cost effectively. This technological platform also enables local businesses and local administrations to add their own services to Infoville with minimum investment (Muro, 2000).

Infoville should be considered not as an information tool but rather as a task performance tool. The distinction between information tool and task performance tool is critical and lies in the interactivity of knowledge platforms. Infoville is clearly not simply a tool for the performance of individual tasks and the meeting of individual needs but is explicitly concerned with the recollection or aggregation of these tasks as the identification of the item 'participate in a discussion about a school's performance' indicates. Infoville shows us the meeting point between modern commerce, modern government and a participating info-polity.

The need to ensure that the distributed character of the technology is properly appreciated and accommodated in the design of 'on-line' government and administration is increasingly recognised. There was, and is, a danger that 'top-down' designs of governmental cyber space will take hold. Instead of joined up government meaning the easy interaction between consumer and business and electorate and government which encompasses a discourse space for the discussion and fine tuning of policy and service provision, it may be conceived as simply a cheaper and more cost effective way of delivering services.

In the UK, as in the rest of Europe, there is no shortage of pronouncements and policy papers about public sector online service delivery, "joined up" government, social inclusion and improving regional competitiveness and modernising public sector business processes using ICT (Information and Communication Technologies). There is also widespread scepticism about the ability of public agencies to deliver on this score (Lake, 2000).

While top down projects i.e. projects promoted by the EU or national (or regional) administration are valuable – not least because they provide funding and a sense of direction – they are likely to underperform because they can not be sufficiently sensitive to local conditions, needs and infrastructure. The power of the web is its ability to link disparate groups or communities of users without forcing them into a 'one size fits all' straitjacket. This is in practice counter-cultural to the ways in which Government organisations behave – and this is the root of the problem ... The Internet challenges hierarchies and most Government institutions retain rigid hierarchical structures (Hall, 2000).

Hall and Lake indicate the potential of the new technology for overturning old task distributions and old task boundaries in government and administration without the disintegration of overall direction, structure or purpose in social and political life. The hierarchical form is for many purposes outdated and indeed restrictive of regional and commercial development.

Lake (2000) in his discussion of FifeDirect, a Scottish equivalent of Infoville, alerts us to the sustainability of web based community information systems: in the case of FifeDirect, a key component of the web-based community information system is an electronic employment exchange:

FifeDirect evolved from a Community Network Project, a telematics based project begun a number of years earlier. This project initially provided access to employment service vacancies and limited other information in an intranet system based on proprietary technology. By 1999, the limitations of this system were evident and partners decided the time was ripe to move ahead using web based technology (Lake, 2000).

Interestingly here the performance of local tasks became more readily accomplishable over a universal technology than they were within a local dedicated technology – the width of distribution of the economic and travel/ transport messages contained within the FifeDirect electronic employment exchange do not affect their recollectability or reintegration into a locally focused site. In the Infoville experience (Muro, 2000), a similar local distance phenomenon is found: within Infoville of the 49 minutes a day average connection of users, 85 per cent of this time is spent inside Infoville web resources and only 15 per cent is spent outside on the World Wide Web. The technology is clearly having the consequence of relocalising (Grieco, 2000) or improving local interactions albeit within a globalised framework: the role of the technology in the stimulating of intra-community discourse and social, economic and political exchanges has social capital consequences. Indeed, the social capital consequences of community nets are a critical component of their contribution to the regeneration of local environments.

Distributed Task and Aggregate Accountability: the Reverse Panopticon

As we have seen, local government is potentially with the availability of knowledge platforms now equipped to consult with its citizenry in a continuous and inexpensive manner which has a high level of transparency; some local governments have already availed themselves of the full range of knowledge platform technology whilst others have confined themselves to web sites which simply provide information, are not interactive and provide no value added in terms of the transparency of local government performance. Where local government and associated public services such as transport have availed themselves of the full range of functions available within the framework of new technology: this will, in time, have consequences for perceptions of accountability.

Rendering performance visible on the click of a button and enabling comment to take place on the click of another enables the development of a reverse panopticon. Instead of big brother observing the citizenry, the citizenry is capable of observing big brother. Traditionally, only the time-resourced and the radically committed have had the necessary wherewithal to participate in politics. The new technology enables the time constrained and the spatially constrained to participate in the task of civic politics and consumer action and surveillance of commerce (see the Keep San Antonio moving campaign at http://www.keepsamoving.com/; Greene, Hogan and Grieco, 2000).

Ensuring local participation in government and in the regulation of commerce outside of the electoral voting window has largely been in terms of the inclusion of representatives: typically, the claim is made that those fulfilling this function rarely share the characteristics of the communities they are meant to represent. Activists have their own agendas and these are not necessarily rendered accountable in terms of the community of representation. The information capabilities of the new technology enable the retrieval of information on voting performance, on attendance or absenteeism at meetings and on issue raising. Within the American national political environment such auditing is already at work. We can expect to see its emergence within trade unions and local government also: the ability to retrieve and review action creates an ability to identify both good and bad processes in organisations. Universal transparency is likely to reveal unexpected tensions in policy and performance.

Within transport in the United Kingdom at the present, there is clearly a tension being revealed, explored and crafted between rail safety and rail speed.

In the context of substantial speed restrictions across a large number of locations, alternative auditing processes are beginning to emerge. For example, if the speed restrictions in order to preserve safety result in passengers moving onto the road in cars where higher accident statistics hold, then should speed levels be set so as to reduce this leakage into a more dangerous environment? At present, these statistics are not yet available in the form of a click of a button status but if public opinion can be brought on board by enabling ready access to such information then it is a development which is already possible and likely to occur. However, providing information in this way has its consequences: for example, a change in the pattern of evidence can result in public opinion moving in a direction in tension with the way in which government wants to move. Transparency once established has no loyalty: removing the policymakers/sensemakers from the data/public interface has consequences for democratisation.

Power Equalisation: the New Relationship Between Organisation and Community

The thrust of this chapter is that there is a new relationship between organisation and community made possible by the new information communication technologies which are essentially relational in their structure and form. This new relationship is emerging in respect of the polity and government, the workforce and the employer and the consumer and commerce. The new information communication technologies dramatically alter roles, ranks and responsibilities: the ability to obscure and to bury 'dangerous knowledge' is severely limited. Time/space constraints of the past restricted knowledge to specific locations and specific holders, electronic adjacency is now a universal property or characteristic and in this context power is equalised through equal access to knowledge and the ability to construct competing knowledge bases.

Transport is a domain in which time/space considerations have been critical in the shaping of services and in the governance of those services. Public service facilities have typically concentrated on the needs of working men with scant regard to the requirements of women and, with the exception of school journeys, children. The new information technology enables the different components of the transport client base to advocate changes in the quality and form of provision: it is likely to be one of the interfaces between government/business:public/private at which we see the links between technology/voice/identity and the pressure for improved service provision occurring. Direct voicing through new technology and the resulting distributed discourse are all set to change the contours of organisational and civic identity.

References

Carter, C. and Grieco, M. (2000), 'New Deals, No Wheels: Social exclusion, teleoptions and electronic ontology', *Urban Studies*, Vol. 37, No. 10, pp. 1724–35.

Cobos, R. and Alaman, X. (2000), 'KnowCat: A knowledge crystallisation tool', in B. Stanford-Smith and P.T. Kidd (eds), *E-Business: Key issues, technologies, applications*, Omashu: IOS Press.

Denning, S. and Grieco, M. (2000), 'Technology, Dialogue and the Development Process', *Urban Studies*, Vol. 37, No. 10, pp. 1865–80.

Green, M., Holmes, L. and Grieco, M. (2000), 'Archiving Social Practice: The management of transport boycotts', presentation to APROS 2000, Sydney.

Greene, A.M., Hogan, J. and Grieco, M. (2000), 'E-Collectivism: Emergent opportunities for renewal', in B. Stanford-Smith and P.T. Kidd (eds), *E-Business: Key issues, technologies, applications*, Omashu: IOS Press.

Grieco, M. (2000), 'Intelligent Urban Development: The emergence of wired government and administration', *Urban Studies*, Vol. 37, No. 10, pp. 1719–22.

Hall, G. (2000), 'Social Inclusion in the Information Society', in B. Stanford-Smith and P.T. Kidd (eds), *E-Business: Key issues, technologies, applications*, Omashu: IOS Press.

Holmes, L. (2000a), 'What can Performance tell us about Learning? Explicating a Troubled Concept', *European Journal of Work and Organizational Psychology*, Vol. 9, No. 2.

Holmes, L. (2000b), 'Reframing Learning: Performance, identity and practice', presented at Critical Contributions to Managing and Learning: 2nd Connecting Learning and Critique Conference, Lancaster University, July 2000.

Jackson, P. and Harris, L. (2000), 'eBusiness and Organisational Change', in B. Stanford-Smith and P.T. Kidd (eds), *E-Business: Key issues, technologies, applications*, Omashu: IOS Press.

Lake, A. (2000), 'FifeDirect – Using the Internet for Regional Economic Development and Social Inclusion', in B. Stanford-Smith and P.T. Kidd (eds), *E-Business: Key issues, technologies, applications*, Omashu: IOS Press.

Little, S. (2000), 'Networks and Neighbourhoods: Household, community and sovereignty in the global economy', *Urban Studies*, Vol. 37, No. 10, pp. 1813–25.

Muro, M.P. (2000), 'A Large Scale Implementation of a Smart Community Model', in B. Stanford-Smith and P.T. Kidd (eds), *E-Business: Key issues, technologies, applications*, Omashu: IOS Press.

Pastor, G. (2000), 'People and Knowledge in the Net Economy', in B. Stanford-Smith, and P.T. Kidd (eds), *E-Business: Key issues, technologies, applications,* IOS Press.

Stanford-Smith, B. and Kidd, P.T. (2000), *E-Business: Key issues, technologies, applications,* Omashu: IOS Press.

Turner, J., Holmes, L. and Hodgson, F.C. (2000), 'Intelligent Urban Development: An introduction to a participatory approach', *Urban Studies,* Vol. 37, No. 10, pp. 1723–34.

Chapter Four

E-communications and Relational Constructionism: Distributed Action, Distributed Leadership and Ecological Possibilities

Dian Marie Hosking

Introduction

This chapter begins by distinguishing two very different constructions of knowledge and relations: entitative and social constructionist. Each of these has very different implications for how new information and communication technologies (ICTs) may be viewed. In the 'entitative' view, people have knowledge about entities that can be codified and digitised, i.e., propositional knowledge or 'knowledge that'. Relatedly, new ICTs are viewed as tools for information transmission and knowledge management. In contrast, the present chapter outlines and explores a more rare, social constructionist, approach. In this view, ongoing processes of relating are considered to make social realities in joint action. For this reason, focus shifts to know*ing* which now is joined with action. In this case, new ICTs become viewed as additional media for making people and worlds – identities and relations – as social realities. This invites questions about *what sorts* of identities and relations become possible. Particular attention is paid to possibilities for multi-voiced *participation* in policy and practice, whether or not invited. Important in this context is the ways in which power is constructed 'warranting' or social validation, 'power to'. One possibility is 'power over': the familiar case of mono-logical, dominance relations in which warrant is achieved for a singular hierarchy of knowledge, responsibility, and status. Another possibility is 'power to' as it might be constructed in multilogical, heterarchical, open processes. We explore possibilities for e-communications to construct 'power to', along with some of the relational skills that might be implicated. In so doing, we discuss multilogical, reflexive ways of relating, distributed leadership, and 'ecological' (rather than 'ego-logical') relations. Illustrations are drawn from recent negotiating events and campaigns where the new technologies were prominent.

Different Views of Persons and Things, Knowledge and Relations

Communications and Knowledge

It has become commonplace to talk of people and things using nouns. They are treated as subjects and objects, their characteristics being described using noun qualifiers (see e.g., Hosking and Morley, 1991). As an acting Subject (S) a person or organisation is assumed to relate to, learn about, and to influence, form, shape, or structure other entities (persons, organisations, markets, etc.). In this way, the latter are treated as if they are knowable and formable 'Objects' (O) in S-O relation. In this view, the implicit *model of communications* presumes a sender and a receiver. The communication process is viewed as a one-way transmission of *information about* someone or something, with feedback to indicate the quality of reception. For example, people (e.g., leaders, managers) and organisations are said to discover what knowledge 'is', and to own, store, manage, and sell 'it'.

Grammars typically require use of *both* nouns *and* verbs in subject-verb--object relation.[1] So users can try to give richness to both noun and verb forms in rather the same way, for example, that research programmes can assume and investigate both particle and wave, both stability and change. However, *both/and practices are rare*. Instead, verbs such as knowing and organising are treated *as if* they were nouns (knowledge, organisation), or they are used as verbs – but verbs capable of doing very little given the richness of the noun (adjective, pronoun, etc.) context.

Elsewhere this has been called an 'entitative' view (Hosking and Morley, 1991) – one that assumes that some entity with knowable, defining and stable characteristics can know and achieve power over another entity – some-one and/or some-thing. What is crucial here is that *entities are given ontology*. These entities are treated as (a) relatively fixed beings and (b) as being what they are *prior to*, and *'outside' of*, processes. This construction has important implications for our present interest in the 'new' 'information and communication technologies' (ICTs). Perhaps the most general implication is that being and knowing are separated. Given this move, knowing is viewed as *knowledge about* some pre-existing Self and Other(s) i.e., 'people and worlds'. This is 'knowledge that' e.g., the world *is* round, e.g., that a good leader *is* charismatic or *has* charisma; noun qualifiers are the tools of description. Relatedly, knowledge is turned into a thing – a property of some storage device that can be physically located in something or someone (mind) – something that can be managed and distributed – as in most constructions of 'knowledge management'. ICTs then become interesting as tools for information transmission and knowledge management.

Of course, these entitative constructions do not exhaust the realm of possibilities. Another approach is one that centres *relational processes* and views these as the moving location in which social realities are constructed. From this point of view 'mind' shifts into the world and becomes viewed as distributed in time, and space, so to speak. Knowledge also enjoys a more processual treatment, being viewed not as knowledge of some pre-existing world, but as an ongoing social construction process. From this perspective, new ICTs provide media for *making self and other* (people and worlds) – for constructing identities (of persons, institutions, artefacts, etc.) and relations. In this context, it makes sense to ask whether the new ICTs offer possibilities for constructing radically different people and worlds. More narrowly, we can ask *if the new ICTs are uniquely or especially capable of supporting distributed ways of organising, distributed leadership and 'ecological' (rather than ego-logical) constructions* (e.g. Bateson, 1972; Hosking, 2000).

Relational Processes of Construction

The present account gives ontology to social construction *processes* and suggests how these might be understood. Self(/ves) and others (people and things) are viewed as ongoing social constructions '*made in*' relational processes. This move gives theoretical bite to *processes* rather than entities. It contrasts with many other 'social constructionisms' that concentrate on socially constructed *products* (see e.g., Pearce, 1992) and contrasts with the entitative view (outlined above) that treats 'self contained individuals' (Sampson, 1993) as the authors of their own social realities.

In the present perspective what is (ontology) and how we know (epistemology) are joined and viewed as social constructions made in ongoing relational processes (methodology). Instead of communications between pre-existing entities with their own identities and other personal characteristics, we speak of relational processes in which 'acts' or 'texts' are coordinated. We use the terms acts and texts very broadly and interchangeably. So, texts (acts) might be written or spoken but also could be gestures, artefacts, and what commonly are understood as objects in nature. Further, coordinations might be achieved in face-to-face relations as in a handshake or a face-to-face conversation, or coordinations may be distributed in time and/or space e.g., using the 'new' information and communication technologies (ICTs).

This *joining of what, and how*, we know means a changed understanding of language. Briefly, conceptual language is no longer emphasised as a tool for representing some independently existing reality[2] – as in entitative conceptions (see, for example, Gergen and Thatchenkerry, 1996). *Conceptual language becomes viewed as one of many possible ways to construct social realities in relation* (e.g., Hosking, Dachler, and Gergen, 1995; LeShan, 1974). Construction processes may be said: (a) to embrace a mix of the already learned (conventional) and the new (emergent); (b) to be ongoing (rather than necessarily fixed) and; (c) to be relational in the sense of inter-relating many simultaneous act-supplement (text-context) connections, many of which are tacit (e.g., Polanyi, 1958; Coulter, 1989).

The present arguments leave aside talk of 'what *is*' the case (some personal identity, organisational structures, etc.), interests in boundaries (separating independent existences), and the long-standing emphasis on propositional *knowledge that* – knowledge which may or may not be true. Now invited is talk of more or less local coordinations that real-ise – that more or less temporarily 'fix' – particular constructions from an infinity of possibilities (see e.g., Slife and Williams, 1995; Woolgar, 1996). Talk of 'what *is*' is no longer so interesting in that 'it' is more or less fleeting and local and, as we shall see, multiple. In this view, social ontologies are socially constructed, in social relational processes, performed in the same or a different time and place, with or without the new ICTs.

Constructing Self-other Relations

The constructionist themes outlined have been developed over many years in many literatures including philosophy of social science, interactionist social psychology, feminisms, postmodernist histories of ideas and cultures, etc. (see e.g., Gergen, 1994, for a review). Writers have had different interests, for example, including the sociology of knowledge, gender relations and ecology. This said, construction is generally viewed as a process of differentiating and relating (e.g., Bateson, 1972) some construction of self from some construction of other(s).

Given this view of social construction, self and other social realities are no longer viewed as singular and relatively fixed entities. Rather, '*self*' *is viewed as a relational construction*, i.e., as made in ongoing act-supplement, self-other relations. The particular construction of self or 'identity' varies in different self-other relations. Relational processes become the moving 'construction site' of *multiple identities* in multiple self-other relations (e.g., Weigert, 1983; Hosking and Morley, 1991).

Many have pursued this line of theorising to focus on identity constructions. In this context, the new ICTs and other post modern developments have been considered interesting in terms of their implications for self constructions (e.g., www.aber.ac.uk/media/Functions/mcs www.acsu.buffalo.edu/~reymers/id-bib.html). For example, the web expands the possibilities for constructing multiple and changing identities and relations. Just as one dramatic instance, there are sites *designed* for assumed 'cyber' identities and play (e.g., www.cycosmos.com). However, identity 'play' can equally go on in multiple local networks of relations e.g., in different Listserves, e-mail relations, web sites, etc. ICTs provide opportunities for moving around multiple self-other relations (Hosking and Morley, 1991). Of course, these possibilities are, in themselves, neither good nor bad. One view argues the increased likelihood of a 'saturated self' (Gergen, 1991) fragmented in multiple changing relations. Another view emphasises the freedom that comes from not being stuck in fixed notions of self and how the world is, not stuck in 'this and that' thinking (Chogyam Trungpa, 1987).

The present view of construction processes sets aside the sender-receiver model of communications. Instead, it becomes more meaningful to ask questions about *relational processes* and the particular identities and relations they (re)construct. Instead of starting with pre-existing and fixed identities such as 'leader' and 'team worker' – who communicate – we may inquire into the processes that construct, maintain, and change particular identities and relations. Returning to our interest in the new ICTs, we may ask if they afford and/or facilitate particular ways of relating that previously were not possible or were just more difficult. Of particular interest is the possibility that these new technologies are especially enabling of *distributed action*, particularly distributed leadership and organisation (e.g., www.taosinstitute.org www.ac.nz/~alock//virtual/welcome.html).

The entitative approach outlined earlier differentiates self and other as Subject and Object (e.g., Fine, 1994). They are related in an *exclusive* and *opposed* logic of *either-or* – an *ego-logical* perspective. Such *ego*-logical constructions offer two differing identities, ways of acting, or 'positions'. The Subject position is active – knowing and influencing – in relation to some differentiated other(s) viewed – *from a subject position* – as knowable and formable. Common constructions of this sort include leader and follower, change agent and organisation, expert and novice.[3] This construction – from a Subject position – treats Others as passive objects (see e.g., Berman, 1981; Hosking, Dachler, and Gergen, 1995; Harding and Hintikka, 1983; Plumwood, 1993).

The entitative perspective, when viewed from our relational constructionist standpoint, offers a very restricted view of identities and relations. One of its many aspects is that, when put to work in discussions of organising, leadership, communications, etc., the knowing scientist/researcher/storyteller is left out of the narrative. He or she is implicit, a raconteur left in the shadows, offering a 'god's eye view from nowhere'. In the present view, the storyteller cannot achieve warrant for his or her claim to be a neutral knower (scientist or leader). Rather, the narrator/theoretician is acting to claim the position of knowing Subject-acts/texts that may be supplemented and socially validated e.g., by other scientists.

When considered in relation to relational constructionist narratives, Subject-Object constructions can be said to be *monological and hierarchical*. It is the subject's acts that (re)construct 'power over' other in the 'doing' of science, the doing of leadership, the doing of organising, etc. Subject-Object ways of relating place limits on possible self-other differentiations and other ways of relating. Most obviously, they place limits on what elsewhere has been called 'eco-logical' relations (Hosking, 2000). These are processes that differentiate self and other in inclusive relations – *both* separate – *and* inseparable. In the absence of the privileged knowing subject, *multilogical, heterarchical* ways of relating become possible, as does 'power to' rather than power over.

Summary of Premises

- relating may be viewed as multiple coordination – as joint and not 'individual' action;
- constructed in conceptual language and other forms of action; by
- coordinating what may be called 'act and supplement' or 'text and context';
- acts (texts) allow many *possible* supplements, some (becoming) conventional;
- relational processes are local, historical, social, etc. but may be widely distributed in space and time;
- coordinating with act-supplement relations already ongoing and constraining how a process is likely to go on; so

- not 'anything goes';
- processes (re)construct some Self in relation to some construction of Other(s); so
- knowing is always from some 'relational position' in ongoing coordinations;
- (re)constructing 'power over' other or 'power to'.

Constructing Cooperation: Ontologies Distributed in Joint Action

One common view of ego-logical relations has been that they are enforced by the world 'as it really is'. However, few now think this construction to be tenable. For example, reflection on scientific practices shows that knowledge of 'the observed' (Object) cannot be entirely separated from 'the observer' or Subject (e.g., Heisenberg, see e.g., Berman, 1981; Knorr Cetina, 1981; Woolgar, 1996). Relatedly, theory cannot be simplistically separated from data (see e.g., Gergen, 1994). Scientific practices may embrace the *assumption* that scientist (S) and Object (O) *are* separate existences and may strive to achieve separateness such that S can achieve knowledge about O and only O. Deviations from such practices then are devalued – as bad science or as unscientific (see e.g., Harding, 1986, 1987; Slife and Williams, 1995). The present arguments indicate *both* that *S-O constructions are made* in social processes *and* open-up the possibility that *non S-O constructions also could be made*. This is just as true of relations conducted via the web or mobile phones as in any other medium.

These considerations invite reflection on how some particular differentiation and relation (S-O or otherwise) becomes conventional. In the present view, this becomes a question of how some construction is reproduced in act-supplement relations. We have seen that coordinations may construct S-O relations e.g., between a chief executive and her many staff, between organisations, or between different local cultures (e.g., between a colonial government and local officials). However, we also have seen that relating can differentiate Self and Other in *inclusive, different but equal, relations*. Constructions of this sort may be made and remade in processes that are open to many coexisting, different but equal, local 'logics'. A fascinating possibility is that the new ICTs may facilitate *multilogical* processes. Current attempts at e-governance (e.g., in Pakistan) might fall a long way short of multiloging in equal relations, but the new ICTs certainly could make a major contribution of this sort.

This inclusive and multilogical view of relations seems very radical indeed when compared with the Cartesian construction of mind, separate from internal and external nature. In the Cartesian view, mind and other personal characteristics are differentiated (set apart), nominalised (made into nouns), and 'spatialised' (viewed as something, in some space, e.g., Jaynes, 1976). In the Cartesian view S is 'outside' of and acts over O to make the latter in some way serviceable – by providing a natural or 'human' resource.

Our relational-constructionist view could be seen to offer a *non-spatialised construction of mind*. More accurately, mind no longer is given independent ontological status. Mind becomes viewed as constructed in action, as distributed in social processes/cultural practices, and as constantly in the making. In such views, 'minding' becomes understood as a world of pattern, of form in process (relating) (see e.g., Hosking, 2000; Reason, 1994b). Given these sorts of shift, some theorists prefer to talk of 'knowing' and to emphasise an 'ecological' rather than 'ego-logical' construction' of relational processes (e.g., Bateson, 1972); others use the language of cooperation, coordination, joint action, or relational processes.

Relational-constructionist arguments offer no firm foundation for the claim that either mono-logical or multilogical ways of relating are more true or better in any universal, transcendental sense. *Particular* local (social-historical) contexts may facilitate or give pragmatic value to one or the other. Equally, the pragmatics of *particular* local cultural processes and relations may seem to call for e.g., inclusive, multilogical relations. These particularities seem to include the 'postmodern' world of 'new' ICTs, globalisation, increasing inequalities in financial wealth and economic infrastructure, the growing power of large corporations, destruction of forests, landscapes and communities. Changed forms of practice seem urgently needed (e.g., Bateson, 1972; Reason, 1994a, b; Dachler and Hosking, 1995; www.oneworld.net/campaigns/wto).

Multilogue – in the narrow sense the expression of marginalised, suppressed and hidden voices – is certainly enabled by the new ICTs (http://www.geocities.com/unionsonline/eventhistory.html). One example is given detailed discussion by Hogan and Green (this volume) in their account of how e-communications are used to challenge dominant voices and hierarchical leadership. It seems that ICTs make available what previously was unavailable or just more difficult. This is relevant to what Cockburn called 'democracy deficit' (Cockburn, 1995). Voices can be raised by anyone with some minimal E-ducation who can get web and/or e-mail access (e.g., http://www.internet-campaigns.nl).

The new ICTs also enable 'loose coupling' (Weick, 1979; Maturana and Varela, 1987). In this context, loose coupling has a number of aspects, each of which may facilitate greater voicing/participation. First, voices that are widely distributed in space, perhaps involving remote geographical locations, now can be brought together. Second, participation can be distributed in time – participants can coordinate when it suits their limited time budgets. Third, 'loose coupling' is achieved in the sense that the 'relational work' that sustains particular relationships is widely distributed amongst all participating voices. For example, many relations may be simultaneously constructed in e-communications involving one (or many) to many, for example, through use of e-petitions, e-voting, one to many 'list' communications (e.g., http:// www.geocities.com/transport_and_society/telegovernance.html).

As the activities around www.rogerlyons.com show, everyone can become a researcher and interventionist (see Hogan and Green, this volume). 'Power to' participate in more open, discursive ways of organising now is, and can be, more widely distributed. Opportunities now are more easily created for achieving warrant or social certification for multiple coexisting 'logics', as well as for contesting some ongoing 'monologic'. It seems that ICTs may facilitate wider and more open participation in policy formation protest – in transformational change work of any kind.

The New ICTs, Multilogical Ways of Relating and Leadership

We now may further explore how '*multiloging*' may 'go on' and, in particular, how e-relations and web-based relational processes might contribute. It is perhaps helpful to repeat that, in the present view, it is *processes of social construction* that are centred, rather than persons. We are asking: how may processes be open to possibilities rather than closed; how may relational processes construct inclusive, different but equal relations, and be open to multiple 'logics' of self, other and relations, and; how might new ICTs figure in this. Such processes seem likely to involve a number of reflexive practices.

Reflection on Knowing 'From Where'

One reflexive practice involves reflecting on the relational position from which some construction is made. That there is always a relational position is well illustrated by, for example, Escher's painting of himself painting a painting.

Many years earlier van Eyck did something similar in his work *The Betrothal of the Arnolfini*. In the latter, van Eyck included a mirror reflecting the newly married couple and the image of himself painting the painting. You could say that van Eyck's painting wonderfully illustrates the view that social reality (self, other, and relations) is always constructed from *some particular* relational position. Other relational positions may construct very different social realities.

This said, it is interesting to ponder on what, if anything, is special when the new ICTs provide the relational medium rather than e.g., same time/same place coordinations. On the one hand, ICTs may be used to author texts and to track or audit authorship, e.g., through e-mail addresses, the name of a web 'master', or tracking a mobile phone. Of course these possibilities *can* be employed for increasing 'power over' other in Subject-Object relations. On the other hand, it may be very hard, if not (practically) impossible, to get much sense of 'the' relational position from which some reality claim is made for example, through a web site. In the present view, *these new technologies make more palpable* the *relational (and therefore multiple and local) quality of social realities*. Given the relational quality of identities, one possibility is (a) to examine *local* relational process to see what identity claims are made and warranted. Another possibility (b) is to treat all voices as (in principle) equal, abandoning the usual desire to determine the authority of some 'voice', relative to others.

Following on from the above, reflecting can be thought of as shifting emphasis from 'what is' (e.g., van Eyck's witnessing of a marriage) to the social processes in which 'thingness' is constructed. As we have just seen (b above), part of what this could involve might be 'letting go' of any fixed sense of self as one who knows and letting go of already fixed notions of 'other'. This can go together with depersonalising texts/acts – including remember what, in an entitative perspective, would be called knowledge. This would involve treating texts/acts as possibilities rather than as fixed facts, or as personal possessions; this would involve treating them as *contributions to a potentially useful process* rather than as identity claims. In these ways, relational processes may give space for non S-O ways of relating and make space for new constructions to emerge.

If we further explore these possibilities in relation to constructions of leadership we can see that the new ICTs can facilitate '*distributed* leadership' (Brown and Hosking, 1986). Leadership can be distributed to the extent that communications are open to ways of relating that construct multiple logics in *both-and, different but equal* relations. Such practices may be especially useful when globalised organisations and media are bringing in to relation many different participants, world making activities, and priorities; we shall return to this issue.

Space Clearing

Any act or 'text' can be made to mean very different things depending on the supplements or con-texts with which it is coordinated. This is how *multiple logics* get to be constructed – perhaps to the frustration of leaders who wish to communicate their 'vision' and manage meanings for others in S-O relation (see e.g., Smircich and Morgan, 1982). Processes often construct exclusive, 'either-or', right-wrong relations between different logics. This is made more likely when different logics are expressed using different jargon (as in relations between different specialist groups), or when different logics are expressed using the same words to mean different things. Furthermore, that many supplements are *implicit* also means that different and perhaps conflicting logics may be constructed without this being apparent to cooperating participants.

This invites the question of how to engage in 'space clearing'. Put slightly differently, this is a question of how to 'make space' for multiple constructions of identities and relations and how to 'make space' for change. In particular, we need to know how to construct self and other in inclusive, cooperative ways – rather than 'from the outside' in separate, Subject-Object relation. In addition to constructing *a* leader, *one* 'vision' (the leader's), and 'power over' others, multiloging allows leader identities and logics to be distributed in relational processes; talk of leader*ship* rather than leaders (Hosking, 1988) becomes more appropriate and useful. We then might investigate how 'social dreaming', involving many 'visions' (dreams) might be performed using new ICTs e.g., using videoconferencing and listserves (see e.g., http://www.newintermediaries.co.uk).

Not Knowing

In addition to reflecting practices, and space clearing, multiloging includes act-supplement relations that feature '*not knowing*' (e.g., Anderson, 1990; Anderson, 1997).[4] Not knowing, in the sense intended here, has a number of aspects. First, it involves acting to supplement some act/text in ways that avoid positioning self as a knowing Subject and Other as not knowing. Part of what this means is coordinating on the basis of as few assumptions as possible, turning assumptions into questions, withholding closed and categorical 'right-wrong' judgements – trying to give space to possibilities (e.g., Bandler and Grinder, 1975; Bass and Hosking, 1998; Friedman, 1995).

Resisting the 'knowing' position also means resisting the imposition of generalised narratives, general theories, stereotypes – as tools for making sense of Other. Resisting the knowing position also means avoiding closure. Closure often is attempted by turning 'inwards' to some separated construction of self, for example, 'as leader I must know better than others (and so not listen to other voices); breaking the relationship – 'letting go' of dissenting voices is, of course, another way. Such courses of action (whether or not using words) will disable multilogue and enable the limited possibilities of *either* stability *or* change through yet more 'power over'.

If we think about ICTs in the context of these arguments we can see that these new technologies have great potential for openness to multiple voices. In particular, the web with its hyperlink facility makes it very easy to move around different 'voices' and relationships. Such processes are potentially unbounded, are always in some sense emergent, and may be more or less open to multiple logics. In addition, ways will need to be found to combine the ICTs with appropriate large scale, participative, policy making methodologies.

Making the 'Here and Now'

An entirely new realm of possibilities arise when relating is viewed as *making social realities* – rather than 'finding out', or sense-*taking* – perceiving some pre-existing reality. Illustrations of the former may be found in the increasing use of change methodologies that set aside notions of problem finding and problem solving (e.g., Weisbord et al., 1992; Cooperrider, Barrett and Srivastva, 1995). These methodologies require letting go of the notion that something exists that has gone wrong and needs to be put right. Instead of constructing pasts to be analysed and changed and futures to be planned, attention shifts to talk and other kinds of action as they construct some 'here and now'. The new ICTs have enormous potential for the conduct of these large scale change methodologies which rely on bringing sometimes hundreds of people (a 'whole system') together in some shared time/space location. Those who wish to facilitate large-scale change efforts and distributed leadership now may use for example, chat rooms, cyberdesks, knowledge boards, web-based video conferencing and the like to assist activities such as Future Search or Appreciative Inquiry (see e.g., www.futuresearch.net).

This focus on action making social realities in the here and now is very congruent with what has become known as virtual reality – usually (and naively) counterposed to 'real' reality. Further, the present relational constructionist framework can be seen to be similar to Buddhist conceptions of 'beginner's mind'. The latter is a reference to coordinating in ways that are open to possibilities – rather than closed and so actively stabilising some particular construction of self, other, and relation. Acting with 'beginner's mind' means holding lightly to (what we take to be) knowledge (including Buddhism and social constructionism) and including generalised narratives of what leadership 'really' *is*.

Reflecting Frames, Reflecting Questions

Many have spoken of the importance of reflecting on the frameworks constructed in language including presuppositions that hold particular constructions or practices in place. Reason (1994a) focused on spoken texts whilst others have emphasised nonconceptual act-supplement coordinations as they frame and reframe (e.g., Bass and Hosking, 1998; Hosking and Bass, 1998; also Bateson, Watzlawick and others). Reflecting on the constraining contributions of language tools, taken-for-granteds, and practices shows that all methods create that which they are 'tuned for' (e.g., Slife and Williams, 1995). Reflecting on frames can open up a world of yet to be imagined, yet to be created possibilities.

Coordinations often involve asking and answering questions. Like any other text or act, questions are connected to narratives (of questioner, other, the former's purposes) and these will constrain possible con-texts or supplements. Of course, this makes perfect sense when questions are thought of as useful for 'finding out' e.g., to identify problems, what happened, and who is to blame. However, this may not seem so helpful once we view questions as literally (re)constructing the world we know, ourselves, and our relations – and not so much as finding out (about some pre-existing reality). As we have seen, multiloging involves asking questions from a 'not knowing' stance. Questions now are used to explore 'from within' the ongoing, here and now, relational process, opening-up possibilities and multiple realities, negotiating locally rather than imposing 'outsider' constructions (e.g., Anderson, 1997; Janov, 1995; also www.publicdialogue.org).

Last, it should be emphasised that, in the present view, distributed leadership is not only a matter of multiple voices and distributed action. Rather *multilogical relational processes* are required, contributing to *local* construction processes, contesting monological constructions, and/or achieving warrant for multiple 'different but equal' logics. So, for example, the fuel tax protest in the UK involved distributed action using ICTs, particularly mobile phones (http://www.geocities.com/the_odyssey_group/fueltaxcrisis/fueltaxcrisis.html). However, there seems little to suggest that this was anything other than multiple participants sharing the same (mono)logic and acting on it. In this sense, the protest could be regarded as imposing a monologic on the government and other dissenting voices that found little way to be heard.

Summary of Multiloging Practices

• Reflection on knowing from where – given multiple standpoints.
• Space clearing – making space for multiple logics.
• Not knowing – staying open to other and to self transformation.
• Making 'here and now' rather than analysing pasts and problems.
• Reflecting frames, reflecting questions – if 'power over' is to be avoided.

Reflecting on Multiloging, E-communications and Distributed Leadership

The new ICTs and virtual realities have made more palpable what, for many, has been hard to imagine i.e., social construction processes, distributed knowledge, multiple identities, and power as an intrinsic quality of relational processes. The difficulties perhaps have arisen for reasons that include: our ordinary (Subject-Object) grammar (see Suzuki, 1979; Korzybski, 1958), along with; the history of ideas to which reference is made – including Cartesian separations, behaviourism, cognitivism and the dualist opposition of person and culture (e.g., Berman, 1981; Sampson, 1993; Gergen, 1994). Web sites, hyperlinks, chat rooms, knowledge platforms or cyberdesks, etc. are perhaps easier-to-grasp illustrations of the view that stability, boundaries, and singularity – the logic of either-or – may not be so self evidently 'the way the world really is'. Furthermore, moves away from such constructions also are moves away from the presumption that organising needs, or can achieve, 'top-down' hierarchical control and one coherent logic. Setting to one side the assumption: of stable entities, of transmitter-receiver models of communications, of language as representation, puts in question the presumption that 'power over' is either needed or, indeed, is possible.[5]

Our talk of *multiple logics* or knowledges is to be understood as a reference to different local 'fixings' of different patterns of possibilities where each fixing affords participants different ways of being and different possible supplements in ongoing relations. Such differences can perfectly well coexist, despite the common notion that e.g., leaders must shape shared notions of reality, or that organising requires shared goals or values.

Of course imposing one dominant voice may 'work' in relation to some reality constructions and values. However, it seems increasingly evident that 'homogenised knowledge' and knowledge that is 'fast' (Orr, 1997) may have disastrous consequences, more quickly and more extensively than ever before – before globalisation, the web, agri-business, worldwide travel, and current notions of development. In this context, some have suggested there might be a 'myth for our times' that could be more useful – in relation to certain projects – than the entitative myth.

A myth of this sort would put to one side the entitative narrative of Subject-Object relations, its reliance and emphasis on language as representation, and its centring of a singular, and in some degree knowable, real world. Another way of people and world making is found in the inclusive and multilogical ways of relating outlined. This said, our relational constructionist arguments[6] also suggest it is wise to avoid becoming too attached to any paradigm (Bateson, 1972; Bandler and Grinder, 1975; Berman, 1981). Acting slowly and inclusively involves living with possibilities rather than certainty, including multiple 'voices' or 'Other' positions, and taking care of patterns; perhaps the new ICTs might help.

Notes

1   Some languages such as English, are much more dualistic than others such as Japanese. See e.g., Suzuki, 1970.

2   This is *not* to be viewed as a relativist stance; these arguments have nothing to say about realism-relativism.

3   We could say that this has become the dominant Self-Other relation, coexisting alongside a more inclusive, participative construction that became 'sub dominant' in different cultures in different historical periods. The emergence and imposition of modern science – what Berman calls 'the Italian heresy' – played a relatively recent role in this (see Berman, 1981).

4   Buddhism speaks of 'beginner's mind' as open and ready – open to many possibilities – while in the experts mind there are few (e.g., Suzuki, 1970).

5   Again, it might be helpful to abandon notions such as being in control of the universe and, instead, developing something like 'right view' of interconnectedness and change.

6   Buddhism also advocates a reflexive position which proposes that Buddhism, like any other framework, should be held lightly.

References

Anderson, H. (1997), *Conversation, Language, and Possibilities: A postmodern approach to therapy*, New York: HarperCollins.

Anderson, T. (ed.) (1990), *The Reflecting Team: Dialogues and dialogues about the dialogues*, Broadstairs: Borgmann Publishing.

Bandler, R. and Grinder, J. (1975), *The Structure of Magic 1*, Palo Alto: Science and Behaviour Books.

Barrett, F.J., Thomas, G.F. and Hocevar, S.P. (1995), 'The Central Role of Discourse in Large Scale Change', *Journal of Applied Behavioural Science*, Vol. 31, No. 3, pp. 352–72.

Bass, A. and Hosking, D.M. (1998), *A Changed Approach to Change*, Aston Business School Research Paper Series RP9808.

Bateson, G. (1972), *Steps to an Ecology of Mind*, New York: Ballantine Books.

Berman, M. (1981), *The Re-enchantment of the World*, Ithaca: Cornell University Press.

Brown, H. and Hosking, D.M., (1986), 'Distributed Leadership and Skilled Performance as Successful Organisation in Social Movements', *Human Relations*, Vol. 39, No. 1, pp. 65–79.

Cockburn, C. (1995), *Strategies for Gender Democracy*, Brussels: European Commission (cited in Hogan, J. and Green, A.-M. (2000), 'E-collectivism: On-line action and on-line mobilisation', draft for APROS conference).

Cooperrider, D., Barrett, F. and Srivastva, S. (1995), 'Social Construction and Appreciative Inquiry: A journey in organisational theory', in D.M. Hosking, H.P. Dachler and K.J. Gergen (eds), *Management and Organization: Relational alternatives to individualism*, Aldershot: Avebury.

Coulter, J. (1989), *Mind in Action*, Cambridge: Polity Press.

Dachler, H.P. and Hosking, D.M. (1995), 'The Primacy of Relations in Socially Constructing Organizational Realities', in D.M. Hosking, H.P. Dachler and K.J. Gergen (eds), *Management and Organization: Relational alternatives to individualism*, Aldershot: Avebury.

Fine, M. (1994), 'Working the Hyphens: Reinventing self and other in qualitative research', in N.K. Denzin and Y.S. Lincoln (eds), *Handbook of Qualitative Research*, London: Sage.

Gergen, K.J. (1991), *The Saturated Self*, New York: Basic Books.

Gergen, K.J. (1994), *Realities and Relationships*, Cambridge, MA: Harvard University Press.

Gergen, K.J. and Thatchenkerry, T.J. (1996), 'Organization Science as Social Construction: Postmodern potentials', *The Journal of Applied Behavioural Science*, Vol. 32, No. 4, pp. 356–77.

Harding, S. (1986), *The Science Question in Feminism*, Milton Keynes: Open University Press.

Harding, S. (1987), *Feminism and Methodology*, Milton Keynes: Open University Press.

Harding, S. and Hintikka, M. (eds) (1983), *Discovering Reality: Feminist perspectives on epistemology, metaphysics, methodology and philosophy of science*, Dordrecht: Reidel.

Hosking, D.M. (2000), 'Ecology in Mind, Mindful Practices', *European Journal of Work and Organisational Psychology*, Vol. 9 (2), pp. 147–58.

Hosking, D.M. and Bass, A. (1998), *Constructing changes through relational dynamics*, Aston Business School Research Paper Series No. RP9813.

Hosking, D.M., Dachler, H.P. and Gergen, K.J. (eds) (1995), *Management and Organization: Relational alternatives to individualism*, Aldershot: Avebury.

Hosking, D.M. and Morley, I.E. (1991), *A Social Psychology of Organising*, Chichester: Harvester Wheatsheaf.

Janov, J. (1995), 'Creating Meaning: The heart of learning communities', *Training and Development*, May, pp. 53–8.

Jaynes, J. (1976), *The Origin of Consciousness in the Breakdown of the Bicameral Mind*, London: Penguin.

Knorr Cetina, K.D. (1981), *The Manufacture of Knowledge: An essay on the constructivist and contextual nature of science*, Oxford: Pergamon.

LeShan, L. (1974), *The Medium, the Mystic, and the Physicist*, New York: Penguin/ Arkana.

Maturana, H.R. and Varella, F.J. (1987), *The Tree of Knowledge: The biological roots of human understanding* (revised edition), Boston: Shambala Publications.

Orr, D. (1997), 'Slow knowledge', *Resurgence*, Vol. 179, pp. 30–32.

Pearce, W.B. (1992), 'A "Camper's Guide" to Constructionisms', *Human Systems: The Journal of Systemic Consultation and Management*, Vol. 3, pp. 139–61.

Plumwood, V. (1993), *Feminism and the Mastery of Nature*, London: RKP.

Polanyi, M. (1958), *Personal Knowledge*, London: RKP.

Reason, P. (1994a), 'Three Approaches to Participative Inquiry', in N.K. Denzin and Y.S. Lincoln (eds), *Handbook of Qualitative Research*, London: Sage.

Reason, P. (ed.) (1994b), *Participation in Human Inquiry*, London: Sage.

Sampson, E.E. (1993), *Celebrating the Other: A dialogic account of human nature*, Hemel Hempstead: Harvester Wheatsheaf.

Slife, B.D. and Williams, R.N. (1995), *What's behind the Research? Discovering Hidden Assumptions in the Behavioural Sciences*, London: Sage.

Smircich, L. and Morgan,G. (1982), 'Leadership: The management of meaning', *The Journal of Applied Behavioural Science*, Vol. 18, pp. 257–73.

Suzuki, S. (1970), *Zen mind, beginner's mind*. NY: Weatherhill.

Trungpa, C. (1987), *Cutting through Spiritual Materialism*, Boston: Shambala Publications.

Watzlawick, P. (ed.) (1984), *The Invented Reality*, New York: W.W. Norton.

Weick, K. (1979), *The Social Psychology of Organising*, Reading, MA: Addison Wesley.

Weigert, A. (1983), *Social Psychology: A sociological approach through interpretive understanding*, Notre Dame: University of Notre Dame Press.

Weisbord, M. et al. (1992), *Discovering Common Ground*, Ontario: Berrett-Koehler.

Woolgar, S. (1996), 'Psychology, Qualitative Methods and the Ideas of Science', in J.T. Richardson (ed.), *Handbook of Qualitative Research Methods for Psychology and the Natural Sciences*, Leicester: BPS Books.

Chapter Five

Personal Dataspace and Organisations: Managing Personal Knowledge and Identity

Marcus Wigan

Introduction

Identity and information ownership are increasingly confused: individuals have electronic identities which are in part the retrievable record of their on-line activities or that information which is held upon them on-line. The individual may seek to manage his or her electronic identity and in this management of identity the ownership of personal data. One of the key aspects of this area of dispute is the personal data space within which people perceive that they operate. This concept allows many of the attitudes and behaviours in organisations to be viewed from a productive angle, where networking, data management, data ownership and identity are reconstructed by individuals. The vulnerabilities of the trade-offs between web-linked identity and more restricted forms of external memory are explored. The implications for leadership and distributed management are considered.

The processes of retaining identity and maintaining corporate citizenship have shifted substantially in the last decade. The social and cultural expectations of business and organisational operation have moved a long way towards shorter term horizons for individuals as members of any particular organisation. This trend has been at least in part due to rising levels of global competition as well as a shift in Western cultural values towards more market driven models of society. Employees now have the potential to both join and to leave with very large amounts of data – which they regard as their own.

This greater fluidity in organisational membership has grown roughly in step with the expansion of information systems and their full integration into organisational structures. Information technology and communications now form a core infrastructure for many businesses, and common and critical infrastructure for many more, and the key tool for government administration.

As Information Technology (IT) has grown in importance and pervasiveness, the ability of individuals to own and leverage their own information and their own computers has also risen. This radically enhanced connectivity creates the space and place for the development of a more extended identity or a larger portfolio of effective identities on the part of the individual: the e-form allows for regular patterns of interaction between an individual and his or her network which were neither supportable nor sustainable on a face-to-face and shared same place basis. Home-based computers and telecommunications have consequences for the social identity of individuals but they also have consequences for workplace identity and for the management of workplace identity by employers and by workers themselves. Since portable computers became widespread in the early 1990s, not only does most of the intellectual assets of an organisation walk out of the door each night – but so to (to the increasing concern of IT managers) does multiple megabytes of critical corporate information. This trend emphasises the need to recognise that it is not only organisations who have gained massive information management capacity – individuals now also have the same capacities in their own right. By the late 1990s the most powerful computers were to be found in homes (running games) rather than on corporate desktops, so even the data processing power within the direct personal ownership of individuals has outstripped their capacities at work.

This chapter uses the concept of Personal Data Space (PDS) enunciated by the author at the first CSCW (Computer Supported and Cooperative Work) meeting (CSCW'86, (Grief, 1986)) held in 1986 in Austin, Texas. This concept is best considered by example. If you are asked at a random time during your working day 'how much information are you carrying?', the answer to this question is a measure of your own personal data space.

This amount of data has risen steadily, to a level where major information resources can be casually carried out without one being fully aware of it. This scale of personal data space has substantial implications for knowledge management, corporate security, and individual productivity and must affect leadership styles and assumptions of trust. Service and knowledge-based industries have grown substantially in the economy, and the differences of view as to who 'owns' data, and how the information that people feel they now wish to carry with them raises serious questions of culture, trust and control.

Personal Data Space

Checking how much data one is carrying about one's person is a good first approximation to personal data space. When this question was raised by the author at CSCW'86, this turned out to be 8Mb of floppy discs. This was a very large amount of data at the time, and was somewhat of a surprise to both the author and to the rest of the meeting. By 1998 this had grown to about a gigabyte, as the one or two CDRoms in one's pocket could easily be overlooked.

By 2000 this has risen to include floppy discs, CDRoms, DVDRoms and personal organisers, compact flash cards, memory sticks, smartcards and palmtop computers. A sample check while this chapter was being written was one DVDRom (5.5Gb), two compressed CDRoms (12.1Gb), a Palm Pilot (4mb), a Compact Flash card (32Mb) and a couple of floppy discs (2.8Mb). The scale has risen sharply – and the 10Gb hard disc of the laptop must also be added.

The amount of information that could be accidentally discovered about one's person in 1986 was enough to handle the critical elements of data on which one might have been working during the day. By 1998 it was enough to hold a critical fraction of a major database, by 2000 – with the addition of the DVDRom – it has grown to be enough to secure a complete corporate database on one or more areas.

The next trend to expand the efficacy of personal data space was the advent in the early 1990s of the genuinely portable laptop computer. This quickly changed not only the scale of the personal data space – but also made the information active and on line. The management of fully indexed documents, databases, and communications that the laptop provided changed two factors:

- data carried about was now immediately searchable and usable;
- communication with others directly from this resource was also now something that could be considered to be part of one's personal portable information resource capacities.

The growth of the Internet has now expanded access to information by several orders of magnitude – but only if one is actually connected to the Net at the time the information is required.

So what is personal data space now? It is now a key element in personal productivity, comprising:

- immediately accessible and fully indexed and searchable materials that you yourself have created, large databases that you have built, major databases others have created – including a large section of any corporate database on which one is working – and the ability to *act* upon it without the need to locate a library or contact other parties.

Arguably personal data space is now an active rather than a passive concept. PDAs (personal digital assistants) have had as much effect as the Internet on this. PDAs are not very powerful, but computer power is an increasingly ambiguous measure. Computational demands now peak in the areas of graphics, image processing, security encoding and encoding, computational physics, geospatial information, data mining and design. The levels of complexity of personal computers has risen steadily, particularly in the case of the market leading WinTel (Intel+Windows) systems.

However a better measure of power might now be considered the bandwidth of the connection to the internet – where the PDA or the WAP telephone both offer valuable immediate interaction irrespective of location or the amount of mass storage on the system which has climbed to 10Gb and more, even on laptops.

The link between immediate communication and PDS is the location of the data storage. We have dramatically expanded the amounts of data that we consider our own. It is not uncommon for people to have data stored on several web sites, each of which offer 100Mb of free storage fee of charge. This distributed personal data space raises further questions of information management, ownership and control. The data on a personal computer has ambiguous status. It is the creation of the user, if a program has been used to create a document, a database, a multimedia presentation or a statistical analysis. Increasingly this production is taking place outside working locations, and often outside 'working hours'. Even the tasks undertaken on home computers tend to overlap workplace tasks, and for many knowledge based workers the more demanding work may well be done at home, or at least outside the workplace. More confusingly, it may also be done on the individual's own personal computer, and at a location far from their place of work.

This personal data space is clearly a critical element in both individuals mode of management of information and the capacity to deploy it – and also a major intellectual property and control issue for organisations. Management now has a choice of methods of dealing with this. One reasonably common – if extreme – measure is to instigate tight controls of programs on desktops at work. Even to the extent of an automatic image refresh each night, so that a 'personal' environment cannot be maintained, the cultural and management aspects of this process are clear, and not necessarily positive. However this strategy cuts PC support cost substantially, but does not allow workers to customise their working environment or to manage their 'personal' caches of data and important resources as a PC now permits one to do.

An organisational response to this has been to move steadily towards workstations that have no floppy discs – and indeed may not even retain the programs in use except in memory, by using Application Server methods for the licensing and supply of programs, and by moving to network computer terminals (Melymuka, 1998) where all the data is resident in a central machine at all times. These strategies represent a sharp shift from the personal world of a well used PC with personalised programs, utilities and data files – but far less expensive for the organisation to deploy. However, the political problems of getting people to give up their own data space on 'their' personal computer is a delicate issue (Anon, 1998).

This management approach relies upon fixed machines always connected to the network, and ensures that data does not escape from the corporate network at all. This example also illustrates the small scale personalised data space represented by a PC set up to the taste of its major user is another area of personal data space that is likely to be challenged or removed. The issue here is not just the control or ownership of data, but personal control of another metaphorical space – the working environment represented by the hard disc and the screen of the PC on one's desk, and all the data one adds to make life a little easier to work with.

Corporate Data Space

This growth on personal control and management of data and processing has created growing risks to corporate knowledge management resources and to information security. Laptop computers are frequently damaged, lost or even stolen containing large amounts of sensitive or valuable information. Even when nothing untoward happens to these laptops, the integrity of the corporate data can easily be compromised by the work done on sections of the organisations' database that are worked on with such laptops.

The central control and synchronisation of Lotus Notes systems provides one way to address such issues. There are now increasing incursions into what is 'personal' in the workplace. Installing small programs on a desktop PC to make one's work easier is now only possible on laptops. The growth of connectivity also means that floppy discs or even CDRom access to the desktop machine may not be possible. Furthermore, in many of the new computer based industries such as call centres, the levels of surveillance and tracking of all keystrokes on computers has become endemic. Every keystroke can be – and often is – recorded and may be automatically analysed. Such an approach redefines what is 'personal' in such an environment.

The expansion of corporate data space beyond the individual computer has also changed almost all personal communication into corporate information. E-mail monitoring is often undertaken under the rubric of filtering for sexual harassment and other abuses for which the company could reasonably be found liable, This is a contentious issue in its own right, but it is not the inspection of the email that is the focus of the expanding capture capacity of corporate data space: it is the structure of the patterns of interchange that has become of real value. The patterns of e-mails are now subject to intelligent automated connection analysis as well as the content, and tools now not only exist to do the necessary tracking and analysis of networking and communication patterns (Wigan, 1991), but are now also marketed.

From a corporate standpoint, the analysis of email content and communication patterns can reasonably be considered to be uncontroversial and necessary steps towards protection from liability and towards building up better knowledge management in the organisation.

From the standpoint of an individual employee the picture may well be seen rather differently. The barriers between work and home activity have become permeable, and this lack of identification between work and workplace and home and private activity makes it difficult for 'private' space to be clearly defined. In the lack of such a definition, the ownership of work, information or other activity becomes inexorably drawn in to being perceived by the employer as all 'company property'. This is not so readily done when formal working at home arrangements are contracted for, as then the employer usually provides equipment, communications, etc., although the individual usually subsidies the costs of space, heating, power, etc.

Every key stroke can be – and these days often is – recorded and analysed, either in real time for performance monitoring or off-line for assessment purposes. The line between surveillance and personal space has been crossed repeatedly by this incremental extension of workplace management. Again, the cultural aspects need closer attention, but in a Human Resources database speciality report Lapointe (1999) points out that over 60 per cent of the data held in Human Resource management databases is in a real and practical sense 'private data' which only the employee can supply and update accurately.

Who owns *this* data (Wigan, 1992)? Who owns it if the employee updates it at work?

The blurring of private and company domains in the case of people working from home has the potential to bring in all the issues of company recording and surveillance of workplace telecommunications and computer activities into communications to and at home. The effects of this osmotic move towards control of private communications has already been tested by a US airline taking legal action including discovery of home e-mail records against workers posting comments on the web about their employer – and e-mail transmission of normal workplace-related union communications at work in Australia as also been challenged.

As such communications have no firm physical locus, these actions and challenges are likely to grow. It is increasingly unclear exactly what domain is personal data space. The distinctions between where data is held, where communications are undertaken, and the concept of personal and company time are changing. The steady growth in importance of tapping the tacit and explicit knowledge of employees is also affected by personal data space perceptions. Examples include those quoted by (Duarte and Snyder, 1999) where knowledge based worker teams avoided having conflict resolution or even any expressions capable of a negative interpretation on email, and restricted this to face to face interchanges – precisely because the data space of email exchange is owned by the employer, and has become an audit trail that can be discovered retrospectively.

Knowledge Capture and Management

The growth of knowledge work has drawn with it the need to master and manage more and more information. The need to respond rapidly, and to make use of the implicit and explicit knowledge built up in organisations is making the concept of knowledge management a real imperative in many companies. The company and the personal are once again blurred in their boundaries, and the modes of company knowledge capital building have critical implications for company culture.

The first signs of this have been the wide recognition that data mining and data warehousing have sparked numerous tensions over ownership of data within the enterprise. Database modelling and database designs now widely acknowledge the necessity of handling such turf wars early if the project is to succeed. Data mining and data warehousing depend more on reorganising existing stores of data and making them more effective for the organisation, and so have to contend with existing cultures that already 'own' different segments of the data. These common issues require careful negotiation and culture management, and many failed projects of this kind have faltered due to the lack of such attention. Different sensitivities and responses apply when knowledge capture techniques are applied to existing communication processes. These are new structures, where patterns of information flow and content analysis of such communications changes are essentially forms of action research which change the nature of the interchanges undertaken. If employees are not brought along carefully in such processes, then the natural reaction is to keep communications off line.

This type of response has been observed in a different form in public service organisations as a response to Freedom of Information legislation, where sticky notes and other forms of impermanent annotation were used to limit the damaging effect of the unknown levels of subsequent disclosure of views and analyses. The analogy for the current era is the use of personal email addresses and channels outside the organisation, anonymisers and other measures to keep a degree often tentative exploration and communication from the permanent record, or simply as a reaction to sustained dataveillance.

One of the most positive aspects of computer-enhanced communication has been the growth of computer supported cooperative work (CSCW). While this has had widely variable results, companies such as IBM and Boeing have gained extremely large improvements in project performance (CODA, 1999). There has been a variability of outcomes, and mixed and often disappointing outcomes from many group decision support and knowledge management deployments of Lotus Notes – perhaps the most widely used tool to date adopted by many organisations for this purpose.

Some Leadership Implications

The detailed management of all the communications and the analysis, content analysis and feedback from the successful CSCW developments are just as intrusive and potentially sensitive as any other dataveillance approach. However, the culture of the decision support and the project applications of these tools may explain some of the signal successes. The levels of trust obtained are a key feature in the IBM and Boeing cases (CODA, 1999). Trust is a critical element in any Knowledge Management, CSCW or any other team working environment. Trust management is central to virtual teams

(Duarte and Snyder, 1999) and this has an impact on leadership approaches and styles.

Cultural factors also play a part. In Australia in particular, close monitoring is not necessarily effective (Parry, 1996), and can affect the balance between maintaining an individuals' personal data space and ensuring that tacit and explicit knowledge is brought into play. The merging of corporate and personal data spaces is beginning to encroach on the 'private' aspects of many professional resources. The need for private data space is growing, as the quantities of information needed to respond effectively to change at even a daily level are rising.

There are differences in philosophy of dealing with this situation. Continued connectivity and capture of all interactions and exchanges is one more in tune with organisational goals, and expanded personal data resources within immediate reach (personal data space) in another. These two are increasingly in fundamental conflict. Organisations need to ensure data integrity, and so reduce the variations created by many different sub-datasources distributed over lap or desktops in many different people's hands, individuals often see their own space as including the computer that they use, even if it is fixed and permanently attached to the organisations' network.

The task of a leader is to ensure effective output from his/her team, but within the organisational constraints. To make effective use of the knowledge resources increasingly requires higher levels of trust across boundaries, and also depends on commonly held, timely and accurate data. The objectives of leaders and managers are similar but not the same, and social influencing factors become more salient for leaders (French and Raven, 1959).

A critical element of interest in this chapter is information power (Raven, 1974; Yukl, Kim, and Falbe, 1991). The use of information withholding strategies is unproductive in knowledge based work, but still is often in the interest of knowledge workers as individuals. The tensions over intellectual property and the use of personal data and intellectual resources increases as the boundaries between work and leisure in home and work locations blur. Many employment agreements require all ideas of intellectual property created by an employee in any way related to his or her primary work as the company's property via the employment relationship. The development of knowledge and skills in other areas has in the past been clearly separated, but in an era of process management where extensive leaning is frequently required, such boundaries are harder to define. This is perhaps more a personal knowledge issue rather than a personal data space issue. However knowledge is a special form of data in this sense, and ownership is a real issue.

The progressive blurring of time use at home and at work also changes the control and application of working time as well as leisure time (McCreary, 1999). The use of leisure time for work is increasingly having to be matched by leisure time inside work as the time trade-off becomes important for practical as well as morale reasons. Major companies such as Ericsson are now specifically addressing this. There are strong pressures to continually retrain and to extend one's personal knowledge and at the same time a widespread loss of traditional loyalty from organisations towards their employees. This is having the effect of many organisations cutting back on training as the rate of return declines with high turnover of those trained, and places the onus on the employee to make up to the full investment in training and development. This makes the issues of own knowledge and own dataspace all the more poignant. Two alternative ways of viewing the employment relationship can therefore be:

- securing the rental of intellectual capital; and
- extracting as much as possible of the capital.

This applies particularly in areas where imported tacit knowledge is important and efforts are made to secure it. Simply paying people for knowledge contributions provides a means of at least acknowledging such issues (Marshall, 2000).

Identity Issues

Identity issues are tightly linked to data ownership and apply equally well within and without organisations. Any processes involving electronically mediated communications and transactions will generate data, and will cumulatively provide closer and closer records of identity. In the extreme case of a digital signature (or a private key in a PKI (Private Key Infrastructure)) such as the OGIT (Office of Government Information Technology) Gatekeeper approach, once either can be secured (if necessary by simply stealing the entire computer, no longer an unusual event) then the identity of the person is severely compromised. Cases of identity theft are already occurring and quarantining the types and amount of data that exists about oneself or held by third parties is probably a prudent reaction.

In concluding on the issue of identity theft in the organisational context, it is important to recognise that employees are not the only possible category of those exposed to identity theft. Customers and clients are also exposed to risk. The internal loss of identity in the employment context may be tempered by the use of secure intranets and complementary security system – but customer relationship management database applications are a cause of unease for many in their role as customers.

Conclusion

This article has identified the emerging tensions between the possibilities of personal data space created through new information technologies and the organisational risks in the permeability of information barriers between private life and workplace presence. At the same time, organisations have much to gain from the time-space flexibilities of knowledge workers as a consequence of the new technologies whilst knowledge workers themselves may experience intensified surveillance as a consequence of the extended electronic monitoring accompanying such time space flexibilities. The concept of personal data space has been used here to bring many of these tensions into focus – the new IT environment contains simultaneously threats and opportunities in the new unfolding electronic drama and mystery.

References

Anon. (1998), 'Post-PC Politics', *Computerworld*, pp. 92, 94.

CODA (1999), 'Intelligence Community Collaboration Base Line Study on Computer Supported Collaborative Work: Final report', at http://collaboration.mitre.org/prail/ IC_Collaboration_Baseline_Study_Final_Report/3_0.htm.

Duarte, D.L. and Snyder, N.T. (1999), *Mastering Virtual Teams*, San Francisco: Jossey-Bass.

French, J.R.P. and Raven, B. (1959), 'The Bases of Social Power', in D. Cartwright (ed.), *Studies in Social Power*, Institute for Social Research University of Michigan: Ann Arbor, pp. 15–67.

Grief, I. (1986), *Proceedings*, CSCW'86, Conference on Computer-Supported and Cooperative Work, Association for Computing Machinery, New York, 3–5 December, Austin, Texas.

Lapointe, J.R. (1999), 'Revise Policies to Clarify Data Ownership', *Workforce*, Vol. 78, No. 10, pp. 103–4.

Marshall, M.P. (2000), 'Managing Your Company's Knowledge', *Agency Sales Magazine*, January, pp. 41–2.

McCreary, L. (1999), 'Guiltless Pleasures?', *CIO*, Vol. 12, No. 10, p. 8.

Melymuka, K. (1998), 'Hey, That's My Desktop: Users and executives can get touchy when you replace PCs with newer devices', *Computerworld*, pp. 93–4.

Mendel, B. (1999), 'Online Identity Crisis', *Infoworld*, 18 October, pp. 36–8.

Parry, K. (1996), *Transformational Leadership: Developing an enterprising management culture*, Melbourne: Pitman.

Raven, B. (1974), 'The Comparative Analysis of Power and Power Preference', in J. Tedeschi (ed.), *Perspectives on Social Power*, Chicago: Aldine.

Wigan, M.R. (1991), 'Cooperative and Distributed Work', in R. Clarke and J. Cameron (eds), *Managing Information Technologies, Organisational Impact*, Vol. 1, Amsterdam: North Holland, pp. 15–28.

Wigan, M.R. (1992), 'Data Ownership', in R. Clarke and J. Cameron (eds), *Managing Information Technologies, Organisational Impact*, Vol. 1, Amsterdam: North Holland, pp. 157–69.

Yukl, G., Kim, H. and Falbe, C.M. (1991), 'Antecedents of Influence Outcomes', *Journal of Applied Psychology*, Vol. 81, pp. 309–17.

Chapter Six

E-collectivism: On-line Action and On-line Mobilisation

John Hogan and Anne Marie Greene

Introduction

Using a case study web site, this chapter illustrates how interactional processes of the Internet have been harnessed by lay trade union activists ·to both challenge the oligarchic practices of the formal leadership of their trade union and give voice to membership interest groups. Such analysis is situated within a framework of trade union renewal thesis (Fairbrother, 1989; Gall, 1999; Heery et al., 2000) and mobilisation theory (Kelly, 1998). We look specifically at the potential of the use of information and communication technologies (ICTs) in contributing to increased internal democracy, representativeness and accountability within trade unions, seen as crucial for the interest formation and identity construction necessary for collective action.

There can be no doubt that unions have become less powerful and less demonstrably effective both in the workplace and at national level across the world. Commentators within the industrial relations field have debated the constituent parts of a trade union renewal thesis, notably Peter Fairbrother (1989) and which has also taken up by Fosh (1993), Gall (1999) and Heery et al. (2000). Renewal thesis strategies can be classified into two main areas (although they are obviously interlinked): the first dealing with recruitment and servicing of members; the second with organising and mobilising. We focus on the latter area of renewal. In addition, there has been some recent attention to the positive role that new information and communication technologies (ICTs) might play within union activity (Greene et al., 2000; Hogan and Grieco, 2000; Lee, 1997; Fiorito, 2000; Shostak, 1999; Pliskin et al., 1997). However, the role of new ICTs has currently been disattended to in the renewal debate in Britain, and therefore, we situate analysis of the potentialities of the use of ICTs firmly within debates about strategies for union renewal and mobilising collective action.

We begin by synthesising debates around union renewal thesis, arguing that organising and mobilising strategies offer most potential for supporting trade unionism in the twenty-first century. We then move to discuss current theorising around mobilisation, most recently developed in John Kelly's (1998) book *Rethinking Industrial Relations: Mobilization, collectivism and long waves*. We argue that this analysis does not elaborate fully enough on the importance of internal union democracy to the formation of collective interest, nor on the significant role played by ordinary members and lay activists. To illustrate our argument, we offer a detailed exposition of the case of the web site www.rogerlyons.com. Such detail is justified as it stands as one of the most extensive examples of the auditing, archiving and mobilising capacity of a contemporary lay activist web site and has been developed in order to force accountability and democratic processes within a trade union hierarchy.

Trade Unions and ICTs

Existing research has pointed to the positive potential offered by new ICTs in terms of aiding organising and organisational effectiveness (Fiorito, 2000; Lee, 1997) and in terms of fostering and enhancing solidarity and collective action (Shostak, 1999; Pliskin et al., 1997). This primarily involves use of the Internet, including such features as e-mail, web sites, chat rooms, bulletin boards, and on-line application and voting mechanisms. We describe such features as e-forms of trade union recruiting, organising, mobilising, and campaigning (Greene et al., 2000). However, research is largely based within the US context and both academics and trade union practitioners in Britain have been slow to respond to the opportunities that ICTs afford for organisation and mobilisation both with and beyond sectors and workplaces. In Britain, we lack the quantitative databases providing information about trade union use of ICTs and application on a national basis, such as exists in the US (Fiorito, 2000).

Such US research indicates universal use of more basic technologies such as word processing, and very widespread use of Internet and web-based technologies at national union level, with statistical analysis demonstrating (overall qualified and tentative) support for a view of ICTs as enhancing organising and organisational effectiveness. However, similar assumptions cannot be made within the British context without comparable data. Lee (1997) offers a useful compendium of the ways in which ICTs might be used as tools of union activity of all kinds, but the analysis is more limited in its theoretical development about the nature of union participation and collective action.

In addition, quantitative data such as that offered by Fiorito (2000) only provides us with a limited picture of the impact of ICTs on trade union activity. For instance, it offers little understanding of the social processes involved in technology use by unions, such as we gain from more qualitative and anecdotal research found in Shostak (1999) and Pliskin et al. (1997). Furthermore, the US quantitative analysis is limited in its exclusive focus on the national union level, rather than also looking at the local and individual level. There is thus a need for much more case study and in depth analysis in the British union context. Elsewhere, we have tried to begin building up a picture of current use of ICTs in the British union context, in particular focusing on the potential offered by ICTs, for increasing the transparency and accountability of union officials, mobilising membership activism and extending solidarity across global arenas (Greene et al., 2000; Hogan and Grieco, 2000). Here, such themes are situated firmly within debates regarding union renewal.

Trade Union Renewal

There has been a distinct move in recent years, away from renewal strategies based around recruitment and servicing of members (designed to increase membership numbers) towards organising and mobilising members (designed to increase participation and activism of members). This is not least because the servicing strategies of the 1980s and early 1990s appear to have been singularly unsuccessful. Additionally, the underlying assumptions of such strategies have been criticised (see summary in Greene et al., 2000; Waddington and Whitson, 1992; Black et al., 1997). Deficiencies in union recruitment have significant consequences for membership retention and participation, and the reforming of union bargaining agendas. That trade union decision-making structures are unrepresentative of membership diversity is widely recognised (Labour Research, 1998; Dickens, 1997), and Cockburn (1995) coins the term 'democracy deficit' to describe the present situation within most British unions. The low participation of women and minority ethnic union members is particularly highlighted and must be increased if more people from such under-represented groups are to be encouraged to join trade unions. Organising has thus emerged as a strategy of trade union renewal.

First, areas of potential membership, which have traditionally not been unionised should be 'organised', either recruiting new members in workplaces or 'in-fill' recruitment of those nonmembers in workplaces with union recognition. The most recent strategies for renewal have focused around the need to develop an 'organising' culture within the trade union movement, drawing on similar trends within the trade union movements in the USA and Australia. Such a strategy has been actively promoted by the British TUC with its Organising Academy, opened in 1998 (Heery et al., 2000). These organisers have been trained to recruit both in traditional and growth areas of the labour market, and therefore nonstandard, women, young, and minority ethnic workers are particular targets. The first batch of academy trainees has only just finished training, and so it is too early to really assess the affects of this particular strategy or of the diffusion of an organising culture throughout the movement.

ICTs offer potential benefits within this area of renewal (Greene et al., 2000). In summary, the use of ICTs can overcome difficulties in recruitment involving distance and cost. In particular, agencies and agents who were traditionally separated by the physical barriers of distance are now highly proximate electronically – they are in daily reach and range of one another. In addition, achieving close physical proximity of union representatives to members is very expensive. Electronic forms change recruitment frontiers because they enable organisation on the basis of informal resources, which is less expensive to organise.

In addition, the TUC Organising Academy is charged with attempting to organise activism within union membership, in other words to mobilise membership: that is to increase participation and activism of membership within the union and foster the willingness of members to take collective action. There is much debate about whether mobilisation should be encouraged (Bacon and Storey, 1996; Kelly, 1996, 1998) and if it should be, what the strategies are for mobilising union members. Within these debates, mobilisation theory has emerged as a salient tool of analysis.

Mobilisation Theory

John Kelly (1998) points out that mobilisation theory (particularly drawn from Tilly, 1978) focuses on the social processes of collective action. Notably this involves how interests come to be defined as common or oppositional, the processes by which groups gain the capacity to act collectively, and the organisation and opportunity requirements for collective action. Kelly's interest in mobilisation theory is in exploring *how* people come to see their interests as a common concern and generate within a group, a feeling of injustice, which is powerful enough to move an individual reaction or attitude to a collective response. Various elements of relationships and social interactions are seen as important in generating this sense of injustice and persuading people to come together in collective action in the trade union context. In particular, the actions of key union activists or union leaders are seen as crucial in promoting group cohesion and identity, persuading members of the costs and benefits of collective action and defending the collective action taken in the face of counter-mobilisation (Kelly, 1998: 35).

Overall, mobilisation theory is useful in its focus on social processes and in highlighting the multifaceted nature of participation and activism in trade unions (see also Fosh, 1993). Kelly points out that mobilisation theory as espoused by Tilly (1978) emphasises the need to try and gauge the extent to which members identify with the union organisation and the degree of interaction, or density of social networks amongst members (1998: 37). However, there are gaps in the analysis. In particular, improving internal union democracy is not specifically mentioned by Kelly (1998), in the context of mobilisation theory. This is even though one might argue that the extent to which someone identifies with a trade union may rest, at least partly, on how far one feels that their interests are represented correctly, and can trust that union leaders act in one's best interests.

Internal Union Democracy

One of the established prerequisites of renewal thesis (see Fairbrother, 1989; Gall, 1999) involves the need for union structures and leadership to be more accountable and more representative, with procedures allowing increased member participation in decision-making and policy formulation. There is thus an explicit concern to revive or revitalise the trade union movement by having decision-making bodies that are more representative of membership. There are of course also links here with the recruitment aspects of renewal: notably the concern for union leadership and structures to be more representative of women and minority ethnic members, such that workers from these social groups might be attracted into membership. This is also significant in aiding membership retention, in making union agendas more representative of membership demands, particularly for those segments particularly under-represented.

Fosh's (1993) research suggested that local union leaders (in our terms not only full-time officials but also lay representatives and activists), by their ability to lead in a way that encourages members to become involved and see the collective implications of issues that arise, can build upon surges of membership participation and interest, thus increasing the strength of workplace unionism. A participatory and collectivist style of union leadership would be more representative (demonstrating commitment to the interests which members express), more accountable (consulting and reporting back to membership and adhering to membership decisions), and more involved (drawing members into workplace decision-making) (Fosh and Heery, 1990). Such democratic processes could thus challenge the oligarchy of union leadership (Michels, 1915). In terms of mobilisation theory, identification with the union, and willingness to take collective action in support of that collective organisation, is thus seen as dependent, at least partly on how accountable, transparent and representative, the leadership of the union is seen to be.

Technological developments may have benefits for unions in this area (Greene et al., 2000). ICTs clearly have the potential to refashion union democracy, reducing the distance between bureaucracy and rank and file that is so harshly criticised. The proximity of union members to local, regional, national and international on-line trade union resources, through ICTs, increases the transparency of the behaviour of union officials to the union membership and enables an independent assessment of performance of officials, in a manner that was never previously possible. E-forms also offer a level of transparency through the use of intelligent auditing and search functions. Such technology is already used by the US electorate and pressure groups in the monitoring of voting records. It could also be used by individual union members or groups of members to muster and manage the performance profiles of key organisational actors and activities, well beyond the traditional surveillance capacity and skills of union membership.

The Lay Union Member

An additional weakness with mobilisation theory is that there is a lot of emphasis on the role of the union leader and one might question, where does such a viewpoint leave the ordinary lay member? Furthermore, much of the existing research has also looked at the use of ICTs by national union organisations and full time officials (Fiorito, 2000). The old adage that 'the union is its members' seems to stand at odds with the dominant debate around the need for union leaders to promote, persuade and transform the interests and identities of members. A different view is to focus on how lay members can play a vital role in defining both substantive issues relevant to the union, and the styles of behaviour that union representatives can adopt (Beynon, 1973; Darlington, 1994). The relationship between union leaders and lay members is thus seen more as a two way process, where the lay membership are considered as an important constraint on leader action. However it is important that the lay membership have sufficient channels to make themselves heard and force union leaders to be accountable and representative.

It is useful to focus in on the local level of trade union organisations: in terms of activists, those at branch and workplace level, whilst also looking at the participation and involvement of ordinary lay members. Such a local or micro focus is found in the US context in the work of Shostak (1999). Such local level analysis then begins to draw out the importance of recognising alternative interests and identities of union members. Indeed, this is a critical point made in John Kelly's final chapter, on postmodernism and the labour movement, where a variety of different interests and identities are seen as 'fusing' with that of workplace-based identity concerns. It is interesting however, that such arguments come late in the volume and are not directly related to the processes of mobilisation, such that we have little understanding of how recognition and representation of these wider interests might contribute to the fostering of collective identity and mobilisation of collective action. Richard Hyman's analysis (1997; 1995) offers some further elaboration, recognising the way in which collective interests as citizens, as well as more personalised life-style concerns are forming part (or should form part) of trade union representation. We argue that trade unions must be seen to offer spaces for the voicing of a variety of interests, and to represent such interests effectively in the name of union democracy (representativeness, accountability, and transparency) if collective mobilisation is possible.

It is interesting to debate how the dispersed methods of communication and information distribution facilitated by new ICTs, might offer benefits in this regard, indeed ICTs are seen as 'providing a material basis for transforming unions into more "discursive" forms of organisation' (Hyman, 1997: 326). ICTs can be used as complementary tools of collective identity to more traditional forms, making it less important to work on a permanent membership basis for many levels of solidarity actions (Greene et al., 2000).

In summary, the need for organising and mobilising members has become a prominent part of trade union strategies for renewal. However existing debate and research has neglected to consider three key areas. The first involves the importance of increased internal union democracy as a tool of mobilisation. Secondly, much analysis has disattended to the important role played by lay members and activists outside of the official union leadership hierarchy, exploring the voicing of varied membership interest groups, necessary for the formation of collective interests. Thirdly, there is a little discussion of the potential of new ICTs in these areas of increased union democracy and interest voicing. We use our case study web site as an illustrative example of how the use of ICTs has enabled activists outside of the central union hierarchy to increase the transparency and accountability of their union leaders.

The Case of www.rogerlyons.com

Methodology

The case study web site has been created by a lay activist of the British trade union Manufacturing, Science, Finance (MSF). MSF is Britain's fifth largest trade union with around 420,000 members. Its membership consists largely of professional and skilled workers drawn from both the private and public sectors, thirty-three per cent of which are women, although the leadership remains white and male dominated. At the time of writing, MSF was in negotiations with the AEEU (Amalgamated Electrical and Engineering Union) for a possible merger, a context which holds greater significance in light of events detailed below.

Material for analysis has been gathered largely on the Internet, surveying the official and unofficial web sites associated with MSF. The chronology of events, proceedings of testimonies and internal union interactions were acquired primarily through the web site www.rogerlyons.com. In addition, analysis has been made of popular media coverage of the events. Finally, contact has been made with MSF officials and the manager of the site www.rogerlyons.com. It should be made clear that we are presenting the data as made available in the public domain at the time of writing. We cannot externally corroborate the authenticity or legality of claims made, or of evidence presented in the web sites and public media we have explored. Thus, any assertions made are based on the evidence available within these public domains and are open to interpretation. In addition, the web sites are updated frequently, and we can only verify the content of web sites at the time of writing.

The background to the creation of the web site revolves around a number of recent allegations of abuses of union resources by officers at the apex of MSF, which have begun to reach the public domain through popular media and web site channels. We present the case through four sections. The first provides a chronology of the main relevant events. We then move on to explore how the allegations of misconduct have been processed within the official union organisation. We then offer detailed analysis of the www.rogerlyons.com web site itself, highlighting the way in which the controversies have been appropriated and mobilised within cyberspace. Finally we reflect upon the significance of the site in light of debate around trade union renewal, mobilisation and internal democracy.

Chronology of Events

The context under discussion begins in early 1999, when Marcia Solomon, who was formerly employed in the MSF Finance Department as PA to the Head of Finance Nelson Mendes, passed on information gained in the course of her employment about the financial behaviour of the General Secretary Roger Lyons and Mendes to the then Assistant General Secretary, John Chowcat. Lyons and Mendes were accused of petty and major fraud. The alleged major fraud consisted of setting up false bank accounts in the name of nonexistent union branches, known as shell accounts, paying union funds into these and then paying it out to Lyons' and Mendes' accounts. In addition, Solomon claimed she had seen mention of accounts relating to these two branches in the official accounts for the union, held by the Unity Trust Bank. The petty fraud allegations involved unauthorised loans, bogus expenses claims and misuse of Lyons' credit card. Amongst the revelations is that Lyons had managed to get the union to pay for household items, quantities of alcohol, and petrol allowance for family holidays. A host of other minor expenses claims have also been revealed, including 'a claim on his credit card for a 25p bun from Patisserie Valerie in Soho' (*The Guardian*, 23 May 2000).

This initial 'whistle-blowing' disclosure then set into motion a whole train of events. In particular, the involvement of the Assistant General Secretary, John Chowcat is highlighted, who brought the allegations to the attention of the union hierarchy. Investigations by the MSF General Purposes and Finance Committee, Personnel Manager and MSF accountants, found no evidence to corroborate the allegations made. Chowcat's reward for raising concerns was the charge of gross misconduct. He was accused of promoting the allegations so as to gain factional advantage. The panel selected for the disciplinary proceedings concluded that Chowcat should be dismissed. However, the decision to dismiss Chowcat was not executed. Instead, a 'compromise agreement' was reached, an undeclared severance deal that is thought to amount to £250,000, along with pension supplements, in exchange for a silent departure.

After a Certification Officer's report had been made, vindicating Lyons and Mendes, Solomon decided to declare to the union the full extent of her involvement in providing Chowcat with information. Her testimony at an investigation meeting (reproduced in full at www.rogerlyons.com), chaired by the personnel manager Tony Ayres, on 26 August 1999, at the office of the MSF, reveals that she was alarmed at the failure of the investigations and was concerned that the union address the allegations properly. Solomon repeated the accusations of serious fraud. She also pointed out that another member of staff could corroborate her claim that cheques had been made out to Lyons and Mendes from the fictitious branch accounts. However, the testimony indicates her concerns that union officials did not investigate the validity of her claims, indeed when she challenged Ayres as to what he proposed to do about investigating this other witness:

> He simply said that he was investigating the affidavit that I had submitted and that this other staff member had not submitted an affidavit. That was where it was left.

This appeared to have caused Solomon alarm, for she went on to state:

> The fact that Tony was so dismissive of the possible relevance of the evidence from another staff member confirmed to me that they were interested only in finding a way to terminate my employment, not to understand why I had made the disclosure.

What is more, Solomon clearly regarded her position as particularly parlous, given that:

> No credence was ever given to the fact that all my other allegations of unauthorised loans, unwarranted expense claims and credit card abuse had been substantiated.

Eventually, a disciplinary hearing was convened on 1 December 1999. It was decided that Solomon was to be dismissed. Solomon appealed against the decision within the specified time limits, but the MSF refused to hear her case. In July 2000 Marcia Solomon, backed by her union the GMB, took the MSF to an Employment Tribunal. As she states in her Witness Statement (also reproduced on www.rogerlyons.com):

> When I was dismissed, I was told that, by making unsubstantiated allegations about financial impropriety taking place at the highest level within MSF, I had breached the trust and confidence expected of a member of staff and had brought MSF into disrepute. By contrast, I will say that the primary reason for my dismissal was that I had 'blown the whistle' on this financial impropriety, specifically because I had alleged it was being perpetrated by Roger Lyons, the

General Secretary, and Nelson Mendes, the Head of Finance ... In making my disclosure to an appropriate person, the Assistant General Secretary John Chowcat (whose employment has also now terminated), I acted in good faith and without any desire for personal gain.

After four days, the Chair of the Employment Tribunal halted proceedings. It was apparent that MSF could not maintain a credible defence. Instead, on the fifth day, an out of court settlement was announced. According to *The Guardian* newspaper:

Marcia Solomon ... won a £50,000 tax-free payment in a £140,000 out of court settlement ... The deal involves the MSF union paying £50,000 plus VAT to cover the legal expenses of the GMB union, which defended its former shop steward. The MSF is also agreeing to take no action against any of its staff who acted as witnesses for Ms Solomon (Hencke, 2000a).

However, the case has not ended here. Since the ruling at Solomon's employment tribunal, MSF has been involved in two other public incidences of what can only be seen as attempts to close down debate about these accusations. This has involved a retirement settlement with a senior official who had threatened to air further accusations at a tribunal (Hencke, 2000b), and the case of Roger Lyon's former chauffeur, who has filed an unfair dismissal suit against the union, due for a hearing in January 2001 (Hencke, 2000c).

Public press coverage has been particularly derogatory of the conduct of the union. Indeed, such is the depth of the crisis of legitimacy, it has been claimed that the General Secretary of the TUC, John Monks, has advised Roger Lyons to resign. What is more, the press have suggested that during the present run up to the proposed merger between the MSF and the AEEU, the Prime Minister Tony Blair has intervened to insist to Ken Jackson, the General Secretary of the latter organisation, that no space be left after merger for Lyons (Hencke, 2000d).

The interesting context of events here is that the motivation for such a demand is unlikely to be due to political differences between the Prime Minister and Lyons, indeed the latter has been a consistent loyalist. What is more, the proposed union merger can be regarded as a manoeuvre that will actually increase the weight of Blairism within the trade union movement. Instead, we would argue on the basis of the evidence in the public domain that it appears that the accusations against Lyons are regarded as so serious and damming as to constitute a potentially long-term embarrassment.

Pressure for action upon the MSF leadership has also been expressed by members of the union in the letter pages of *The Guardian*. Of particular note is the petition posted in the letters page of the paper on 20 July 2000. Headed by the former Labour MP, Dave Nellist and signed by 133 MSF members, the letter read as follows:

> We have followed your articles on our union with horror and regret ... There is only one course of action which can restore the union's good name. That is to conduct a new investigation by people with no previous connection with MSF. We call on the MSF executive to arrange for such an investigation to be carried out without delay and to publish the findings in full to MSF members and to the general public. And if it is discovered that wrongdoing has taken place, to ensure the perpetrators are removed from their posts.

Away from the terrain of the mass media, there is considerable evidence that there are significant sections of the union that are not satisfied with the performance of their leadership in relation to the substance and processing of the allegations. Attention has been considerably sharpened by the fact that the union was going through a dramatic financial crisis. It was estimated that MSF was in midst of a financial shortfall of some £3 million (Hencke, 2000c). Activities were threatened with suspension and union staff faced the possibility of redundancy. Yet, the union paid out nearly £1 million in 2000 in pursuing failed legal battles connected with the aftermath of the allegations of corruption. The latter part of 2000 saw a proliferation of motions passed by MSF branches calling for the reopening of investigations into the allegations made by Solomon and others. In addition, eight of the MSF's 14 regional councils have demanded that Lyons resign and that the union hold an inquiry (Hencke, 2000e). It has even been claimed that up to 20 MSF full time officials, many of whom are identified as having been traditionally loyal to Lyons, have joined the GMB, the union responsible for representing Solomon. Finally, the Certification Officer has been approached once more and called upon to reinvestigate the accusations of malpractice.

Despite this, the General Secretary continues to assert his innocence and refuses to step down. On 5 August 2000, Lyons and his allies won a 26–1 vote for a motion that condemned 'recent misrepresentations in the media' – and appealed to rank and file critics to give their leader 'the same right to fair treatment as they would expect themselves' (White, 2000). However, the campaigns to reopen investigations and force the resignation of the General Secretary continue.

The Struggle for Accountability: the Official Processing of Account

Beyond the events just discussed, critics of Lyons and the leadership of MSF have pointed to a number of incidents that they believe indicate a lack of willingness to investigate allegations thoroughly and reveal marked tendencies towards the suppression of free debate and disclosure. These incidents fall into three areas: attempts to remove dissenting voices, attempts to cover up discrepancies and attempts to shut down discussion.

i) The removal of dissenting voices Attention has been drawn to the way in which Chowcat was treated. That he alone should be suspended, while the accused should remain at post has been heavily criticised for being inexplicable in terms of due process or fair treatment. It conveys the impression that Chowcat was at fault and that Lyons and Mendes were not. What is interesting is the consequence of these actions for the management of opinion in the union:

> Lyons made good use of the advantage he had achieved, organising a series of meetings for full-time officers and staff round the country. At these meetings he or a close associate briefed the others on the Lyons' version of events. This was clearly important in influencing the overall response within the union. It is reputed that Mendes also made good use of his time, with reports that he was seen leaving Head Office in the early hours carrying boxes of documents (MacGrillen, 2000).

ii) Covering up discrepancies The conduct of the investigations by the union accountants has also been called into question. In short, the objectivity and independence of the investigation is called into question due to the fact that the company has a long history of relations with MSF, which has seen the firm go beyond the provision of accountancy services, with intricate involvement in financial and personnel policy making. So, although the investigation was conducted by a department of the firm with no previous involvement with MSF, the extensive and intensive relationship between the company and union has provoked, in some quarters, serious disquiet about the capacity of the former to impartially judge the behaviour of officials within the latter. That doubt might prevail was given extra impetus when Solomon took the MSF to the Employment Tribunal in July 2000. Her expert witness, a forensic accountant, heavily criticised the accountants' report, indicating that the investigations had been far from exhaustive or comprehensive.

iii) Shutting down discussion   When dissenters within the union tried to question the process of investigation and discipline, it was made abundantly clear that critical scrutiny was unwelcome. For instance, Hugh MacGillen, the Secretary of the London Regional Council of MSF, wrote on behalf of the London Management Committee, voicing dissatisfaction with the dismissal of John Chowcat and demanding an open investigation of all claims. However the President's reply does not convey a spirit of open discussion:

> I believe that your letter indicates a gross interference in matters concerning relations with MSF employees, officers and staff, and violates their rights to agreed procedures. I shall be referring your letter and its contents to the next NEC meeting for the NEC to consider whether any further action is necessary (MacGrillen, 2000).

What is more, Cooke subsequently sent two more circulars to branches and regions strongly advising them not to discuss the matter at all.

Restrictions upon discussion were also experienced at the union's 1999 Annual Conference. Here is one account of how the leadership processed the issue:

> Conference did not discuss the current allegations of corruption in the union after a ruling by the President. The events had generated intense interest in the run-up to Conference. A large number of emergency motions were submitted. When the Standing Orders Committee sifted through these, they declared that only two were in order, from London branches as it happens. But before Conference could decide what it wanted to do with these, the President took matters into his own hands. He made a lengthy statement, as he had previously notified the Conference he would do. The gist of his argument was that the circumstances were governed by Rule 47(c) on disciplinary action against full-time officials and it would prejudice the procedures to discuss the matter in Conference. He therefore ruled that no discussion could take place (MacGrillen, 2000).

The drive to remove Chowcat and the processing of his departure are also suggestive of a desire to manage and conceal information. A decision had been made to dismiss Chowcat for 'gross misconduct'. Yet, a 'compromise agreement' was found that saw the union provide what is widely thought to be generous package of financial benefits in exchange for a muted departure. This course seems contradictory, unless one acknowledges that fear of public disclosure of the allegations weighed more heavily upon the minds of the union leadership than the apparent incompatibility of providing generous financial benefits to an officer who *they* had claimed was deemed unfit for office.

When members and activists attempted to challenge the secrecy surrounding the terms of the Chowcat severance deal, it is alleged that their inquiries were simply brushed aside and in some cases met with threats of legal action. One particular incident is worthy of note. An article appeared in the London Region Bulletin of MSF towards the end of 1999, entitled 'Scandal in MSF', which highlighted that allegations of corruption had been made and that a lack of openness prevailed within the union. Lyons instructed his solicitors to respond. Colin Ettinger of Irwin Mitchell wrote:

> ... there is an article called 'Scandal in MSF.' This concerns allegations concerning 'misconduct in MSF over the last several years.' Again this does not relate to local issues or indeed advance the interests and policies of the union ... There is an issue relating to the costs of this publication. I would anticipate that the union is already committed into a contract to pay the publication costs and these would have to be met. However, those who may have sanctioned the printing of this journal will have done so beyond their remit. In such circumstances it may well be the case that they should be responsible for any of the publication costs ... I would also draw your attention to rules concerning disciplinary action to take against individuals. In particular an individual can be removed from office if they have been found to be 'guilty of defalcation of the union's funds.' Defalcation of course means misappropriation. Payment for a journal/newsletter which has been commissioned in breach of the union rules may well, in my view, amount to such a breach (MacGrillen, 2000).

Apparently, Roger Lyons read this letter out to the Regional Council. He also received the support of the NEC in preventing publication of the bulletin. What is more, it is claimed that the General Secretary went so far as to contact the bulletin printers to tell them that they would not be paid for their work (MacGrillen, 2000).

In many ways Solomon's Tribunal hearing and the growing interest of the press in the corruption allegations, which accompanied the build up to and aftermath of the case, are thought to be the most significant forces bringing the details of the case to the attention of the MSF membership. Yet, the press was not the only communicative arena in which members of the union have begun to gain greater access to the allegations about the conduct of their leadership. One of the consequences of the Solomon case was finally to place some core documents in the hands of MSF members. We now move on to look at the way in which the controversies in MSF have been processed on an unofficial web site set up by a lay activist.

Challenge, Appropriation and Mobilisation in Cyberspace: the Web Site www.rogerlyons.com

This site is at the centre of the cyber campaign against the leadership of MSF and was set up by David Beaumont, a lay activist within the union. He created the site after reading the first *Guardian* article to expose the allegations:

> I was outraged when I read the *Guardian* article … I only buy *The Guardian* occasionally, but I use email every day. Other union members would email me newspaper stories as they came out and I began collating links to them. When I had a dozen or so it occurred to me that I could publish them on a web site … The site is there mainly to let people know what is going on by providing links to legal documents, details of Lyons' expenses and newspaper articles (www.rogerlyons.com).

The main features of the site (at time of writing) are as follows. The home page greets the visitor with a colour cartoon figure of Roger Lyons, a caricature of one of the figures from the TV cartoon series, *The Simpsons*. Out of the mouth of the figure comes the speech bubble, '*Mmmm … buns*', a humorous reference to the claim he made on his credit card for a 25p bun from Patisserie Valerie in Soho. The home page also has graphics of beer, food and hi-fi equipment swirling around the page, present at all times, to remind the reader of the goods and services that the union's general secretary is suggested to have availed himself of. In order to help assess the readership of the site, and the impact that it has made, there is also a specification of the number of visits that the site has received. In only six months of operating the site claimed over ten thousand hits.

Frequently throughout the pages of the site, the reader is invited to email the author to make comments on the site itself or on the issues discussed. There are also invitations to participate in electronic discussions, at one point, readers are invited to write to MPs who are MSF members. A feature that was added in November 2000 is an invitation to the visitor to register an on-line vote on two key questions. First, 'Should Roger Lyons resign?'; second, 'Do you think that MSF should merge with AEEU?'. In addition, the visitor can inspect how the votes are progressing. On 20 November, the votes in favour of resignation stood at nearly 90 per cent, whilst a similar proportion rejected the proposed merger. Thus, wider issues and concerns are brought into the discussion. Although sight has not been lost of the principal aim: the exposure and removal of Lyons and others implicated in the alleged corruption, it has also begun to widen its remit to provide a critique of the forthcoming proposed merger with the AEEU. To this end, there are links to detailed articles and commentaries that call into question the value of the merger and raise questions about the ways in which the MSF leadership is trying to mobilise and justify support.

One of the site's principal strengths is in providing a detailed archive of events, associated materials and connected links. Indeed, the chronology of events presented in this chapter would have been much more difficult and time-consuming without the resources offered by this site. For example, there is a link to 'Roger in the News'. In this section the visitor can see at a glance that the allegations of corruption have featured in at least 27 national newspaper articles in the previous six months. Each of these pieces, bar one, can be viewed electronically, at the click of a button. The stories cover the allegations, the denials by Lyons and other senior figures in MSF, as well as reports about the proceedings and outcome of the various Employment Tribunal cases, along with references to the dissent expressed within sections of the union. As a resource, this centralised referencing, combined with the automated links to the source materials, is highly valuable in providing a means to gain an overview of events at high speed and low cost.

In particular, the site contains a link devoted to the case between Marcia Solomon and MSF. This is an amazingly detailed resource. Here, one can see an affidavit by Solomon, along with a 13,000-word, highly-detailed Witness Statement submitted at the London North Employment Tribunal for her case held in July 2000. There is also the opportunity to read the aide memoire provided by Chowcat for the case. In addition, there is a day-by-day account of the tribunal, with accounts of the conduct of witnesses, lawyers and Tribunal members, as well as reports of stories and rumours circulating around the court. Added to this is a further link entitled 'Lyons Defence'. This contains a paper that details a document that was circulated by MSF to the NEC, branch secretaries and delegates to conference. The document is alleged to be the work of the MSF Public Relations Department, although it contains no specification of author. It contains a systematic rebuttal of the accusations made against Lyons. The paper analyses the case for the defence and disputes each point. In addition, there are links to documents that provide lengthy and detailed analysis of the alleged corruption and also provide a precise description of the union General Secretary's expenses.

David Beaumont is clear about the objectives of the site, which can be gained through links to Frequently Asked Questions (FAQs). Analysis of this rationale indicates firstly, concerns of the costs, both financial and in terms of reputation, of the way that the union leadership appeared to be covering up the accusations detailed above: 'My ultimate aim is to get rid of what I see as the corruption in this union that oozes from the top down'. Secondly, concerns for the union leadership to be more accountable to and representative of membership views, taking into consideration the participation of lay members are presented:

> I would like the union to be more accountable to its lay (unpaid) members. In the rules the Annual Conference of lay members is the supreme governing body of the union, in practice the NEC just ignores or subverts it. The lay members' democracy is constructed into regional councils. By the end of July more than half the Regional Councils had passed motions for Lyons to resign or face a new, independent inquiry. The NEC have refused to print these motions in their minutes, let alone discuss them.

Thirdly, David Beaumont highlights some of the advantages offered by electronic forms of communication, supporting existing research. In particular, speed of dissemination and interaction facilitated by new ICTs is emphasised:

> I find maintaining the web site relatively quick and easy. Email is particularly useful, with 10 minutes work I managed to email every single MSF employee last week and all 79 MSF MPs this week. I just wouldn't consider writing paper letters for that.

At the centre of the message disseminated on the site is a rejection of Roger Lyon's defence, supported with reference to official and internal documents (also reproduced in full for the visitor). David Beaumont claims to have no party political affiliation. Instead, his activity centres upon the union: 'I just want to be a member of an open, democratic and honest union. Is that too much?'.

Significance of the Site

Although the online documentation is significant, there are a number of other features that are particularly noteworthy. Firstly, the site provides space for those who are marginalised within the union. In a sense, the whole theme of the site is that of providing information to, along with a voice for, the blinded and gagged. Secondly, the site demonstrates the capabilities inherent within the new ICTs to allow for the rapid and cheap posting of sophisticated mobilisation materials. On the home page, there was an invitation to 'Meet Roger'. On clicking this link, the visitor was notified of a meeting:

> Roger Lyons is coming to the Yorkshire and Humberside regional meeting on Saturday 18 November at 10:30 a.m. in Wakefield Town Hall opposite the Prison. The meeting is open all MSF members. Ask him to autograph your expense claim.

The notice contained a high resolution picture of Lyons, thus making him more readily identifiable, but also it contained a further link to Wakefield Town Hall, which if clicked brought up a detailed Ordinance Survey map, so that all those who might wish to go to the meeting could find the venue more easily.

The site also contains reference to activities that indicate an awareness of the potential for the 'e-form' to break through organisational boundaries and to be used as a distinct weapon of insurgency. Here, particular attention needs to be paid to the link 'Staff Edition', which when opened revealed an e-mailed memo sent to all MSF staff encouraging them to visit the site. The significance of this communication is that given one can assume access to the at least near complete list of staff email addresses, the campaign to publicise the case against Lyons can reach the target audience in a matter of minutes. Furthermore, the rich content of the e-mailed memo, with direct hyperlinks to different parts of the www.rogerlyons.com site effectively places an opportunity to view the contents of the web site of the site in every e-mail in-tray.

Discussion and Implications

The implications of the www.rogerlyons.com site are hard to measure with precision, especially at this early stage. However, there is little doubt that it is important. It has already received coverage in local and national press, it has been featured in protests organised and reported at this the 2000 TUC conference, and has received a remarkably high number of visits. What is more, it has been reported that MSF have instructed lawyers to take action to close down the site (Hencke, 2000c) illustrating the significance of the threat that the site is seen to pose. As an aside, it is worth noting that the threat of closing down the www.rogerlyons.com site has already been anticipated and guarded against. Visitors have been warned that the site might not be there when they next log on, but that all they have to do is go to www.

notrogerlyons.com, a mirror site where all the materials will be transferred. Given the centrality of forcing greater openness to the site's campaign, the threat of being banned gives the site even greater cache.

The significance of the debate around this site is that it clearly links into our previous discussions regarding union democracy, voicing of interests and mobilisation of collective action. Arguments about oligarchy, have focused on the way that information can become the exclusive property of a small group of 'elite' union officials at the apex of the union hierarchy. The www.rogerlyons.com web site challenges this exclusivity, in a context where there appear to have been official efforts to prevent the disclosure of information and to clamp down on discussion. The web site provides a space for the voicing of grievances and the creative manipulation and presentation of information, which allow people to make up their own minds about the events occurring within their own union domain. It also allows particular events and issues to be linked to wider concerns and interest groups. It demonstrates clearly the way in which ICTs can more easily facilitate the two-way interaction processes within the union hierarchy, with ordinary members and lay activists finding the spaces to make their opinions and views heard amongst a wider audience, cheaply and very quickly.

The documents reproduced on the web site are not ordinarily and easily available to the lay member. While some clandestine circulation obviously would, and did occur, this web site places the material within easy access of a much wider audience. We can therefore reiterate our arguments that the proximity of union members to local, regional, national and international on-line trade union resources, through ICTs, increases the transparency of the behaviour of union officials to the union membership and enables an independent assessment of performance of officials, in a manner that was never previously possible. In addition, through a well constructed archive, lay members can trace and track through the unfolding of events; assessing the activities of the leadership over time, and preventing external agencies from breaking their history by disrupting the social relationships which constitute union solidarity. It is as repositories of collective memory that unions can give shape to conceptions of the past, present and future and in doing so construct sustainable worker identity.

What gives the site its greatest meaning is perhaps what it represents in abstraction. It may well be the case that the insurgency fails. After all, the internal machinations of any union, no matter how bizarre or dramatic, will more often than not pass the ordinary member by: it is highly probable that for the time being this drama is one that is going to exercise the passions of only a small group of activists and full-time officials. It is difficult at this early stage to assess what the real impact of the site has been in terms of the playing out of events around the accusations made against Roger Lyons. One may argue for example that events became too serious, and too wide-reaching to be covered up by officials and public coverage was inevitable. Indeed, it must be remembered that the initial impetus for the web site derived from the author reading about details of the case in a national newspaper article. However, the site has had more impact since then, allowing the speedy and most up to date coverage of events, providing a detailed archive and repository of documents and opinion, and providing easy, cheap and fast means of responding and participating in the discussion.

There is little doubt that such cyberspaces will become increasingly important in the future, as Internet use increases and electronic forms of communication become more and more habitual. At this point in time, what the www.rogerlyons.com site indicates is that cyberspace is a place where traditional patterns of cognitive policing cannot be exercised. What is interesting therefore, is that academics and practitioners, in the trade union arena have not really come to fully discuss the implications of new ICT developments for trade union action, particularly at lay activist level. Further research into the use of electronic forms could provide useful spaces for theorising about the nature of collective participation and mobilisation.

References

Bacon N. and Storey, J. (1996), 'Individualism, Collectivism and the Changing Role of Trade Unions', in P. Ackers, C. Smith and P. Smith (eds), *The New Workplace and Trade Unionism*, London: Routledge.

Batstone, E., Boraston, I. and Frenkel, S. (1977), *Shop Stewards in Action: The organisation of workplace conflict and accommodation*, Oxford: Basil Blackwell.

Beynon, H. (1973), *Working for Ford*, Harmondsworth: Penguin.

Black, J., Greene, A.M. and Ackers, P. (1997) 'Size and Effectiveness: A case study of a small union', *Industrial Relations Journal*, Vol. 28, No. 2, pp. 136–48.

Cockburn, C. (1995), *Strategies for Gender Democracy*, Brussels: European Commission.

Darlington, R. (1994), *The Dynamics of Work Place Unionism: Shop stewards' organisation in three Merseyside plants*, London: Mansell.

Dickens, L (1997), 'Gender, Race and Employment Equality in Britain: Inadequate Strategies and the Role of Industrial Relations Actors', *Industrial Relations Journal*, Vol. 28, No. 4, pp. 282–9.

Fairbrother, P. (1989), 'Work Place Trade Unionism in the 1980s: A process of renewal', *Studies for Trade Unionists*, Vol. 15, No. 57, London: Workers' Educational Association.

Fiorito, J. (2000), 'IT, Union Organising and Detours along the Way', paper presented at the LSE industrial relations seminar series, November 2000.

Fosh, P. (1993), 'Membership Participation and Work Place Trade Unionism: The possibility of renewal', *British Journal of Industrial Relations*, December, pp. 577–92.

Fosh, P. and Heery, E. (1990), *Trade Unions and their Members: Studies in trade union democracy and organisation*, London: Macmillan.

Gall, G. (1999), 'The Prospects for Workplace Trade Unionism: Evaluating Fairbrother's union renewal thesis', *Capital and Class*, Vol. 66, pp. 149–57.

Greene, A.M., Hogan, J. and Grieco, M. (2000), 'E-Collectivism: Emergent opportunities for renewal', in B. Stanford-Smith and P.K. Kidd (eds), *E-Business: Key applications, processes and technologies*, Omashu: IOS Press, pp. 845–53.

Heery, E., Simms, M., Delbridge, R., Salmon, J. and Simpson, D. (2000), 'The Organising Academy: An assessment', paper presented to the 18th Annual International Labour Process Conference, April, Glasgow.

Hencke, D. (2000a), 'Union pays £140,000 over Expenses Case', *The Guardian*, Saturday 8 July.

Hencke, D. (2000b), 'Third Tribunal Payout gags MSF Allegations: Union official drops victimisation case for £200,000 retirement deal', *The Guardian*, Tuesday 18 July.

Hencke, D. (2000c), 'Lavish Spending Union told to make £3m Savings', *The Guardian*, Friday 22 September.

Hencke, D. (2000d), 'No. 10 Tries to bar Lyons', *The Guardian*, Friday 22 September.

Hencke, D. (2000e), 'MSF Chief in No. 10 Talks', *The Guardian*, Saturday 2 September.

Hogan J. and Grieco. M.S. (2000), 'Trade Unions On-line: Technology, transparency and bargaining power', in M. Donnelly and S. Roberts (eds), *Working Together for Change, Proceedings of the Second Scottish Trade Union Research Network Conference*.

Hyman, R. (1995), 'Changing Union Identities in Europe', in P. Leisink, J. Van Leemput and J. Vilrokx (eds), *The Challenges to Trade Unions in Europe*, Aldershot: Edward Elgar.

Hyman, R. (1997), 'The Future of Employee Representation', *British Journal of Industrial Relations*, Vol. 35, No. 3, pp. 309–36.

Kelly, J. (1996), 'Union Militancy and Social Partnership', in P. Ackers, C. Smith and P. Smith (eds), *The New Workplace and Trade Unionism*, London: Routledge.

Kelly, J. (1998), *Rethinking Industrial Relations: Mobilisation, collectivism and long waves*, London: Routledge.

Labour Research (1998), 'Are Women out of Proportion?', March, London: LRD, pp. 12–14.

Lee, E. (1997), *The Labour Movement and the Internet: The new internationalism*, London: Pluto Press.

MacGrillen, H. (2000), 'Is MSF a corrupt Organisation?', http://www.londondefence campaign.freeserve.co.uk/msfcorrupt.htm.

Michels, R. (1915), *Political Parties: A sociological study of oligarchical tendencies in modern democracy*, Glencoe: Free Press.

Pliskin, N., Romm, C.T. and Markey, R. (1997), 'E-mail as a Weapon in an Industrial Dispute', *New technology, Work and Employment*, Vol. 12, No. 1, pp. 3–12.

Shostak, A.B. (1999), *Cyberunion: Empowering labor through computer technology*, London: M.E. Sharpe.

Tilly, C. (1978), *From Mobilization to Revolution*, New York: McGraw Hill.

Waddington, J. and Whitson, C. (1992), 'Why Sign Up? New Trade Union Members Reasons for Joining', *IRRR Research Review*, No. 6.

White, M. (2000), 'Union Leader Apologises for Flawed Judgement but Refuses to Quit', *The Guardian*, Monday 7 August.

Chapter Seven

Archiving Social Practice: the Management of Transport Boycotts

Miriam Green, Margaret Grieco and Len Holmes

Introduction

This chapter explores the capability of the new information technology to 'archive' social practice through its global access and infinite storage capabilities. The new information communication technologies move knowledge management away from a depository or repository model and into a network mode. Communities can as a consequence of global access reintegrate their identities through recollecting materials on their existence which have become distributed through history. The chapter examines the social archiving of transport boycotts and fuel tax protests and explores the implications of such archiving capabilities for the development of political negotiation and bargaining skills.

Montgomery, the Home of the Civil Rights Movement

Exploring the history of transport boycotts and their role in civil protest, we made use of the Internet and the World Wide Web to enable our search for materials (http://www.geocities.com/the_odyssey_group/boycotts.html). We knew of the importance of the Montgomery bus boycott in Alabama (1955/ 1956), of Rosa Parks and of the centrality of this bus boycott to the development of the United States Civil Rights movement. Our interests in and experience of Africa alerted us to the use of transport boycotts by African workers and communities to challenge their working and living conditions in colonial Africa in Salisbury, Rhodesia (1956) and Alexandra, South Africa (1957) – the Salisbury transport boycott was a key component of Miriam Green's Master's thesis at SOAS (Green, 1968, 1983).

As we examined and explored the Web for materials and began to grapple with the question of whether the Montgomery boycott (http://socsci.colorado.

edu/~jonesem/montgomery.html) informed the Salisbury boycott or vice versa or whether the two events were independent, we became aware of the capabilities contained within the new information technology for communities to assemble, collect and retrieve 'knowledge materials' which would better allow them to both continue with and recontextualise their past.[1] As we used the web to put together the story of transport boycotts and their significance in civil rights movements – we discovered that we had been missing an important part of the puzzle, the 1957 transport boycott in Alexandra had its precursors in previous transport boycotts in the 1940s in Alexandra itself. These boycotts were located inside the general strategy of boycotts and nonviolent struggle which emerged within the Gandhian frame of resistance to apartheid in South Africa.

The resources of the web could lend a new turn to the construction of *event histories* (http://www.geocities.com/unionsonline/eventhistory.html): event histories could now be constructed through multiple voicing where voices could remain distinct and separate rather than being submerged in the summary forms of experts and clerics whose job it was/is to record and preserve history.

At this point we were exploring the capabilities and competencies of the new technology in assembling popular or grass roots' history. We had not thought forward to the role the technology could play in the organisation, maintenance and broadcasting of contemporary transport boycotts. But as we explored the range of materials available on the Internet and World Wide Web on transport boycotts and started to engage with the question of why transport boycotts are chosen as a form of civic protest and what makes them such an effective tool in developing solidarity and gaining attention, we realised that we were now looking at a whole host of contemporary transport boycotts or transport related boycotts where the Internet and the World Wide Web were being used in the organisation, maintenance and archiving of social disputes.

Just as we begun to put our traditional transport boycott materials together with our new form IT transport boycott practices for development into an article, the fuel tax protests occurred in the United Kingdom. The fuel tax protests in the United Kingdom (http://www.geocities.com/the_odyssey_group/fueltaxcrisis/fueltaxcrisis.html) have made major use of the Internet and web sites – in taking this approach, they have followed on from the use of information technology in similar campaigns in the United States (http://www.gasolineprotest.com/; http://madaboutgas.com).The new information technology has enabled a new form of distributed leadership (Brown and Hosking, 1986; Brown, 1992; http://www.geocities.com/dian_marie_hosking/ldrship.html) whereby the coordinated action of large numbers of people can be organised through an immediate, easily operated electronic forum. Indeed, government action has focused upon destroying the credibility of these electronic forums in the public mind. The fuel tax protest web sites operate as contemporary chronicles of the action and interaction with government and in this way parallel the role of the Montgomery bus boycott web site in chronicling the history of the civil rights movement.

There is an important difference: the current chronicling of the actions in respect of government and the interactions with government of the fuel tax protestors is aimed at increasing the immediate bargaining power of that lobby.

This chapter explores the capability of the new information technology to 'archive' social practice through its global access and infinite storage capabilities. It argues that the new information communication technologies move knowledge management away from a depository or repository model and into a network mode. Communities can as a consequence of global access reintegrate their identities through recollecting materials on their existence which have become distributed through history. The chapter examines the social archiving of transport boycotts from the Montgomery bus boycott to the UK fuel tax protests and explores the implications of such archiving capabilities for the development of political negotiation and bargaining skills.

Repository, Depository or Knowledge Network?

The new information technologies have an infinite capability for the archiving of social practice: the smallest of agencies can now hold detailed archives of its activities and indeed detailed archives of the activities of all relevant others (the reverse panopticon). In the next section, we will explore the consequences of these detailed archive capabilities and the consequent capacity for social archiving in respect of emergent identity. Here we want to move in the simpler ground of indicating that the virtual archiving of knowledge enables a movement out of the traditional repository or depository knowledge model into knowledge network mode.

Historically, archiving knowledge was the domain of the privileged and the secluded. Acquiring, reproducing, replicating and storing information and knowledge required special premises and special skills. Only the resource rich, or those endowed by the resource rich, could establish the special facilities necessary for the storage of precious knowledge. The physical constraints and limitations of knowledge acquisition and knowledge storage generated a repository or depository model of knowledge management.

Accessing knowledge meant journeying to or inhabiting places of learning or having sufficient personal material resources to establish independent, private archives. The physical morphology of the distribution of learning, teaching or knowledge materials had consequences for power structures: the concentration of knowledge resources in urban locations advantaged those urban locations in respect of rural populations – the concentration of knowledge resources at the centre of colonial powers advantaged those colonial powers over colonised peoples. Distance from knowledge resources has consequences for the ability to bargain for social, political and economic resources. To give a concrete and current example of the implications of the geographical distribution and centralisation of knowledge before the advent of global information communication technologies, local researchers in countries such as Ghana were disadvantaged in the development of their 'authority' and 'expertise' by the holding of a greater volume of recorded knowledge on Ghana outside Ghana by colonial powers[2] and modern development agencies (communication, Professor Nana Apt, 1996).

The development of a public library system, a universal education system and working class literacy movements and the associated enfranchisement of working people in developed countries adjusted some of the social distance which had grown between urban and national educated elites and the majority of citizens. But still the walls around specialist knowledge and its relationship to elite training remained relatively unchanged – and the depository/repository structure of knowledge holding maintained the conditions for the persistence of elites, experts and the self-evidence of the need for leadership.

The development of distributed technologies which are available in the domestic location and which enable individuals, groups and movements to cooperate over distance with the minimum of scheduling and coordinatory requirements permit a new relationship to knowledge. The creation of virtual libraries and the globalisation of virtual knowledge locations enable the most remote individual and most remote community to be involved not only in accessing knowledge but in shaping and creating its form and enabling the access of others to that viewpoint, paradigm or perspective (http://www.geocities.com/transport_and_society/enlightenment.html). Indeed, African NGOs and institutions in countries such as Ghana have begun to make use of the distributed technologies to 'mark up' their own contributions to debates in development rather than simply using technology to access the 'expert' views of other locations and cultures – whilst there are many difficulties remaining in the attempt to describe alternative views through the use of the new technologies, institutions such as the Centre for Social Policy

Studies in Ghana have begun the task – indeed, Professor Nana Apt of the University of Ghana has begun to pull together the materials produced by the Centre but 'broadcast' through other institutions onto the one site, csps_ghana (http://www.geocities.com/csps_ghana/). This re-collection of materials is accomplished through the essentially distributed or network character of the new technology.

There are a number of dimensions in which new knowledge forms can be regarded as 'network' in character. Firstly, the ability of individuals or groups or organisations to construct knowledge sites which can link to one another in such a manner as to facilitate ready access to similar or contrasting sites whilst preserving independent editing and autonomy of publication is new: the on line 'linking' of knowledge sites is a relational knowledge form capable of distributing leadership. This first dimension can be thought of as a network of knowledge sites or a knowledge network. Network measures can be developed to explore the boundaries of such structures: reciprocal linking; overlapping contents; shared activities.

Secondly, the ability of individuals or groups to share a common cyber space or cyber desk allows for levels of iteration and incremental contribution to knowledge building not readily achievable in a physical environment – '10 minute activism' is the label already used to describe small inputs made by individuals into campaigns through on line forms, electronic petitions and bulletin boards, '10 minute contributions to knowledge development' would not be an essentially different concept. The second form of network we are talking about is then a network of knowledge contributors. Imagine for a moment, communities scattered around the seaboard of Scotland wanting to capture and record the history of the herring girls and their travels around the coastline of Scotland before the domestic presence of on-line technologies – it would have been a very difficult task. Imagine the same task with on-line technologies, family photographs and old letters readily scanned in and developed as personal pages with an 'index' location which groups and displays the total set of links. Indeed, such projects have already begun to develop – the *Digital Clubhouse Network* (http://www.digiclub.org/) in the United States creates cross generational linkages between older persons and youths where the older persons provide access to their memories and memorabilia of the Second World War and the youths record the history for on-line videostreaming and display within a virtual museum.

There are key features of the new knowledge environment which require registration: firstly, whereas historically identifying where knowledge was resourced and archived did not ensure ease of access – difficulties of accessibility and mobility were as great as difficulties of identifying the location of information 'holdings' – in the on-line environment, access is relatively simple when the location of 'holding' is known but identifying the relevant locations can be a time-consuming business given the proliferation of locations. The range of new information holding options and the healthy proliferation of distinct 'voices' in this on line environment is creating a higher round of network developments – the creation of meta databases and search engines to sift and sort the environment. This 'indexing' function might be viewed as in some way similar to the boundary management function of discrete repository or depository holdings.

Secondly, globalised information communication technologies and structures enable a readier contact and exploration of the distinct and diverse. It is easier to penetrate the on-line cultural environment than the physical social environment: the normal barriers of social type and social adjacency in respect of exploring the social framework of an alternative view are reduced in their significance. Put in social network terms, reachabilities are transformed. Local action or protest has enriched reachibility characteristics as a consequence of the new information technologies. The cost of globally distributed but parallel protests or knowledge building being coordinated is greatly reduced through the use of web enabling a higher level of effectiveness.

Reintegrating and Projecting Identity: Collective Identity in an Information Age

'*Azikwelwa*' or 'We Shall Not Ride' (Slogan of the Alexandra bus boycott, South Africa, 1957).

The new information technology enables a new relationship in the shaping and promoting of social identity: individual contributions can be converted into collective resources and collective tools with the minimum of coordination, correspondence or cooperation. For example, the simple indexing of on-line memoires or materials around specific events, institutions or processes can generate substantial resources for the reinforcement, development and display of collective memory.

In exploring the materials available on the Montgomery bus boycott (1955/1956), we came across a range of sites that can be integrated into a collective virtual archive. For example, the account of Congressman Lewis, an activist in the Civil Rights Movement, of the significance of the Montgomery bus boycott for the Civil Rights Movement provides an insider view of the social practices and processes of that time and movement – a voice from the civil rights movement on the significance of the Montgomery bus boycott (http://www.state.gov/www/dept/openforum/proceedings/2000/000320_lewis.html).

Although the Montgomery bus boycott preceded the African bus boycotts of Salisbury and Alexandra, the Civil Rights Movement did indeed have its eyes on events in Africa. Lewis tells us:

> Some of you may recall the March on Washington on August 28, 1963, when I spoke there at the age of 23. A few days before the March, I had been reading the New York Times and saw a photograph from what was Northern Rhodesia a group of black omen, in this part of Africa carrying a sign saying, 'One Man, One Vote.' For my March on Washington speech I said, 'One man, one vote is Africa's cry, it is ours too, it must be ours.' That became the slogan for the Student Nonviolent Coordinating Committee. And as students in Nashville, in Atlanta and other places around the South there were people saying the whole of Africa would be free and liberated and we couldn't get a coke and hamburger at a lunch counter and we could not register to vote.

The search for web material on the Alexandra bus boycott generated less detailed and less personal accounts (http://data.fas.harvard.edu/cfia/pnscs/DOCS/Struggle/geography.htm#Southern Africa) – but the material is sufficient to indicate the scale of the civil disobedience.

Sutherland suggested that the success of the bus boycotts in Alexandra, where thousands of people organised against a raise in the bus fare, demonstrated that a strategy which combines economic leverage with self-respect can mobilise and maintain a large scale uprising (from the Geography of NonViolent Struggles – http://data.fas.harvard.edu/cfia/pnscs/DOCS/Struggle/geography.htm#Southern Africa).

The web materials on Alexandra indicate, however, that bus boycotts were used in South Africa before the Montgomery bus boycott:

> Bus boycotts were carried out by the African people as early as 1945 in Alexandra township and 1949 in New Brighton; both were successful in preventing the imposition of increased transportation costs. In Chapter 5 we have described in detail the historic Alexandra bus boycott of 1957 where the combined might of the masses succeeded in halting the state in its attempt to place the burden of increased transportation costs on the backs of the poorly-paid African workers. Other campaigns include the boycott of beer-halls and dipping tanks, initiated by the militant women of Natal and documented in Chapter 9 (Luckhardt and

Wall, 1980; cited from on-line version, http://www.anc.org.za/ancdocs/history/congress/sactu/organsta10.html).

The Alexandra bus boycott was both a consumer and a political protest: the problems of transport organisation and transport costs from the townships to places of work (http://www.geocities.com/township_transport) placed a daily living burden on Africans:

> The overcrowding of the townships (and the complete lack of new houses) erupted into the shanty towns movement started by Sofosonko Mpanza; the problems of transport led to the first great bus boycott in Alexandra; the new Political awareness was expressed by the formation of the African National Congress Youth League under Lembedi, the starvation wages led to the series of illegal strikes among the VFP (power) workers, the milling workers, the coal distributive workers, the timber workers, and the building of the Powerful Non-European council of Trade Unions under Makabeni, Tlooma, Marks and others. These wage struggles culminated in the great Mineworkers' strike in 1946 and tentative plans for a general strike in sympathy (from http://www.revolutionary-history.co.uk/supplem/Hirson/Sthome1.html).[3]

So far we have seen no material which shows that the Montgomery bus boycotters were aware of the African practice but it does seem that the home of the bus boycott is Africa rather than Montgomery.

At present, the web materials around the Montgomery bus boycott experience and events are the richest in terms of available personal accounts and consequent multiplicity of perspectives. This is to be expected in a context where US levels of access to in-home communication technologies are higher, where community history initiatives are more common and more developed, where ensuring the availability of Afro-American history is a social priority. But there is nothing to prevent the use of low cost, hand held information communication tools being used to promote, protect and project community identities in Africa. Technology can power and empower identity. The power of identity takes on new significance in a world of distributed technology, distributed leadership and distributed social definition. At present, Gauteng province (http://www.gauteng.net/) in South Africa, in which Alexandra is situated, has developed a web site which broadcasts Alexandra as the home of past boycotts and struggles and invites inhabitants to make their contributions to its living history pages: the necessary index for collecting together experience and recognising identity is now present in this African location.

The bus boycotts were an important device for black South African leaders in their efforts to achieve solidarity and reference to the bus boycotts and their role in the independence struggle is now to be found in the obituaries of these past leaders:

> The obituary of John Pule published in Sechaba, 1989 and reproduced on the Web: During the Alexandra bus boycott in 1957, at the time of the historic Treason Trial, it became John Pule's main task to coordinate with other areas in conducting a solidarity boycott in Soweto. Political activist, organiser and fighter, he was in the centre of the whirlwind (http://www.sacp.org.za/biographies/ jpmotshabi.html).

An obituary also reproduced and relayed on the web provides us with the information on the leader of the 1957 Alexandra bus boycott – the obituary of Alfred Nzo (http://www.mg.co.za/mg/za/archive/2000jan/13janpm-news. html#nzo):

> Nzo has a long and distinguished career as a leader in the liberation struggle, he was behind the 1957 Alexandra bus boycott and was a key figure in the ANC delegation that was [*sic*] participated in talks with the apartheid government in the negotiations leading up to the 1994 elections.

Obituaries are not personal accounts of lived experience, nor are the obituaries of leaders likely to give access to the lived experience of rank and file – but these materials clearly represent a beginning and a new way of collecting together history and making a claim on identity within a global communication space (Little, Holmes and Grieco, 2000).

Holding the Front of the Stage: Distributed Technology, Knowledge Building and the Maintenance of Dispute

The earlier sections of this chapter indicated that the importance of the new technology is not simply in its infinite archive capability nor is it located simply in the ability to access knowledge from remote locations rather the importance of the new technology may very well lie in its ability to knowledge build from remote locations. Knowledge building has been neglected in the context where the focus has fallen upon access to 'expert' knowledge – knowledge which may be impaired by the lack of adequate feedback.

Here, we will explore some of the on-line tools and protocols that transport activists have used in knowledge building in recent consumer/electorate versus government/international business disputes but before moving to this bustling and thriving sector of on-line politics in the developed world, we want to return to South Africa.

The bus boycotts formed very important tools for the development of solidarity in the liberation movements of Africa and of Afro-Americans in the United States. With the emergence of black African leadership in Africa and improved equity arrangements in the United States, the strength of the transport boycott tool for manifesting civic protest does not disappear. Boycotts provide visible public outcomes, remain within the law and often have readily actionable enforcement dynamics: it is easy to see who breaks the boycott and uses public transport rather than walk – they are visible for the duration of their journey. Shunning the offending party is a dynamic which communities can and do enact. The new South Africa aware of its own history on transport boycotts has built into its *policy documents* devices and procedures for combatting unauthorised transport boycotts (http://www.transport.gov.za/docs/ annual/section5.html): a quick review of the tasks of the Road Task Inspectorate is instructive: 'Road task inspectorate: … Combatting unauthorised road transport, bus boycotts and taxi violence'.

Maintaining collective memory of struggle has a sting in its tale. The archiving of social practice is a political activity and the archiving of local political voice represents a challenge which is already visible on the web.

Fuel charge and tax protests have now taken place in the United States, Australia, Europe and the United Kingdom. There is clearly global learning going on in respect of social and political practice. A key strategy is of knowledge building detailed information on the variations in fuel prices across the whole geography of any particular country. 'Eye on the pump' campaigns (http://www.geocities.com/the_odyssey_group/fueltaxcrisis/fueltaxcrisis. html) are to be found from Scotland across the Atlantic to Wisconsin. Each individual simply enters the local details on a common on-line form and the information aggregates to a collective national picture automatically: the information search costs are dramatically reduced and political campaigns effectively informed and able to enhance their bargaining stance.

Comparable with the aggregated information arrangements, transport activists have been making use of *electronic petitioning* technology (http:// www.lowerpricedfuel.co.uk/) – a technology which enables the transport activist lobbies to demonstrate the scale of their support both before government and in front of the general public.

The updating or daily chronicling of activities is another function performed effectively by the distributed, globalised technology. The technology provides an ability to counter the claims of government and international business with on-line real time streamed images of action – a consistent UK site in this respect was http://www.fuelprotest.com/. Characterising peaceful protest as overly aggressive or criminal is more difficult when web-cam technology is in use.[4]

These are but a few of the features of the new world of transport boycotts and protests: taken together, they demonstrate an ability to maintain global presence, knowledge building and the context for the enhancement of popular bargaining and politics. 'Ten minute' activism on a network model can generate information and personnel resources which match those of the very large agencies in society. It is a new landscape with an old history of collective action: the dimensions of restricting of mobility and overcoming difficulties of accessibility are old political tools. The prospect of virtual mobility and accessibility has consequences for the political terrain of the physical: tele-assembly, an association tool which was inconceivable is now a reality. Tolpuddle Martyrs to tele-assembly: it is a transport journey worth considering.

Conclusion: Archiving Social Practice, a Future for Community Information Technology

The time dimension of political action and of framing that action has developed a critical significance within the politics afforded by the new technologies: through archiving, action can be recontextualised. Agents and agencies which at the point of initiation of political action seemed doomed to lose can readily broadcast their triumph and request of others a more careful reconsideration of prospects for collective action in the future – consider the Liverpool dockers (http://www.labournet.net/docks2/other/update.htm#Liverpool).

Within the new time relationships and political relationships of electronic adjacency, the phenomenon of collective memory is heightened (Grieco, 1996). Protests can now be linked across time as well as space. Technology developers, grass root organisations and government agencies have all become aware of the potential of the new technologies to 'join up' communities which are in disrepair and which have become fragmented by the severance of urban design and modern scheduling pressures: '10 minute' link ups to social activities in a technology which offers both 'real time' and asynchronous modes will increasingly be on offer.

In such a frame, 10 minute activism is likely find a significant place: organising boycotts in such a context is, as we have seen here, a relatively simple business. Historically, campaigns and political activities required a high degree of coordination and administration: through new technology effective campaigns can be pursued with a lesser requirement for continuous and constant coordination.

On-line consumer campaigns to pressure industry and government are the order of the day; similarly, on-line community campaigns to promote and protect neighbourhoods have begun to emerge (see, for example, the case of the Craigmillar estate in Edinburgh, http://www.ccis.org.uk/; http://www. partnerships.org.uk/articles/ccis1.html). The development and refinement of community information technologies which enable the indexing, broadcasting and strategising of community experience and preferences are clearly not far away.

The Digital Clubhouse Network (http://www.digiclub.org/) with its heavy involvement of technology developers, opens the door on what the future might look like: imagine the Montgomery bus boycott and the Civil Rights movement streamed on-line, real-time globally.

I have a dream ...

Notes

1   'Recontextualisation' is here taken to mean the reframing of the context of past action in the light of knowledge of outcomes. Argyris and Schon (1974, 1978) use the term 'double loop learning', broadly similar in meaning to Bateson's notion of 'deuterolearning' (Bateson, 1972) in respect of managerial and organisational learning. The issue we wish to call attention to here is the archiving and retrieval potential of the web for hitherto poorly resourced and subordinated groups to challenge the dominant modes of framing of the contexts in which they engaged (Grieco and Holmes, 1990; Holmes and Grieco, 1991).

2   See also Law (1986) on methods of long-distance control, which are central to the dominance of the West since the sixteenth century, also Latour (1987) on 'centres of calculation' (Chapter 6).

3   See the ANC's archive of historical documents for the webpage on the miners' strike of 1946 (http://www.anc.org.za/ancdocs/history/misc/miners.html).

4   Web-cam technology provides live streaming of digital images from a camera connected to a PC, linked to the internet. Such technology is now robust and inexpensive, often bundled with entry-level personal computer systems.

References

Brown, H. (1992), *Women Organising*, London: Routledge.

Brown, H. and Hosking, D.M. (1986), 'Distributed Leadership and Skilled Performance as Successful Organisation in Social Movements', *Human Relations*, No. 1.

Green, M. (1968), 'The Bus Boycott, Salisbury, 1956', unpublished MA dissertation, London: School of African Studies.

Green, M. (1983), 'The Salisbury Bus Boycott, 1956', *History in Zambia, Journal of the Historical Association of Zambia*, No. 13.

Grieco, M. (1996), *Workers' Dilemmas*, London: Routledge.

Grieco, M. and Holmes, L. (1990) 'Radical Beginnings, Conventional Ends? Organizational Transformation – a Problem in the Development of Radical Organizations', in G. Jenkins and M. Poole (eds), *New Forms of Ownership*, London: Routledge.

Holmes, L. and Grieco, M. (1991), 'Overt Funding, Buried Goals, and Moral Turnover: The organizational transformation of radical experiments', *Human Relations*, Vol. 44, No. 7, 1991.

Latour, B. (1987), *Science in Action*, Milton Keynes: Open University Press.

Law, J. (1986), 'On the Methods of Long-distance Control: Vessels, navigation and the Portuguese route to India', in J. Law (ed.), *Power, Action and Belief: A New Sociology of Knowledge?*, London: Routledge & Kegan Paul.

Lewis, Congressman John (D-5, GA) Chief Deputy Democratic Whip, US House of Representatives (2000), 'Winds of Change: Civil Rights and Democratic Progress', Secretary's Open Forum, 20 March.

Little, S., Holmes, L. and Grieco, M. (2000), 'Calling up Culture: Information spaces and information flows as the virtual dynamics of inclusion and exclusion', paper presented at IFIP WG9.4 Conference: *Information Flows, Local Improvisations and Work Practices*, Cape Town, May.

Luckhardt and Wall (1980), Organize ... or starve!: The History of the South African Congress of Trade Unions, London: Lawrence and Wishart (on-line version at http://www.anc.org.za/ancdocs/history/congress/sactu/organsta00.html).

Mokonyane, D. (1994), 'The Bus Boycott in South Africa: Lessons of Azikwelwa', 2nd edn, London: Nakong Ya Rena.

Living Links

Archiving social practice (http://www.geocities.com/the_odyssey_group/boycotts.html).

Calling up culture: information spaces and information flows as the virtual dynamics of inclusion and exclusion, by Len Holmes, Steve Little and Margaret Grieco delivered in Cape Town, SA at IFIP 2000 (http://www.geocities.com/stephen_e_little/callup.html).

Digital Clubhouse Network (http://www.digiclub.org/) http://www.geocities.com/
    the_odyssey_group/fueltaxcrisis/fueltaxcrisis.htmlevent histories: multiple voicing
    (http://www.geocities.com/unionsonline/eventhistory.html).
Fuel tax protests 2000 (http://www.geocities.com/the_odyssey_group/fueltaxcrisis/
    fueltaxcrisis.html).
Montgomery boycott (http://socsci.colorado.edu/~jonesem/montgomery.html).
Transport and Society Network (http://www.geocities.com/transport_and_society).

Chapter Eight

Changing Contours, Changing Technology: Aboriginal Participation in Administration in the Northern Territory

Perry Morrison

The literature on grassroots participation in electronic administration and governance has been scant with much dependence and citing of a few well known cases. The case study presented here aims to begin the enlargement of the case study literature in respect of the grassroots experience, opportunities and potential in electronic administration and governance (Forester and Morrison, 1993). A number of federally-funded projects are now underway in the Northern Territory with the common task of improving access and usage of Internet, e-mail and broadband applications such as videoconferencing. Indeed, Australia is in the interesting situation of possessing virtually First World communication infrastructure over much of the continent while simultaneously having Third World health and living conditions amongst its remote Aboriginal peoples. This combination is an interesting test case of the promise of modern telecommunications to kick start e-commerce and communications mediated development in the Developing World. However, as this chapter will demonstrate, technofixes for complex political, economic and social problems are not as simple as they seem, and the issues revealed in the Australian context have a strong resonance with the promises of the Green Revolution and earlier 'trickle down' models of economic development based on innovation diffusion.

Introduction

Many international bodies and agencies such as UNDP and the World Bank are embracing information technology (IT), telecommunications and the Internet in particular as promising new vehicles for accelerating development of the least developed countries.[1] In part, this support is based on the need for such countries to move beyond primary production and cash economies and for them to partake in the opportunities afforded by e-commerce and the emerging cyber-economy. In addition, Internet and related technologies are being investigated as more efficient mechanisms for delivery of government services, health care and a huge range of civil administration in remote areas.

A number of federally-funded projects are now underway in the Northern Territory with the common task of improving access and usage of Internet, e-mail and broadband applications such as videoconferencing. Indeed, Australia is in the interesting situation of possessing virtually first world communication infrastructure over much of the continent while simultaneously having Third World health and living conditions amongst its remote Aboriginal peoples. This combination is an interesting test case of the promise of modern telecommunications to kick start e-commerce and communications mediated development in the Developing World. However, as this chapter will demonstrate, technofixes for complex political, economic and social problems are not as simple as they seem (Forester and Morrison, 1993), and the issues revealed in the Australian context have a strong resonance with the promises of the green revolution and earlier 'trickle down' models of economic development based on innovation diffusion.

Background

The physical geography and human demography of Australia's Northern Territory are extreme to say the least. It occupies 1.35m km² and yet holds people 195,000[2] or approximately 6 per cent of the national population. Aboriginal people make up 28 per cent of the Northern Territory and 70 per cent of them live in communities of less than 1,000 people. Many communities hold fewer than 50 people and consist of sheds without power, reliable water sources or road access.

These indigenous people exhibit social indicators that place them at Third World levels. Their average life span is approximately 20 years less than non-Aboriginal Australians and, like Indigenous populations elsewhere, the incidence of heart disease, diabetes and chronic obstructive airborne disease is at epidemic levels.[3] On the Tiwi Islands, north of Darwin, the Menzies School of Health research has reported that the local population exhibits the highest rate of kidney disease of any population on the planet.

In terms of communications, quite obviously these communities face extreme challenges. Poor infrastructure, low skill bases, climatic extremes, cultural issues and simple remoteness make the establishment and maintenance of facilities very difficult. Very high levels of staff turnover also undermines the long term effectiveness of training efforts. In some communities, staff last a matter of weeks and the average stay for local government personnel is between six and 12 months.

In general, what urban dwellers would reject as unacceptable in communications capability is usually the norm in remote parts of Northern Australia. Very low bandwidth, unreliable terrestrial links and slow, expensive satellite links make Internet connectivity impossible for a large percentage of Australians who need it the most to help overcome the practical and emotional problems that go hand in hand with extreme isolation.

Although none of these problems can be solved in the immediate future, nevertheless, it is obvious that there must be an on-going effort to incorporate remote regions of Australia into the medium of Internet/e-mail and higher bandwidth communications.

Community Context

The structure of remote Aboriginal communities in the Northern Territory generally involves a clinic, school, essential services officer (power generation, sanitation, etc.), women's centre or arts centre, sports/recreation club and community council. The council is mainly comprised of community representatives (elders, traditional land owners and others) but is headed by a council clerk who is appointed by the Northern Territory government. Often a Community Development Employment Program (CDEP) officer is appointed. The Community Development Employment Program is the equivalent of a 'work for the dole' scheme for people living in Aboriginal communities, although those enrolled are not regarded as unemployed for the purposes of federal government statistics.

In terms of the actual running and physical characteristics of these communities, it is an understatement to regard them as places of extremes. Many are cut off by road for up to half the year by flooding in the wet season. Cyclones are a regular feature between November and March each year and the central part of the Territory experiences the temperature extremes common to sandy deserts.

Northern Territory Communications Projects

A number of communications projects have been undertaken in the Northern Territory over the last two to three years – all funded under the Regional Telecommunications Infrastructure Fund from the sale of Telstra.

The Outback Digital Network is a 'federated' arrangement of five Aboriginal media organisations based in Darwin, Broome, Alice Springs, Cape York and Tennant Creek. The Outback Digital Network is tasked with improving communications in 'up to 200 communities' across Northern Australia with approximately A$15m in funding set aside from the Regional Telecommunications Infrastructure Fund for this purpose. The range of services to be provided by the Outback Digital Network is not specific and potentially incorporates phone access, Internet access, videoconferencing capabilities, local area networks, mobile phone and wireless local loop, and satellite and terrestrial links of various kinds, as well as the range of terminal equipment needed to support these services. At this point, the Outback Digital Network has undertaken a lengthy community consultation process and has been engaged in on-going discussions over the selection of a carrier since January 2000.

The Electronic Outback Project is a Northern Territory government project funded to the tune of approximately A$3m from the Regional Telecommunications Infrastructure Fund and tasked with providing improved communications capabilities in four to six Northern Territory communities initially. The Electronic Outback Project is also in the process of finalising its carrier negotiations.

The Local Government Association of the Northern Territory have completed a number of pilot projects aimed at providing Internet access and appropriate training for community council staff. They are now about to undertake an A$800,000 Regional Telecommunications Infrastructure Fund funded project to extend these services to all 66 local government bodies in the Northern Territory (Morrison, 2000). By any measure, the Local Government Association of the Northern Territory projects have all been outstanding successes – partly because their objectives are clear and achievable and partly because they can be implemented without the need for complex carrier negotiations to deliver commercial viability.

In cooperation with the Local Government Association of the Northern Territory, Northern Territory Library Services have also provided Internet access and training in Internet usage as well as an introduction to web page design for librarians in rural and remote communities. The author has been involved in all of these projects (except EOP) as either an implementer or evaluator.

Basic Objectives

Although each of the above projects have addressed specific groups and needs, there is a common objective in providing increased access to the Internet as well as expertise in its usage. ODN and EOP have had larger objectives – including the provision of bandwidth and equipment to deliver more advanced services.

In general, using communications technology to assist in the development of remote parts of Australia and to address the particular problems faced by remote Aboriginal people is a very attractive notion. Current service delivery to these communities is usually based on a 'fly-in/fly-out' mode where bureaucrats and administrators rarely stay for longer than a day or two. This mode of service delivery is horrendously expensive in terms of aircraft hire, salaries and expenses and quite often yields no measurable outcomes because cultural events, funerals and other community priorities can conflict with the fly-in visit. Therefore, the notion of remote forms of administration and interaction which allow communities to engage as their priorities permit, and which may also deliver substantial cost savings, is a highly attractive option for stakeholders. In addition, there is also the possibility of not only demonstrating new service efficiencies, but also introducing completely new kinds of services such as:

- live on-line access to medical specialists;
- advanced health administration and patient care via distributed health information systems;
- face-to-face interviews and group meetings conducted by videoconference;
- application of these capabilities to a whole range of educational, judicial/legal, medical and civil administrative needs.

Finally, even with unsophisticated web-based technologies, there is the opportunity to provide direct access to world markets for local and regional businesses such as art sales, eco- and cultural-tourism operators, etc. And this possibility also offers a form of commercial independence from middlemen and agents which has never been previously possible for Aboriginal people.

Issues and Obstacles

Culture

All cultures need to evolve, yet they also need preservation and maintenance and this paradox is as relevant to indigenous cultures in Northern Australia as anywhere. The cultural and social impact of new communication technologies has a vast literature and if that literature reveals anything at all, then it shows that technological impacts are not predictable in any deterministic sense. Small differences in implementation, social structures, practices and values can bring about vast differences in the impact of a given technology (Tyler and Morrison, 1996).

Nevertheless, there is an implicit tensions between various groups concerned with the long term social impacts of these technologies – and with good reason. All technologies can have negative impacts and in the case of remote Aboriginal communities these may include Internet gambling, access to pornography and even exposure to people and groups who would seek to exploit them over that medium. Ultimately, there is no doubt that these technologies *will* bring about changes in quite unpredictable ways. For example, experiences with the Tanami network and trials with ODN have already shown that Aboriginal people adapt very quickly to videoconferencing whereas bureaucrats are much more uncomfortable with the format – often voicing the concern that they are afraid of appearing 'stupid' or incompetent with the medium. Similarly, we have *not* found low literacy levels to be problematic for browsing the Internet and Aboriginal people appear to become confident users very quickly. In addition, we have elicited a great deal of enthusiasm for community web pages and web sites advertising both a community's profile and its community business enterprises.

Therefore, the issue is perhaps not whether these technologies will have cultural and social impacts – that they clearly will is perfectly obvious – nor even so much what the exact nature of these changes will be (because ultimately I believe they are unpredictable). What is more important is the simple acceptance that these technologies will inevitably be implemented anyway, as well as the importance of Aboriginal people having *control and involvement* in how these technologies are applied from the earliest moment. This is the only possible mechanism for ensuring that advanced communication capabilities have more positive outcomes for these regions than negative ones.

Politics

The Australian telecommunications industry is a political arena with domestic and international dimensions. Under international law, all Australian citizens have the right to a phone service – the so called Universal Service Obligation or USO and Telstra has the primary responsibility to meet this obligation. In addition, all carriers are required to meet specified levels of performance and service quality. However, it is clear that these obligations are not met in many areas and in many instances. Telecommunications services and assets in regional Australia are very expensive to support and maintain because of the distances involved, climatic conditions and simple access. Hence, maintaining and upgrading services in these regions is an expensive activity for Telstra – an obligation which may not provide an acceptable return on capital – and yet one which Telstra cannot simply abandon merely for the sake of commercial viability.

In addition, although these issues are complex enough as they stand, the Australian telecommunications environment itself is changing rapidly as a result of political, commercial and technological developments. The issues of local call charging, the further sale of Telstra, the loss of large capital investments such as the Iridium satellites, the growth of the Internet and bandwidth provision via cable modem, ADSL, and small diameter dishes for satellite downlinks, are merely some of the developments impacting on communications in Australia at the present time. Superimposed on this is the larger political dimension of regional Australia generally – the withdrawal of banking and government services, falling commodities prices and growing unemployment and the general 'ghost towning' of previously viable regional communities. In this context, effective and affordable telecommunications is an important political issue since it offers at least the potential to reverse some of this decline by providing better access to markets, delivering new efficiencies in transport and management and even creating new employment niches such as regional call centres.

Obviously, remote Aboriginal Australians are affected by these regional political issues simply because they live there, and at the same time evidence severe levels of social disadvantage that can be partially redressed by technological means. But their context is nevertheless quite different from other regional Australians. Aboriginal people are not large, direct consumers of services and bandwidth in the way that farmers and many mainstream regional businesses are. Instead, large bureaucracies and dozens of organisations deliver services on their behalf (e.g. ATSIC, health, housing and education departments, etc.) and consume bandwidth in provision of these services, or else find community groups and projects to pay for their communication needs.

For example, although many Internet connections exist in remote communities, they are primarily used by government and government funded agencies or by private non-Aboriginal individuals and businesses. The concept of disposable income is not applicable to Aboriginal community residents receiving the equivalent of the unemployment benefit and having goods at the community store that are often marked up by 200 per cent or more. Certainly, although Aboriginal people are avid users of Internet and other services when they are free, they are unable to afford these services at conceivable commercial cost. This is an important point, because it raises the issue of control and involvement and the real possibility of service delivery agencies driving the communications agenda of these communities and even their infrastructure developments, unless Aboriginal community members are a genuine component of the planning, delivery and usage of these services.

Costs and Who Pays?

The last point is important because it identifies the major client groups in remote communities as centralised bureaucracies or their community based representatives. In either case, it is predominantly federal and state budgets that will be major purchasers of communications funding for remote Aboriginal communities.

In all of this, the primary issue is who pays for the infrastructure to provide advanced services and the interesting chicken and egg situation it elicits. That is, adequate infrastructure does not already exist in these communities because the return on capital is low. To be blunt, if there was a dollar to be made, the services and infrastructure would already be there. In addition to the climate extremes, social dysfunctionality in some communities can destroy or damage installations and equipment overnight. The notion of providing expanded capabilities and infrastructure in such a difficult scenario would need substantial evidence of a sizeable untapped or emerging market. Yet that market cannot be demonstrated until the infrastructure and capabilities have been provided. Hence we have a chicken and egg scenario that needs resolution.

From some quarters, the ODN and EOP projects have been identified as mechanisms for breaking this impasse. That is, EOP and ODN have funding which may allow them to build or lease equipment and infrastructure to allow a 'proof of concept' that there is sufficient demand for advanced services to justify greater infrastructure investment by carriers. However, the scale of funding provided to these projects severely limits the amount of infrastructure they can provide for such a test. In addition, these projects are sandwiched by the perception that they exist to deliver the access to phone services that Telstra cannot or will not provide under the USO, and the more radical concept that their role is to experiment and trial new communications services that bureaucracies and service delivery agencies will take up because their efficiency is neglected. That is, there is a tension between RTIF funds simply being used to address unmet USO obligations on the one hand, and on the other hand providing a more adventurous test bed for the practical administrative potential of advanced communications (Morrison, 1999), the potential demand from government (primarily) for these services and consequently the market specifications needed for carriers to build more infrastructure in these remote regions.

Technological Utopianism

New communications technologies can deliver new efficiencies in old services as well as completely new services. And we have an in-built belief that these possibilities will inevitably benefit everyone equally. Unfortunately, the history of technological innovation and innovation diffusion do not support this assertion. In the 1960s, the so called 'green revolution' of new hybrid crops was meant to end the famines of the third world by producing record yields from more abundant hybrid species that were resistant to pests and disease. It was believed that the benefits of such innovations would inevitably 'trickle down' to the poorest and least powerful members of society.

Unfortunately, the outcomes were much more complex and certainly quite unexpected. These new crops did indeed produce record yields, but only the wealthier farmers could afford the fertilisers and tractors that hybrid seeds needed. And having produced huge harvests, these farmers could make substantial profits – even from a market glut. However, with their historical yields, the poorest farmers without the technology could not survive lower prices and were quickly bought out by the wealthier farmers. The net effect in some countries was a migration of displaced farmers joining the population of urban poor and a class of wealthy and increasingly powerful landed aristocracy.

Indeed, the potential for 'early adopters' of new technologies to benefit is a well recognised phenomenon – as well as the tendency for early adopters to already be in financially and socially advantaged positions in the first place. The relevance of this to communications capabilities in remote Aboriginal communities appears somewhat partial. To begin with, it is difficult to identify who the early adopters really are or will be. Are they government agencies, or individual communities or key people within communities, or even certain carriers who made an early commitment? Will certain communities with certain communications success stories be flooded with ancillary funding, while others receive little additional funding or even experience funding cuts? In short, there is a lot of potential empire building to consider, and the notion that these empires will inevitably have the interests of the 'lowliest' members of society at heart may be a little naive.

Secondly, although technologies can certainly redress some of the disadvantages evidenced amongst remote Aboriginal populations, there are many dimensions to the disadvantage and a purely technological approach can be used as a vehicle for ignoring them. For example, a great deal of ill-health amongst Aboriginal people is a function of poor nutrition (amongst a host of other factors). Menzies School of Health Research, for example, has shown that most malnourished babies in the womb have damaged nephrons (the filter units in the kidney) and those babies are highly predisposed to developing renal disease in later life – and, as already mentioned, certain communities in the Northern Territory have the highest cost of renal failure on the planet. The average dialysis patient in Australia costs about A$100,000 per annum in treatment and generally dies within five years. While it would appear that addressing malnutrition is a simple and solvable problem, the social factors determining malnutrition in Aboriginal mothers are many and complex. They include unemployment and very low income levels, non-nutritious foods provided by community stores (at outrageous prices), the effects of gambling and alcohol on family incomes (although in many instances, large card games are an important socialising component in communities) and gender roles that limit women's authority. In addition, simple interventions such as 'institutionalised' feeding programs of people – especially pregnant women – would possibly attract significant criticisms from a number of quarters.

In short, many problems in these communities are an expression of highly interlocked social, cultural and economic realities that are not amenable to change in the short or medium term. Therefore, although new technologies do indeed have an important role in providing better and different forms of services and opportunities, it would be rather naive to expect them to bring about massive improvements. Essentially, we should not substitute technofixes as a band aid for deep, complex problems, but nor should we deny the opportunity to work with these communities in new and potentially better ways, or deny them the opportunity to be part of the new literacy and economy sweeping the world.

Notes

1   For World Bank projects see http://www.worldbank.org/infodev.htm, its IT strategy can be found at http://www.worldbank.org/infodev/projects/funded.htm. For imminent and past international conferences on IT/telecoms in equitable and sustainable development see http://www.tasknet.nic.in as well as http://wwwiiod.org/index.ap and http://www.un.org/Depts/eca/adf/adf99m.htm.
2   Australian Bureau of Statistics, 1996 Census.
3   'The Aboriginal and Torres Strait Islander Health Information Plan', a report prepared for the Australian Health Minister's Advisory Council, Aboriginal and Torres Strait Islander Health and Welfare Information Unit, Australian Bureau of Statistics, October 1997.

References

Forester, T. and Morrison, P. (1993), *Computer Ethics: Cautionary tales and ethical dilemmas in computing*, 2nd edn, Cambridge, MA: MIT Press.

Morrison, P. (1999), 'The Internet Pilot Project of the Local Government Association of the Northern Territory', UNDP http://www.undp.org/info21/telecom99/8.html.

Morrison, P. (2000), 'A Pilot Implementation of Internet Access for Remote Aboriginal Communities in the "Top End" of Australia', *Urban Studies*, Vol. 37, pp. 1781–92.

Tyler, W. and Morrison, P. (1996), 'Dimensions of Disadvantage Developing Small Area Indicators for Remote Australia', *The Australian Journal of Social Research*, Vol. 2, No. 1.

Chapter Nine

Distributed Globalisation: Identity, Virtuality and Adjacency

Stephen Little

Introduction

This chapter examines those processes of globalisation in the world economy which are impacting on the choices facing individuals, organisations and communities seeking a role and an identity within a complex global system. While the global economy is not an entirely new phenomenon, the speed of communications and transactions, and the increasingly seamless nature of the emerging media are unique. The key role of information and communication technologies (ICTs) in globalisation creates new forms of locational and functional differentiation. These result in new inequities as communities in both 'under' and 'over' developed economies are opened to direct competition from across national and cultural boundaries. The pressure on local communities also operates at the level of region and national state. Appropriate information and communication infrastructure is becoming as significant as physical location in accessing the global economy.

In examining 'strong globalisation' arguments the chapter draws attention to the Technocrat Movement of 1930s North America. In exploring the relationship between place, space, community and technology, the chapter makes use of Melvin Webber's definitions of 'non-place urban realm' from 1964. The aim is to identify issues of relevance to the emergent situation which have already been addressed by observers and critics of earlier change and to ensure that the genuinely unique features of current trends are appreciated.

Technology in a Global Context

The conjunction of an immense military establishment and a huge arms industry is new in the American experience. The total influence – economic, political, and even spiritual – is felt in every city, every state house, and every office of the federal government ... In the councils of government, we must guard against the acquisition of unwarranted influence, whether sought or unsought, by the military-industrial complex (President Dwight D. Eisenhower, Farewell Address to the Nation, 17 January 1961).

In the final quarter of the twentieth century following the end of the Cold War, and of what Ohmae (1995) terms the 'bi-polar discipline' which constrained relationships between ideological blocs, global economic integration grew rapidly. This accelerating change had its roots in conditions at the outset of the Cold War. J.K. Galbraith articulated Eisenhower's concerns in his book 'The New Industrial State' by defining the emergence of the 'technostructure' of the industrial state as the necessary consequence of a change in the locus of power from land via capital to knowledge and technique (Galbraith, 1967). The technical experts delivering the calculative rationality necessary to the industrial state becomes the new locus of knowledge and power.

Internationalisation of trade can be traced deep into history, back beyond the Silk Route. The Western mercantile tradition developed around a set of technologies which Hirst and Thompson (1996) argue reached a functional plateau with the reliability and regularity of the steamship and electric telegraph. While pre-First World War international trade shares characteristics with later forms of transnational commerce, the new organisational forms created by the merging of computer and communication technologies (ICTs) have provided the potential for new forms of networked organisation and 'virtual workplace' unlike anything previously possible. The electronic mobility now available to the formal and informal labour force creates a two-way street, with electronic access to and from the home redefining a sphere of both production and consumption. This coalescence of domestic and working space recalls the pre-industrial household which was a locus of production. In regions where the shift away from household and family centred production has not occurred, however, the globalisation process entails disruption of family networks, as in the use of Export Processing Zones to filter out local practices described by Klein (2000).

The top-down 'strong globalisation' view of global production and consumption reflects experience of a series of complementary flows of materials from periphery to centre and products from centre to periphery. These were followed by the development of multi-domestic production close to the peripheral markets (Dicken, 1998). This centripetal model still holds sway but the subsequent driver of globalisation has been the reduction of transaction costs achieved through ICTs. Globalisation in its current form can be seen as a consequence of the rapid development of ICTs during the Cold War period and this chapter argues that this informational shift implies a new distributed paradigm for globalisation. The strong globalisation argument that globalisation is disseminating a single mode of production from a coherent centre to an increasingly uniform periphery is no longer viable.

The initial development of both electronic computers and associated network technologies was driven by military requirements some of which remained secret for three decades.[1] One consequence of this secrecy was the concealment of the true sequence of innovation, to the detriment of the UK in particular. More importantly, the central role of state intervention and the generous provision of public resources has been edited from the history peddled by exponents of a technology driven view of development.

Proponents of the 'strong globalisation' thesis, typified by Kenichi Ohmae, suggest that there is a coherent and irresistible logic of globalisation (Ohmae, 1990). For Ohmae, globalisation is dominated by a core 'triad' of economic regions: North America, Western Europe and North East Asia, predominantly Japan which share the bulk of international trade. As attention shifted from flows of material to flows of information and knowledge, disparate national and regional cultures became increasingly interlinked within networked and globalised organisations. Production and consumption of goods and services take place in an increasingly complex web, where both sophisticated and commodified products may be produced and consumed at centre and periphery. However, this complexity is far removed from the bland, uniform global culture that is often assumed to be the consequence of top-down globalisation. Any erosion of difference and identity is countered by the reverse colonisation of the information infrastructures by the periphery. This chapter touches on this tension later but first it examines the contestation between two paradigms.

Shifting Paradigms

Most descriptions of the emergent 'information society' place a strong emphasis on the uniqueness of the present situation, and suggest seamless, integrated technical change, leading to a globalisation of social life and economic opportunity. However, by the last quarter of the twentieth century massive investment in technology and its production had produced significant changes in the dominant model of the transnational corporation. By the seventies, multinational corporations were prominent in the economic landscape, and being identified as significant investors in and exploiters of knowledge (e.g. Galbraith 1967; Tugendhat, 1971; Vernon, 1971) but subsequent developments were poorly anticipated. Tugendhat, for example, does not examine the Third World, arguing that its problems are separate and distinct from those of the developed economies. Thirty years ago Asian involvement in the multinational arena was minimal, Tugendhat's data for 1969 shows that Japanese investment in the USA was smaller than that from Belgium and Luxembourg. Understandably, a centripetal model of international flows is unable to account for the intensely networked and distributed global system which had emerged by the turn of the century. The vertically integrated multinational corporation, under unified ownership, has been superseded by networks of externalised relationships between associated but often autonomous firms. Following a variety of state sanctioned developments, East Asia has become an integral part of this global network, a source of markets and resources, and a contributor of innovations in both products and processes. A network of distributed resources has replaced the vertical integration of the earlier phase of economic internationalisation.

This paradigm shift is encapsulated in Saxenian's comparison between Route 128 around Boston and its associated high technology industries and Silicon Valley in Northern California (Saxenian, 1994). The East Coast paradigm relied upon established companies and a new relationship with universities and central government, the core of Eisenhower's 'military–industrial complex' (the phrase was modified from 'military–industrial–congressional complex' in a late draft). This geographical and organisational shift in the US economy was also reflected in a shift in the nature of transnational economic activity.

The closed nature of these large, individual organisations contrasts with the densely networked environment of the more dynamic West Coast firms. Silicon Valley is dominated by companies which grew up with the new technologies they promote. Manuel Castells (1989) describes the complex web of relationships necessary to sustain this level of multidisciplinary knowledge creation as a 'creative milieu'. Such a milieu extends beyond the boundaries of the high-tech firms themselves into a hinterland of rich knowledge resources, involving universities, sympathetic financial institutions and a highly sophisticated labour market.

Silicon Valley start-up companies can secure both finance and personnel from their environment and draw upon a highly skilled and mobile workforce. However, the highly specialised labour market was originally created by an outflow of personnel from the larger, established companies and from universities, particularly Stanford. These older companies provided a form of internal quarantine, with unstructured and dynamic knowledge creation taking place in customised research laboratories, carefully separated from the routine production of their stable products and services. Such separation was both overt, as with the Bell Laboratories, and covert, as with the Lockheed Skunkworks, where cutting-edge military products were pursued in conditions close to the fabled Silicon Valley 'garage start-up' (see Rich and Janos, 1995). The Silicon Valley model has become an almost subconscious archetype for innovation although today established Silicon Valley firms are as likely to innovate through the acquisition of promising start-up companies as through internal development.

> Silicon Valley is the only place on Earth not trying to figure out how to become Silicon Valley (Robert Metcalfe, *InfoWorld*, 2 March 1998).

Castells and Hall (1994), in their extensive analysis of numerous attempts to replicate the dynamics of Silicon Valley, through science parks or science cities catalogue mixed results, both within the original Anglo-Saxon business culture and beyond. Massey, Quintas and Wield (1992) argue that many such attempts fail to take account of the particular historical circumstances of Silicon Valley, and rely instead on simplistic notions of innovative activity in relation to space, and divisions of labour science parks and cities, This is unsurprising, given that the fundamental conditions which gave rise to the phenomenon are not well understood, even by some of the key participants whose anti-statist, free enterprise rhetoric ignores this key ingredient of the recipe. Despite its freewheeling entrepreneurial milieu, Silicon Valley was as dependent upon public sector, defence related expenditure for its genesis as Route 128 had been a decade earlier. The Internet was derived from the ARPANet, named after the Advanced Research Projects Agency of the US Department of Defense. The intention was to share expensive research resources efficiently, and in a cold-war frame, to ensure the survivability of a fragmented or degraded network under physical attack. The World Wide Web originated with a project to share documentation and other materials seamlessly among the staff involved in basic science at CERN, the European Centre for Nuclear Research. The NCSA, the National Center for Supercomputing Applications at the University of Illinois at Urbana-Champaign contributed the Mosaic browser that underpinned its commercial counterparts from Netscape and Microsoft. The Silicon Valley paradox is that much of the robustness and ease of use of Internet based applications, a key to their rapid commercial dissemination in the run up to the millennium, can be traced to the requirements of large public sector institutions. This was a lesson better learned by the developmental nation states of East Asia, Singapore, Taiwan and Korea in particular (see Thorpe and Little, 2001).

However, even informed and sincere imitators of Silicon Valley face the problems of reproducing an adequate or equivalent set of conditions as described by Castells and Hall (1994). Regional and national disparities in access to resources and capabilities still present real problems, as in the case of Malaysia's bold attempt at the creation of a Multi-Media Super-Corridor to connect the country to global high technology production (Wilkinson et al., 2001). The move from high quality but relatively low value routine production to cutting-edge innovation is one that requires both technical and cultural reorientation and a shift in perception by both actors and observers. The Malaysian government itself is ambivalent about the impact on national identity and cohesion of the level of Internet access expected by potential inward investors. Little, Holmes and Grieco (forthcoming) describe some of the social and political impacts on Malaysia's economy.

In order to understand the degree of autonomy possible for countries such as Malaysia which wish to benefit from participation in the global and informational economy, it is necessary to examine the underpinning ideology of the two contesting paradigms of globalisation.

Technocracy as a Global Form

In the United States during the 1930s, and in the political flux immediately before the implementation of the Roosevelt administration's 'New Deal' programme, the Technocrat Movement rose to short-lived national prominence on a programme of technical rationality. It claimed that the economy would prosper in the hands of engineers, further developing Veblen's (1904) conception of the role of technical workers. Ultimately, according to Akin (1977), the movement withered precisely because its narrow technicism precluded the formulation of a programme of political action. However, the notion of the power of technical rationality to deal with almost any economic or social problem has proved an enduring one, linking F.W. Taylor (1911) to former Technocrats like Richard Buckminster Fuller, still active at the end of the 1960s. It received reinforcement through the comparative success of the New Deal policies and the successful application of new management techniques during the Second World War. The rapid advances in military and other technologies ensured a continuing acceptance of such views in the postwar period. The career of Robert MacNamara, as narrated by Halberstam (1971), offers a paradigm of this postwar flowering of technocratic consciousness. Hughes and Hughes (2000) provide evidence of its extensive influence, via the systems paradigm, which in both management and engineering underpinned the drive to globalisation from the Second World War onwards.

The Technocrat Movement adopted energy consumption as a single unifying metric through which the rational management of economy and society could be achieved (Akin, 1977). Inappropriate definitions of performance, stemming from the narrowness of the technocratic view lead to the assumption that a single, valid metric can be found for any system under consideration, and to the denial of any discourse on the framework necessary to account for conflicting views.

J.K. Galbraith's (1967) formulation of 'technostructure' may describe the apogee of the technocracy. According to Galbraith, with the onset of increased capitalisation and technical content there is a loss of flexibility, a growing demand for more specialised personnel, requiring in turn more specific organisation. Planning becomes a crucial function and the technostructure constitutes a group intellect capable of tackling the new scale of organisational problems. Both Veblen and Galbraith speak of a shift in the locus of power towards those with technical skills, although this is a debatable assumption, given the shifts in cost and accessibility of the relevant technologies over subsequent decades. Galbraith's assumption of economic dominance by large corporations through their superior planning facilities, has been challenged by the relative performance of smaller organisations better able to innovate and adopt emerging techniques. However, DeLamarter (1988) argues that market dominance is the prerogative of large and established corporations, and demonstrates the control IBM was once able to exercise over an emergent technology. The principal interest here is in the impact of the technocratic views of technical skills on those exercising them. It brings an understanding of knowledge as explicit and commodified, it requires a reductionist view which sits increasingly uncomfortably with the nature of the knowledge work entailed by ICTs and with the particular demands of a networked form of globalisation.

Place and Non-place in a World of Flows

In response to developments in organisational technologies, organisation theorists have produced a number of descriptions of the new organisational forms that have resulted. The rise of the Internet and e-commerce as facilitators of transnational commerce has led to a range of formulations of 'networked organisation'. Castells has described such networks in *The Informational City*, as a 'space of flows', arguing that access to flows of information and resources is the key to participation in the wider economy (Castells, 1989). However, two decades earlier Webber proposed the 'city as communications system', (Webber; 1964, p. 84) in order to move from the physical bias of established planning conceptions. He switched the emphasis of urbanity from physical built form to the quality of interaction in cultural life through the exchange of information.

Webber formulates 'non-place community' in terms of Interest-Communities, accessibility, rather than the propinquity aspect of 'place' being the necessary condition for this form of community (Webber, 1964). He argues that this definition implies that suburban and exurban dwellers enjoy a measure of urbanity not previously acknowledged: the traditional 'place community' was in fact a special case of a larger genus of association. For Webber individuals are involved in an overlapping set of communities which involve different social and physical spaces. He ends by suggesting that emerging institutional changes and technological developments coupled with ever increasing mobility and specialisation are likely to involve urban dwellers in increasingly wide area communications. Identity and community become a quality of networking activities.

The shifting balance between physical and electronic adjacency facilitated by information and communications technologies reflects Webber's formulation of 'non-space realms'. Webber adds that certain approaches to the classification of urban centres were more amenable to the consideration of the range of interactions which he identifies, but that any reconsideration of definitions of centrality in the terms outlined by him would call into question the traditional notions of centre and hinterland.

Webber influenced and was influenced by an orientation towards nonphysical aspects of community, and a participatory approach to design which emerged strongly during the seventies. The result of Webber's arguments is a relationship between urbanity, density and community radically at variance with that being advanced by Jacobs in her influential *Death and Life of Great American Cities* (Jacobs, 1961) at the same period. Webber prefigured the celebration of Southern Californian urbanism by Banham (1971) and subsequent commentators yet although he anticipated the distributed social identity made possible by subsequent technical developments, he anticipated that this would be the province of a knowledge elite, rather than a more widely available mode.

Distributed Opportunities

The balance between the two paradigms derived from the thinking described above can be judged by responses to the opportunities provided by the technologies of globalisation. The Internet offers smaller players to access resources from and to compete within global networks, and there are examples of such successful interventions. Inoue (1998) describes a 'virtual village' in which small enterprises are able to form and reform alliances in order to provide high technology services to larger companies. Their physical co-location across a number of inner suburbs of Tokyo is enhanced by electronic exchange. Such electronic adjacency is stretched further by the London-based supporters of Sohonet. A group of specialised media companies shares high capacity data links in order to participate in the creative milieu based around Hollywood and West Los Angeles. The high-speed digital exchange of film, video and sound enables post production operations to be carried out in London, in direct competition with Californian companies. The open networked nature of the entertainment industry of Southern California is a lower-tech version of the IT networks in Northern California which, through rapidly increasing use of technologies such as computer generated images (CGI) and the on-line promotion and delivery of content, is moving towards convergence with its northern neighbours.

Such striking innovations appear to alter the relationship between organisational size and performance. However, the additional accessibility and flexibility available to smaller players also allows larger firms to restructure into networks which can enter niche markets yet still draw on their wider resource base. Castells (1996) describes a form of 'network enterprise' which is composed of components of larger corporations, collaborating in specific spatial and temporal circumstances, while the main companies are still pursuing global strategies of direct competition. Castells is describing a mechanism by which larger corporations can achieve some of the agility of smaller competitors. The larger firms are able to de-couple key business units better to target customers and markets traditionally served by much smaller firms. This sophisticated understanding of distributed opportunities by large corporations presents a formidable challenge to smaller and medium scale players.

The newer entrants to the global marketplace quickly became aware of the need to maintain value through a knowledge-intensive approach to the delivery and support of goods, and have themselves invested in the established economies. James and Howell (2001) show that Asian companies are establishing or acquiring research and development (R&D) facilities within the UK and the USA. There are two motives for this. Knowledge of regional markets can be obtained by the route of partnership or part ownership followed by acquisition, as with Fujitsu and ICL. It can also be captured through R&D focussed on local product development, informed by feedback from local customers and incorporated in regionally targeted products, such as the Nissan Primera, a model developed for the European market. At the same time, access to a broader intellectual capital base can be obtained though tapping into regional knowledge which might enhance home-based operations. Both Malaysian and Korean automotive companies have acquired British-based engineering and design companies to further develop their home capabilities. Silicon Valley itself has attracted not just North American but Asian and European entrepreneurs. The incomers' strategy is to create a point of presence for networks that reach back to their home locations in India, Taiwan or France. These previously disconnected networks can then access the core milieu.

Both the British government and the European Commission are encouraging companies to seek alliances and opportunities in the opposite direction, to the less developed economies of South East Asia. This is presented both as a means of accessing the market potential of these growing economies and as a means of improving offshore manufacturing resources in relation to both home and export markets (EC/UNCTAD, 1996). In some instances complementary manufacturing takes place at both ends of such relationships. Overseas plants are increasingly selling to both local and home markets. Recently Japan has conceded the logic of serving at least the lower value end of the domestic consumer electronics markets from overseas plants initially developed to serve offshore markets.

Modelling a Distributed System

Dicken (1998) uses a generic production chain to analyse the dynamics of the global economy by focussing on the globalisation of production. In common with Porter's representation of the value chain (Porter, 1990), a range of critical support activities is modelled at each stage of this generic model. Dicken separates these into flows of materials, personnel and information on the one hand and technology and research and development functions on the other. The centripetal model of the flows and practice of global production reflect these essentially linear models. Vernon (1971) developed a model of increasing product maturity. Once processes become familiar and routine, production can be transferred from the centre, via overseas subsidiaries to less developed regions where in the final stages of product life, the output is sent back to the original source. However, the very success of such approaches to international production by established manufacturers stimulated a range of imitators. The globalisation of productive resources brings new competitors to the markets previously dominated by the most developed economies. Nor is the rate of diffusion any longer a prerogative of the centre. As the distributed form displaces the centripetal, transnational companies have to make complex location decisions for each part of their production chain. Dunning presents a more complex model of the choices facing investors seeking to establish international production (Dunning, 1993). This identifies a variety of motives for seeking overseas location, ranging from investment directed at securing natural resources, at securing new markets or at securing synergy with existing assets or activities.

In a distributed system ICTs allow a two-way traffic between centre and erstwhile periphery. Locations selected from a centripetal perspective as suitable for offshore low cost, relatively routine production have, transformed themselves into globally competitive players, as exemplified by Taiwan. The response from the beleaguered centre has been to seek increased added value by moving towards the end of the production chain. Product differentiation and customer support can maintain demand for goods and services and maintain premium prices for them. Significantly, such a shift makes the distinction between products and services less meaningful. It also represents an intensification of knowledge requirements since a focus at end of the chain requires closer adjustment to cultural variation among users and customers. While the shift is intended to regain central control over the periphery, it simultaneously requires either an accommodation with or incorporation of the local. This paradoxically allows a reinforcement of local identity within the global network and stimulates the exchanges between erstwhile core and periphery described in the previous section.

ICL (International Computers Limited), now owned by Fujitsu, provides an example of this effect. It has moved further from it original manufacturing hardware base to position itself as an information services provider that can support the specificities of a European business environment. The service end of the chain is more culturally variable and success reflects specific local or regional knowledge. ICL resulted from a series of mergers in the UK computer industry running from 1959 to 1968. These produced an integrated national champion and these European credentials allow a Japanese company to maintain a convincing presence in a key market and to deliver products and services tailored to regional practices and requirements.

This 'value chain' approach (Porter 1990) can be seen in a very different industry. In the production chain linking bulk and specialist chemicals to consumer packaged goods, both ICI and Unilever have been engaged in moving to the area of higher added value. In 1997 Unilever passed its specialist chemical division to ICI in order to concentrate on the delivery of differentiated brands based on these feedstocks. Unilever went on to concentrate on the management of a subset of its original portfolio of brands, via an extensive culling operation (BBC World Service, 2000). This aimed to reduce 1,600 brands to 400 in order the increase the value of the retained brands. ICI off-loaded its bulk chemical business to firms content to compete primarily on price at the commodity end of this chain, while retaining its established brands, such as Dulux paint.

Distributed Contestation

Naomi Klein characterises focus on higher value activities by what were formerly manufacturing organisations as a shift from material production to a form of cultural production (Klein, 2000). She argues that the apparent global expansion of high profile brands is in fact accompanied by a downsizing or hollowing out in which all functions except the management and development of the brand itself are subcontracted. This represents the apotheosis of outsourcing facilitated by both a reduction of transaction costs and the alteration of the relative advantages and economies of size. Production of whatever artefact is chosen to re-embody the disembodied brand can be undertaken at the most cost advantageous location, remoter from its ultimate consumers. Ultimately brands may become the carrier of the core values and emotional capital of what were once physically extensive organisations that have been reduced to sets of networked relationships. The brand, commodified through franchise operations may represent the core resource of such a global network, the only means by which it can be readily recognised by the target consumer. The management of organisational values and brand equity and value are likely to become a central issue for the maintenance of communities of practice and coherence of networked organisations.

The growing separation between cultural and physical production has a further consequence for core as well as peripheral economies. Lipietz (1992) argues that the ability to separate production from consumption in these systems signals the end of the 'Fordist compromise' which underpinned the Keynsian social-democratic paradigm. Harvey (1990) points out that Ford significantly increased wages when he introduced his five-dollar, eight-hour day in 1914 in conjunction with his production line. He saw the workers as an integral part of a production and consumption process. Production workers remote from the destination market no longer need to be paid sufficiently well to consume the products of their own labour. The result of these changes is a complex layering of labour markets, both internal and external to the developed economies driving the globalisation process. Harvey regards this post-Fordist situation as a regime of flexible accumulation which is tightly organised through its geographical dispersal and flexible responses to labour markets, and which is even more reliant on the creation of scientific and technical knowledge.

A key issue in any consideration of distributed identity is the relationship between individual and the organisation. The nature of employment has been changed in both the established and the newly participating economies in the evolving global system. Castells (1996) characterises this as the replacement of *organisational man* with *flexible woman*, and Beck (2000) speaks of the 'Brazilianisation of the West'. Castells is arguing that the North American fifties stereotype of the white-collar worker with the Western equivalent of lifetime employment in a large corporation is being replaced by the short-term contract worker, often female, who may gain some advantage from flexible working hours, but who is inevitably on a lower level of remuneration and benefits. Beck goes further to argue that the patterns of employment, common to semi-industrialised countries typified by Brazil are the future for developed countries. He bases this judgement on the impact of the current neo-liberal economic policies which deny any developmental role for the national state, relying instead entirely on market mechanisms. Bond, for example, analyses the implications of adherence to such policies in post-apartheid South Africa (Bond, 2000). A minority of waged or salaried full time workers will coexist with a majority of multi-activity workers following a variety of discontinuous and unregulated sources of income. Such a scenario is far removed from the lifetime employment model of the major Japanese corporations, or even of recent western practice and assumptions.

The demonstrations against the World Trade Organisation in Seattle, and subsequent events in Prague and Stockholm represent one set of reactions to these shifts in employment practices and the impact on communities which derive their identity from economic activities now under threat. Kanbur (2001) argues that they also reflect a perception that the activities of the Bretton Woods institutions, the World Bank and International Monetary Fund, are regarded as increasing rather than reducing global poverty and inequality.

For Kanbur a Group A mentality on the part of the governments and international institutions clashes with a Group B view of the nongovernmental opponents (NGOs). Conflicting views of the appropriate level of aggregation at which to gauge progress, of the appropriate time horizon that should be addressed, and of the nature of markets structures and power relationships ensure that agreement is impossible. NGOs stress the short-term effects on actual communities of medium-term focussed policies, while environmentalists stress the much longer-term sustainability of policies. Both sides disagree open the nature and function of market mechanisms, with the NGOs perceiving substantial market power accruing to large scale established players. The Group A and B positions can be seen to correspond in part to centripetal and distributed understandings of global processes.

Distributed Futures: Identity

This chapter has described an assumption that a diffusion of innovation and technology from centre to periphery along the lines set out by Rogers (1983). However, the information and communication technologies that underpin the global system enabled a reconfiguring or disaggregation of the production chain into a distributed network. Each activity can be located at its point of greatest comparative advantage, while a degree of oversight and control not previously possible can be maintained. For example, in the 1980s North American automotive manufacturers elected to control production lines in their Canadian component plants through data links from the US side of the border. More significantly, and in line with Lipietz' (1992) arguments, in all but the highest technology undertakings, the divergent, creative activities which produce intellectual capital can be disaggregated from the convergent, focused and increasingly marginalised production process.

Despite the dependence on global information flows to achieve this disaggregation, work and employment must still take place in some physical space, however electronically connected that space may be. Increasingly, however, even in developed economies, that space is the household (Little, 2000). At the micro-level consideration has been given to the physical requirements of creative work, as well as the social needs of group formation and interaction.

At the meso-level of space and location, the problems of physical absence for distance workers, and of the split between high and low value work into front and back office functions have been recognised for some time (e.g.

Nelson, 1988), but at the macro level communications between front and back office can cross cultural and national boundaries.

The difficulty of achieving effective communities of practice across both spatial and cultural distance is already being identified in studies of attempts by Western firms to capitalise on the resources of the Indian software industry (Nicholson, Sahay and Krishna, 2000). The centripetal view of seamless interoperability between remote locations fell foul of the definitions and practices demanded of a local identity. There were significant changes in the Indian economy during the 1990s, with a change in government policy towards participation in the world economy. Indian firms are successfully providing services in Europe and North America. However, these either have key staff in place in the client culture in order to ensure the alignment that ICL provides for Fujitsu, or operate via partnerships. One Indian software company approaches the North American market under the brand of its Swedish partner, confident of the quality of its own products, but aware of the image of Indian products and their perceived quality. In approaching the Japanese markets Indian firms are taking care to align with local practices (Nikkei, 2001).

Re-examination of both the Technocratic frame and Webber's understanding of place against the dynamics of current information technology offers insight into immediate issues of the redefinition of centre and periphery and the implications for identity in a distributed economy. ICTs offer a potential for participation in the 'information economy' to peripheral areas. However, in the distributed context 'periphery' is defined by access to these very technologies. There are disadvantaged regions and localities within developed economies as well as in the so-called 'Third World' or between the European core and the so-called 'accession states'.

Applying Webber's work to our current situation offers insight into broad issues such as globalisation and consequent redefinitions of centre and periphery and the implications for existing urban infrastructures. While the work offers a framework against which to assess the many claims made for IT as a panacea for marginalised or peripheral groups, its predominantly North American framework must be opened out to accommodate the multicultural nature of a global economy.

Castells has described 'informational politics in action' (Castells, 1997, p. 333). He is concerned that one aspect of globalisation, the reliance on simplified mass communication, inevitably reduces the complexity of political discourse. However, in the same volume he describes very different and complex forms of electronically mediated communication by dissident minorities: Zapatista rebels in Mexico and militia groups in the USA. In both cases movements premised on the championing of the local and specific and a rejection of the global economy are achieving a presence and a voice in a global arena through the appropriation of the technologies of globalisation. The key technologies of the Internet and World Wide Web do offer opportunities for voices and visions voices from geographically disparate locations to enter the world of global communication. These can build a dynamic between traditional cultural practices, modern communication forms to provide an enrichment of global symbolic life. There is a symbiosis between the use of the Internet for e-commerce purposes and the maintenance of living and differentiated cultures, a pattern which is already evident in Canada, Africa and Indonesia (Little, Holmes and Grieco, 2000).

Many discussions of the impact of the Internet and the globalisation of communication on local culture and material practice focus on the 'Macdonaldisation' of symbolic life (Ritzer, 2000). Global communication is seen as flattening the cultural terrain in the direction of the dominance of the modes and material practices of the global economic leaders, most particularly the United States. The US ownership of the strategic components of global communication technology, most particularly the dominance of Microsoft, is seen as an important element in this flattening of the terrain. Equally important in this doomsday scenario of the destruction of a rich and varied cultural and symbolic life is the emergence of English as a global language. Whilst it would be foolhardy to deny the validity of this scenario as a potential state of the future world of global communications, it ignores many of the new cultural capacities of new forms of global communication. Just as Crystal (1997) argues that the global English language is no longer under the control of its original native speakers, so are the technologies of globalisation appropriated by users at the margins.

In this context, the rise of the portal metaphor as an organiser of web access has allowed countries such as Estonia, to provide public access in its own Finno-Ugric language (Abbate, 2000). The use of 'front-end' translation software can now overcome the language barrier. The portal is a home page which provides structured links into resources appropriate to its users. As an organising device it can reduce search time for newer users. The World Bank recognised the role of knowledge in the 1998–99 *World Development Report* (World Bank, 1998) and is currently re-branding as the Knowledge Bank. Stephen Denning, as Director of Knowledge Management for the Bank has presented this as a necessary dialogue between all parties concerned with development process (Denning and Grieco, 2000). A component of this realignment is the development of a web portal for Global Development

Knowledge. The Bank has opened a web based debate with nongovernmental organisations which has inevitably raised the issue of power relationships. These can be seen in the framing of access pathways by the resource rich on behalf of the resource poor.

The emerging global system is far from complete and far from determined, but it has already had a profound impact on social and working life in the regions included within and excluded from it. Information and communication technologies are driving the distributed processes of globalisation. By providing new forms of adjacency they are also providing avenues of entry for excluded constituencies and the means to refine and develop the management of the knowledge which has been foregrounded by the new relationships.

The speed of change in markets, competition and technology means that there is a socio-institutional lag as the new techno-economic paradigm emerges (Perez, 1983). For example, e-commerce is already mutating into m-commerce: mobile delivery of services. Despite the relative inadequacy of current WAP (wireless application protocol) mobile telephony, the combination of low earth orbit (LEO) satellites with global positioning systems (GPS) in proposed systems such as the European Galileo GPS will allow location-sensitive services to be delivered to individuals and groups on the move (Taplin, 2000). New forms of community of practice may arise, together with a reassessment of the spatial dynamics of knowledge creation and application. With LEO direct satellite systems, the network coverage will of necessity be equally dense and universal across the majority of the planet's surface beneath the hundreds of orbiting satellites.

Whether these and other opportunities lead to robust and effective communication between adherents of centripetal views and proponents of distributed strategies or the reintegration or redefinition of core and periphery will only be discovered though emerging practice.

Note

1   Winterbotham (1974) revealed the massive British Second World War code-breaking system which at its peak employed 8,000 workers, using state-of-the-art business technology and the specially designed Colossus computer. By this time, however, much of the early history of computing had already been framed around the requirements of the post-Manhattan project nuclear weapons programme of the USA. The von Neumann architecture which specified the relationship of computer hardware and program was formulated with weapons calculations in mind.

References

Abbate, J. (2000), 'Virtual Nation-building in Estonia: Reshaping space, place, and identity in a newly independent state', paper presented at *Virtual Society? Get Real!* Conference, Ashridge House, Hertfordshire May.

Akin, W.E. (1977), *Technocracy and the American Dream: the Technocrat Movement 1900–1941*, Berkeley: University of California Press.

Banham, R. (1971), *Los Angeles: The architecture of four ecologies*, Harmondsworth: Allen Lane Architectural Press.

BBC World Service (2000), 'Range Slashed As Unilever Culls Brands', *World Business Analysis*, broadcast 24 March.

Beck U. (2000), *The Brave New World of Work*, Cambridge: Polity Press.

Bond P. (2000), *Elite Transition: From Apartheid to neoliberalism in South Africa*, London: Pluto Press.

Castells, M. (1989), *The Informational City: Information technology, economic restructuring and the urban-regional process*, Oxford: Blackwells.

Castells, M. (1996), *The Rise of the Network Society: The Information Age: Economy Society and Culture Vol. I*, Oxford: Blackwell.

Castells, M. (1997b), *The Power of Identity: The Information Age: Economy Society and Culture Vol. II*, Oxford: Blackwell.

Castells, M. and Hall, P. (1994), *Technopoles of the World: The making of 21st century industrial complexes*, London: Routledge.

Crystal, D. (1997), *English as a Global Language*, Cambridge: Cambridge University Press.

DeLamarter, R.T. (1988), *Big Blue: IBM's use and abuse of power*, London: Pan.

Denning, S. and Grieco, M. (2000), 'Technology, Dialogue and the Development Process', *Urban Studies*, Vol. 37, No. 10, September, pp. 1065–879.

Dicken, P. (1998), *Global Shift: Transforming the world's economy*, 3rd edn, London: Paul Chapman.

Dreyfus, H.L. and Dreyfus, S.E. (1986), *Mind over Machine*, New York: Free Press.

Dunning, J.H. (1993), *Multinational Enterprises and the Global Economy*, Reading, MA: Addison-Wesley.

EC/UNCTAD (1996), *Investing in Asia's Dynamism: European Union direct investment in Asia*, European Commission/UNCTAD Division on Transnational Corporations and Investment, Office for Official Publications of the EC, Luxembourg.

Feigenbaum, E.A. and McCorduck, P. (1983), *The Fifth Generation: Artificial intelligence and Japan's computer challenge to the world*, Reading, MA: Addison-Wesley.

Galbraith, J.K. (1976), *The New Industrial State*, 4th edn, New York: Mentor.

Galbraith, J.K. (1977), *Organization Design*, Reading, MA: Addison-Wesley.

Halberstam, D. (1971), 'The Programming of Robert McNamara', *Harper's Magazine*, February.

Harvey, D. (1990), *The Condition of Postmodernity*, Oxford: Basil Blackwell.

Hirst, P. and Thompson, G. (1996), *Globalization in Question*, Cambridge: Polity Press.

Hughes, A.C. and Hughes, T.P. (2000), *Systems Experts and Computers: The systems approach in management and engineering, World War II and after*, MIT Press: Cambridge.

Inoue, T. (1998), 'Small Businesses Flourish in Virtual Village', *Nikkei Weekly*, 26 January, p. 1.

Jacobs (1961), *The Death and Life of Great American Cities*, New York: Random House.

James, A.D. and Howells, J. (2001), 'Global Companies and Local Markets: The internationalisation of product design and development', in R. Thorpe and S. Little (eds), *Global Change: The impact of Asia in the 21st Century*, London: Palgrave.

Kanbur, R. (2001), 'Economic Policy, Distribution and Poverty: The nature of disagreements', *World Development*, June.

Klein, N. (2000), *No Logo*, London: HarperCollins.

Lamberton, D. (1995), 'Communications', in P. Troy (ed.), *Technological Change and Urban Development*, Sydney: Federation Press.

Lipietz, A. (1992), *Towards a New Economic Order: Postfordism, ecology and democracy*, Cambridge: Polity Press.

Little, S.E. (2000), 'Networks and Neighbourhoods: Household, community and sovereignty in the global economy', *Urban Studies*, Vol. 37, No. 10, September, pp. 1813–26.

Little, S., Holmes, L. and Grieco, M. (2000), 'Island Histories, Open Cultures? The Electronic Transformation of Adjacency', *Southern African Business Review*, Vol. 4, No. 2.

Little, S., Holmes, L. and Grieco, M. (forthcoming), 'Calling up Culture: Information spaces and information flows as the virtual dynamics of inclusion and exclusion', *Information Technology and People*.

Marvin, C. (1988), *When Old Technologies were New: Thinking about electric communication in the late nineteenth century*, New York: Oxford University Press.

Massey, D., Quintas, P. and Wield, D. (1992), *High Tech Fantasies: Science parks in society, science and space*, London: Routledge.

Nelson, K. (1988), 'Labor Demand, Labor Supply and the Suburbanization of Low-wage Office Work', in A.J. Scott and M. Storper (eds), *Production Work and Territory: The geographical anatomy of industrial capitalism*, Boston: Unwin-Hyman.

Nicholson, B., Sahay, S. and Krishna, S. (2000), 'Work Practices and Local Improvisations within Global Software Teams: A case study of a UK subsidiary in India', in *Proceedings of IFIP WG9.4*, Conference on Information Flows, Local Improvisations and Work Practices, Cape Town, May.

Ohmae, K. (1990), *The Borderless World: Power and strategy in the interlinked economy*, London: Collins.

Ohmae, K. (1995), *The End of the Nation State: The rise of regional economics*, New York: Free Press.

Perez, C. (1983), 'Structural Change and the Assimilation of New Technologies in the Economic and Social Systems', *Futures*, Vol. 15, No. 5 pp. 357–75.

Porter, M.E. (1990), *The Competitive Advantage of Nations*, London: Macmillan.

Rich, B.R. and Janos, L. (1995), *Skunk Works*, London: Warner Books.

Ritzer, G. (2000), *The Macdonaldisation of Society: An Investigation into the Changing Character of Contemporary Social Life*, 2nd edn, Thousand Oaks: Pine Forge Press.

Rogers, E.M. (1983), *Diffusion of Innovations*, 3rd edn, New York: Free Press.

Saxenian, A. (1994), *Regional Advantage: Culture and competition in Silicon Valley and Route 128*, Cambridge, MA: Harvard University Press.

Sproull, L. and Kiesler, S. (1991), *Connections: New ways of working in the networked organization*, Cambridge, MA: MIT Press.

Taplin, R. (2000), 'Perfect Guidance for the Stars', *The Times*, 3 October, p. 17.

Taylor, F.W. (1911), *Principles of Scientific Management*, New York: Harper.

Thorpe, R. and Little, S. (eds) (2001), *Global Change: the Impact of Asia in the 21st century*, London: Palgrave.

Tugendhat, C. (1971), *The Multinationals*, Harmonsdsworth: Penguin.

Veblen, T. (1904), *The Theory of the Business Enterprise*, New York: New American Library.

Vernon, R. (1971), *Sovereignty at Bay: the multinational spread of US enterprises*, New York: Basic Books.

Webber, M. (1964), 'The Urban Place and the Non-place Urban Realm', in M.M. Webber, J.W. Dyckman, D.L. Foley, A.Z. Gutenberg, W.L.C. Wheaton and C.B. Wurster (eds), *Explorations in Urban Structure*, Philadelphia: University of Pennsylvania.

Wilkinson, B., Gamble, J., Humphrey, J. and Morris, J. (2001), 'International Production Networks and Human Resources: The case of the Malaysia electronics industry', in R. Thorpe and S. Little (eds), *Global Change: The impact of Asia in the 21st century*, London: Palgrave.

Winterbotham, F.W. (1974), *The Ultra Secret*, London: Weidenfeld and Nicholson.

World Bank (1998), *World Development Report, 1998/99 Knowledge for Development*, Oxford: Oxford University Press.

Chapter Ten

Globalisation – Trash or Treasure? The Experience of the Cancer Support Association of Western Australia

Peter Daale

This short chapter makes the case for open public access to health knowledge in a context where knowledge imbalances between patient and specialist currently accentuate the negative context of those experiencing cancer and those most closely connected with them. It describes some of the activities and the role of the Cancer Support Association of Western Australia. It provides a case study of the new social relationships which the new information technologies permit in the domain of health, treatment and patient participation.

Introduction

What can globalisation contribute to the effective functioning of non-governmental organisations? Is it trash or treasure? I represent the Cancer Support Association of Western Australia and the topic of globalisation is of particular interest to us. Well you might ask, why? I'll attempt to answer that question in these allocated pages as succinctly as I can.

There are many issues which impact on our Association's approach to cancer support, but primarily they are:

1) a long-term strategic interest to deliver support services to geographically remote areas in Australia and Asia;
2) the empowerment of individuals, achieved through information access and knowledge;
3) the very limited financial resources of the Cancer Support Association of Western Australia and of individuals in rural areas, particularly in developing and Third World countries.

Retaining Personal Control and Time Limited Consultation

To highlight the importance of these three issues and in particular the concept of *empowerment through knowledge* with respect to health care and global access to information, I would like you to consider the following experience common to most of our Association's members and visitors from the general public.

When diagnosed with cancer, most individuals receive their diagnosis during a time-limited consultation (say 30 minutes) and corresponding pathology results are often received by phone. This information leaves the individual with a sinking feeling, a sense of powerlessness and fear. The fear is very real and loss of personal control and a dependency on the oncology establishment most often results.

The diagnosis, often complex, is given by physician oncologists who are primarily focused on one of or a combination of surgery, chemotherapy and radiotherapy as the recommended option of treatment. Serious questions remain about the effectiveness of each mainstream approach and many patients face their cancer while under the care of a specialist who uses only one approach. It is true that if your only tool is a hammer, everything begins to look like a nail! Dr Charles Myers, a very well known US physician with a formidable reputation for his involvement in cancer research, puts it very clearly:

> The patient hears the specialist passionately champion a single approach and takes the recommended course without considering the alternatives. Later the patient may discover that another approach might have suited his needs and personal goals much better. This process has created many angry patients.

Our Association's members are no exception. For example, when a patient has enough courage and presence of mind, once a diagnosis is made and treatment is being discussed and possibly already in progress (considering his/her state of initial shock and on-going anxiety), to ask a simple but very pertinent question 'Should I change my diet?' the specialist usually answers 'Just eat what you usually eat'. The patient should immediately speak out and say 'But that's the diet on which I got cancer!'. Sadly, most individuals don't feel empowered and informed enough to challenge whatever is presented to them by what is traditionally considered a very well respected medical establishment. However, it is well documented today that external factors play a *very significant causal role* in cancer and nutrition is one of those factors. Now try an even less reasonable question such as 'meditation or positive thinking' and you are likely to see the bamboo turn into a real iron curtain! Take it one step further and ask yourself: *how* can I ask this specialist *intelligent questions* so that his/her answers become informative, full of support and with referral to appropriate information and cancer support services, possibly outside the specialist's direct control? Don't even think about suggesting a second, third or fourth medical opinion!

Why Did it Happen: the Search for Answers

One further note: many cancer specialists never bother to find out *why* the patient came down with the cancer in the first place. They are mostly concerned with the *prospective treatment* of the disease through surgery, chemotherapy or radiotherapy.

A real patient, whom I will not name, wrote the following:

> I was totally ignorant about cancer, full stop. I didn't know that there was a family history of breast cancer in our family or that I was carrying the breast cancer gene – I didn't know that a gene even existed! But after the initial shock, I began to learn – and learn very quickly – what everything meant, and in particular what to ask and to be more forceful in understanding what was happening to me and around me. Knowledge is power – if you understand something, you lose your fear of it. To me, it was so important to know what was going on so that I felt I had at least some level of control over my treatment, my body, my life!

In an ideal world, the physician will acknowledge that he/she *does not have all* the knowledge, the *only intelligent* brain and that understanding and competent decision-making is not the *sole prerogative* of medical practitioners. The patient should be acknowledged as an intelligent, able human being and physicians should be willing to acknowledge their own limitations and readily refer patients in their quest for information, be it to mainstream, complementary or alternative sources.

Let us just ponder for a moment that in this world, on a global basis, there is an enormous asymmetry of power, capital and knowledge between advanced economies (such as the G7 and Australia) and developing/Third World countries (such as Indonesia, China, Sub-Saharan Africa). All three (power, capital and knowledge) are interlinked and at different times are hidden from the public-view, also within a civil society. Of the three however, *the exclusivity of information and knowledge* is steadily being worn away and has started to empower significant – previously disenfranchised – sections in our global community. Their tool (among others) is the Internet.

Regulating Information and Self-diagnosis

This risk of unrestricted and global information access has been recognised by governments. Governments appear to be prepared to save the public – or should I say 'prevent the public' – and in this instance their banner of disguise is *online censorship and regulation for the greater common good*. I mention guise, because the debate uses access to pornographic material by minors as the justification. In fact the Australian government did something late last year – it amended the Broadcasting Services Act to allow regulation of online content and *requiring* ISPs (Internet Server Providers) to provide filters for users. The US Congress is travelling the same path but on a considerably more sophisticated basis, focusing on *e-rate money transactions*. However, they similarly try and use the concept of a Child Online Protection Act as essential within a civil society.

In *The Australian* newspaper we also read in 'Fear of Freedom' (Dearne, 2000) the warning of doctors against the perils of web self-diagnosis. I don't think I need to explain the meaning of this comment, particularly within the context of the Cancer Support Association. However, individuals are clearly aware that asymmetry of information and knowledge derived from information, which is not easily accessible, equals asymmetry of power and empowerment, and that this asymmetry presents itself along the continuum from macro to micro level, globally and down into every individual society, civil or less so. Controlling forces are equally aware, *and afraid*, that access to information and knowledge is not only becoming much easier but also *astonishingly cheaper*.

An On-line Gateway to Cancer Information: an Australian Model

On a very modest basis and in response to the three strategic issues affecting the Cancer Support Association of Western Australia Inc., which I outlined at the start of my discussion, the Association developed CSA On-Line (www. cancersupportwa.org.au). CSA On-Line is an Internet-based cancer information gateway with the aim *to empower individuals to regain control over their life after a cancer diagnosis*, by providing easy and cost-effective information access to leading cancer sites on a global basis. Information gates selected cover mainstream, complementary and alternative treatments. Early in 2002 it will incorporate a world-class diagnostic cancer information and support tool developed by a US based medical research body, to assist cancer patients and their physician, jointly or *individually*, to make considerably more informed decisions.

Access to CSA On-Line is mostly free of charge, so that as an information tool it can reach any community anywhere in the world in line with Internet connection networks under development. CSA On-Line has also embarked on a strategy of translating the site culturally and linguistically into Mandarin and Indonesian/Malay in recognition of our multi-cultural society locally, and our neighbours in Asia.

Conclusion

In this light, *information empowers* and I have to endorse globalisation as a treasure: it provides universal access to key information on health matters.

Reference

Dearne, K. (2000), 'Fear of Freedom', *The Australian*, 24 October.

Chapter Eleven

The Psychoanalysis of On-line Auditing

David Crowther

The development of the Internet, and the increasing access to it by individuals, has the potential of increasing the extent of accountability of a firm, has provided individuals with increasing power to make their respective voices heard, and has made auditing a current activity rather than an examination of the past. Indeed that auditing has becomes a means whereby the various stakeholders to the organisation can influence, or at least comment upon, the activities of the organisation (Crowther, 2001a). Thus auditing has changed not just in scope, nor in range of stakeholders involved but also in its temporal immediacy. In doing so it has affected the way in which managers can make use of accounting information, and the annual reporting thereof, for their own purposes. It is the purpose of this chapter to explore the uses made of such reporting and the effects of the changed nature of auditing upon organisations and their managers through the use of psychoanalytic theory, and in doing so to throw some light upon the changing nature of managerial accountability.

Introduction

While important from the viewpoint of monitoring stewardship on behalf of shareholders, the audit of the activities of an organisation has tended to be an activity of relatively little importance in the life of the organisation. Such auditing has tended to be mostly in financial terms, on the basis that it was only shareholders as the legal owners of the business who mattered to the managers (in accordance with agency theory), and carried out in arrears (Crowther, 2000a). Indeed for most stakeholders to an organisation the only mechanism for that audit was the annual report of the organisation which was published some period of time after the activity it recorded had taken place. Thus auditing, like accounting, was an activity which happened after the action had taken place and merely provided confirmation that this action was acceptable. Thus very often in the past such an audit was a token verification which at the same time, provided a validation of the efforts of the management of the firm. In this respect auditing serves both a legitimating purpose for managerial activity and a focus upon that activity.

More recently the activity of firms, and hence of their managers, has become of concern to a wider range of stakeholders to the firm, particularly with respect to the social and environmental effects of that activity. In this way the auditing of the activities of a firm has been extended both in terms of the scope of these activities and in terms of the number of stakeholders demanding accountability from the firm and its managers for their activity. Thus auditing has been considerably extended in its scope. The development of the Internet, and the increasing access to it by individuals, has the potential of increasing the extent of accountability of a firm, has provided individuals with increasing power to make their respective voices heard, and has made auditing a current activity rather than an examination of the past. Indeed that auditing has becomes a means whereby the various stakeholders to the organisation can influence, or at least comment upon, the activities of the organisation (Crowther, 2001a). Thus auditing has changed not just in scope, nor in range of stakeholders involved but also in its temporal immediacy. In doing so it has affected the way in which managers can make use of accounting information, and the annual reporting thereof, for their own purposes. It is the purpose of this paper to explore the uses made of such reporting and the effects of the changed nature of auditing upon organisations and their managers through the use of psychoanalytic theory, and in doing so to throw some light upon the changing nature of managerial accountability.

The Audit Script

For most stakeholders the script of organisational activity which forms the basis of audit has tended to be the annual report of that organisation. It has been argued (Crowther, 2001a) that the authors of the annual report of an organisation have created a dialectic between the internal perspective on corporate performance, as epitomised by traditional financial reporting of performance, and the external perspective on corporate reporting, as epitomised by social and environmental reporting. These two aspects of performance have tended to be reported separately in the annual report and accompanying environmental report.

In considering such auditing through the annual report, agency theory argues that managers merely act as custodians of the organisation and its operational activities (Emmanuel, Otley and Merchant, 1985) and places upon them the burden of managing in the best interest of the owners of that business. According to agency theory all other stakeholders of the business are largely irrelevant and if they benefit from the business then this is coincidental to the activities of management in running the business to serve shareholders. This focus upon shareholders alone as the intended beneficiaries of a business has been questioned considerably from many perspectives (e.g. Crowther, 2000b; Cooper et al., 2001), which argue that it is either not the way in which a business is actually run or that it is a view which does not meet the needs of society in general.

Conversely stakeholder theory argues that there are a whole variety of stakeholders involved in the organisation and each deserves some return for their involvement. According to stakeholder theory therefore benefit is maximised if the business is operated by its management on behalf of all stakeholders and returns are divided appropriately amongst those stakeholders, in some way which is acceptable to all. Unfortunately a mechanism, which has universal acceptance, for dividing returns amongst all stakeholders does not exist, and stakeholder theory is significantly lacking in suggestions in this respect. Nevertheless this theory has some acceptance and is based upon the premise that operating a business in this manner achieves as one of its outcomes the maximisation of returns to shareholders, as part of the process of maximising returns to all other stakeholders. This maximisation of returns is achieved in the long run through the optimisation of performance for the business to achieve maximal returns to all stakeholders (see, for example, Rappaport, 1986, 1992). Consequently the role of management is to optimise the long term performance of the business in order to achieve this end and thereby reward all stakeholders, including themselves as one stakeholder community, appropriately.

These two theories can be regarded as competing explanations of the operations of a firm which lead to different operational foci and to different implications for the measurement and reporting of performance. It is significant however that both theories have one feature in common. This is that the management of the firm is believed to be acting on behalf of others, either shareholders or stakeholders more generally. They do so, not because they are the kind of people who behave altruistically, but because they are rewarded appropriately and much effort is therefore devoted to the creation of reward schemes which motivate these managers to achieve the desired ends. Similarly much literature is devoted to the consideration of the effects of reward schemes on managerial behaviour (see, for example, Briers and Hirst, 1990; Child, 1974, 1975) and suggestion for improvements.

The advent of the World Wide Web has enabled other stakeholders to an organisation to participate in the running of that organisation through their ability to undertake immediate on-line auditing of the activities of the organisation and to communicate their opinions to the managers of the organisation. At the same time organisations have supplemented the published, paper-based reporting of performance with on-line reporting. Such reporting is different from the annual report in that more detail is provided concerning performance, with much more nonfinancial data being provided. This has been done by organisations as part of the governance procedures to make their activities more transparent and therefore the organisation more accountable. More significantly however, for the purposes of this paper, such reporting is readily available to anyone who cares to look and is provided more immediately than the retrospective annual report. This has the potential of opening up the discourse of corporate accountability to a much wider range of stakeholders and to facilitate a demand for accountability in a time frame which enables future actions of the organisation to be more readily affected by those stakeholders. More specifically it potentially holds the managers of an organisation more directly accountable for the actions of the organisation.

Although many approaches to understanding the implications for those managers can be adopted, it is argued that the application of psychoanalytic theory provides one valuable mechanism for developing that understanding. Thus this theory is used to help understand managerial motivations involved in corporate reporting and the implications of on-line auditing.

The Motivation of Managers

In considering the way in which corporate reporting impacts upon managerial accountability it is essential to consider the motivations of managers (Crowther, 2001b). This paper therefore considers the motivations of managers in terms of psychoanalytic theory from the Freudian and Lacanian perspectives to consider the implications for managerial needs for individuation. It has been argued (Crowther, 2001a) that this drive for individuation leads to the managerial motivation for the usurpation of primacy and more specifically to the need for the myth creation part of corporate reporting.

The management of an organisation is often treated as a discrete entity but it is important to remember that this entity actually comprises a set of individuals with their own drives motivations and desires. Thus every individual has a desire to fulfil his/her needs and one of these is self-actualisation (Maslow, 1954). This need is the one at the top of Maslow's hierarchy of needs and consequently perhaps the one most considered in terms of motivation. The next two most important needs – the need for esteem (as reflected in self respect and the respect of others) and the need for love and belonging (as reflected in the need for being an integral part of a community) – are however more important for the understanding of the behaviour of the members of the dominant coalition of management within an organisation. These two needs help explain why managers, in common with other individuals, need to feel important, skilled and essential to organisational performance.

A more suitable basis for arriving at a deeper understanding of the drivers of management behaviour, when considered from the point of view of the behaviour and motivations of individual managers of the organisation, is however based upon a psychoanalytic interpretation. Psychoanalytic theory was created initially by Freud but has been widely adapted by others. In a general sense such theory can be considered to be a theory of human emotional behaviour. An investigation of some of the major perspectives is necessary in order to understand the implications for managerial behaviour.

A Freudian Analysis – the Drive for Individuation

In his psychoanalytic theory Freud (1984) argues that the real motivation for any act undertaken by a person may be disguised and not apparent even to the person who performs that act. Thus for Freud the underlying basis for identity, and therefore for an explanation of individual behaviour, was based in the unconscious. He argued that an individual's identity was based upon past experience which was largely unconscious and that behaviour was largely dependant upon an attempt to resolve the conflicts and motivations inherent in the unconscious (Freud, 1975). Furthermore, he stated (1976, 1977) that most aspects of identity are laid down in early childhood and that it is an attempt to integrate the various facets of childhood experience which leads a person to act in particular ways. Part of this conflict is based upon parental influence, which leads to the development within the child of the concept of the ideal self as the perfect being to strive to become in order to win parental approval. This ideal self is of course unattainable but adult life, and the actions undertaken by adults, is based upon an unconscious motivation to achieve this ideal self and thereby secure respect. This motivation has been expressed by psychoanalysts as the drive towards individuation and explains the continual need for reassurance and the gaining of both self-respect and the respect of others.[1]

This drive for individuation is manifest in different ways by different individuals and in different ways at different times by the same individual. This has been interpreted by Bettelheim (1976) as part of the search for meaning to life through the reintegration of the conscious and the unconscious (Bettelheim, 1984). It has been described (Fromm, 1974) as a battle between the opposing instincts of life and death or between the idealist and materialist strivings of the individual (Fromm, 1980). For some people this can be reflected in a drive towards conformity as a means of escaping from the isolation of the self (Fromm, 1957). In extreme circumstances this can result in a person resorting to madness by attempting to hold what Laing (1961) describes as an untenable position. They can also result in paranoid behaviour through the dominance of feelings of guilt (Klein, 1932) or in psychosis (Lawrence, 1995).

All these arguments naturally have consequences for an individual which affect the behaviour of that individual. When these individuals are managers of an organisation they also naturally have implications for the organisation as well and Sievers (1994) has described this as leading to organisational psychotic behaviour. These interpretations of individual behaviour naturally apply to all people. As far as individual managers are concerned however the implication of these Freudian arguments is that managers are motivated by unconscious conflicts and desires which they seek to reconcile through acting out these conflicts as part of their desire for individuation. One way in which they can act out these desires which differs from other people is through their role within the organisation.[2] Furthermore these arguments imply that all individuals are anxious and insecure and seek to reduce anxiety and increase security through their actions. Thus the drive to reduce anxiety is manifest in the desire to seek confirmation of worth from others in order to increase self-esteem. Managers of large organisations are in a particularly powerful position to achieve this end through their actions as they are in a position to influence a large number of people. Employees of the organisation can be directly influenced by such managers but greater self-esteem can be gained from the respect of peers rather than subordinates.[3] Thus the respect of other managers in comparable positions in other organisations is particularly desirable as a means of reinforcing self-esteem.

One of the inevitable consequences of the insecurities surrounding a person's estimation of his/her own worth is that others in comparable positions are deemed to be more worthy than is oneself. Consequently it is argued that each manager deems other managers in other comparable organisations as more worthy of respect than is his/herself. Thus all managers are therefore seeking to compare themselves favourably with the other managers in other comparable organisations, who are always deemed more worthy. One way to attract this respect is to surround oneself with the material trappings of success. As far as the manager in the organisation is concerned this can be interpreted as such things as salaries and bonuses, share options, cars, chauffeurs and company planes. Another way to achieve this favourable comparison however is to earn the respect of the owners of the business, in other words the shareholders – or more specifically the respect of the major shareholders, City analysts and investors. The annual report provides a mechanism for earning this respect of others through the creation of the appropriate semiotic. This semiotic is of course one of success – but more particularly of success at a particularly difficult task. The provision of performance information over the web gives an opportunity to inform more people of the success of those managers in their task and thereby to enhance the semiotic of success and consequent self esteem.

Thus, for example, the following statements are made in annual reports:

> I am pleased to report another successful year for the Group, with our water and sewerage business making excellent progress and our other subsidiaries operating well.

and:

> The benefits of the improvements we have delivered and planned for the future are now becoming apparent (South West Water plc, Annual Report and Accounts, 1994).

These statements are of course made about past performance and in the era of on-line auditing it is only current and future performance which is important (Crowther, 2001a). It therefore becomes much harder for managers to use performance reporting as a mechanism for gaining self respect through the respect of others which, according to Freudian theory, is the main motivation for human behaviour.

The Lacanian View – the Reassertion of the Individual

Since the development of psychoanalysis by Freud, critiques of this theory have been prevalent in the discourses of social theory and of Marxism. Indeed, the intertwining of Marxist and Freudian theory as a means of understanding organisational behaviour and the distribution of power within society is a recurrent theme within many discourses. Thus for example Marcuse (1956) argues that rather than the foundations of civilisation being built upon the subjugation of human instincts in the assuagement of guilt it is instead built upon the way in which power is distributed and the consequent suppression of labour. Similarly Habermas (1971) argues that Freudian psychoanalysis is based upon the voluntary self-deception of individuals as part of their anxiety reducing mechanisms; moreover he argues that corporate organisations are also involved in this deception. Baudrillard (1993, 1999) is equally critical of psychoanalysis.

Possibly the most significant critique of psychoanalysis has been undertaken by Lacan, who developed an alternative interpretation of Freudian theory which has permeated popular culture, while at the same time providing a basis for an understanding of the role of managers as individuals in the development of the semiology of corporate reporting. Lacanian interpretations incorporate both structuralist and post-structuralist arguments to extend the value of Freudian theory. Its limitations from this perspective can be encapsulated in the work of Harris (1979) who stated that the Freudian attempts to understand pan-human psychodynamic processes were sufficient to understand and explain the similarities but not the differences in such processes.

Lacan argues that the formation of the ego is concerned with a fascination with one's own image. For him the external world merely represents a mirror upon which the self is displayed and the concern of the individual is to create a reflection in this mirror. This reflection must of course support that person's desire to see the most flattering reflection, but in such a way that it appears as reality. This is brought about by every person's inherent insecurity and seeking for the ideal self (Lacan, 1977, 1988, 1991) and thus every action which a person undertakes is derived from this motivation. It is accepted however that this motivation may not be overt and may not even be recognised by the individual him/herself. Like Freud therefore Lacan accepts that an individual's motivation may not be transparent even to him/herself but nevertheless that motivation becomes inseparable from the actions undertaken, and those actions have a motivation which is based upon the seeking of personal individuation.

This motivation applies to every individual but some, almost inevitably, have more scope for playing out their individuation drive upon the mirror of the world. In this respect the managers of any organisation have a large mirror to act upon, with this mirror being the organisation which they can shape, either consciously or unconsciously to their needs. Thus a manager, in producing the corporate reporting script, is attempting through the creation of that script to represent him/herself to the external world and to make that representation reflect him/herself as (s)he would wish to appear. That wish is of course to appear as a highly competent and capable person and the more difficult the activity in which (s)he is perceived to be engaged the closer that image relates to the ideal self. Thus the creation of the dialectic in the management of corporate affairs, between managing financial performance and managing environmental performance, leads to an enhanced image of the author as a competent and capable person. If this image is accepted by the readers of the script then, because the author determines and perceives his/her identity from viewing it upon the mirror of the world, the author also can accept this image. Thus the creation of an appropriate semiotic is essential to the individuation process and to the creation of the desired self-image. For example:

> If we are to become truly customer focused we will have to reduce our costs so that we can minimise price increases while maintaining a value added services. The service our customers receive must not only be the best but also be seen to be the best. We aim to make Anglian Water a benchmark company against which others will be judged.
>
> The rationale of the strategic systems review is therefore to focus ourselves on our customers, streamline decision making by reducing bureaucracy, and reduce costs by removing duplication and unnecessary activities in order to encourage an approach that is flexible and responsive to changing demands ...
>
> The process will involve a substantial change in company culture as well as in its structure ...
>
> There have to be job losses over the next two to three years but we will endeavour to achieve this on a voluntary basis (Anglian Water, Annual Report, 1994).

That wish is of course to appear as a highly competent and capable person and the more difficult the activity in which (s)he is perceived to be engaged the closer that image relates to the ideal self. The managers of an organisation are of course not unique in having these motivations driving their behaviour (Bettelheim, 1976). They are present in all of us and consequently form one of the underlying themes of individual existence and organisational behaviour (Mitroff, 1983). The managers of an organisation are however unique in that their position within the organisation gives them the power to act out these motivations through the creation of the myth of their necessity. The creation of the corporate reporting script provides one mechanism for the creation and reinforcement of this myth of their necessity as individuals to the future of that organisation.

The opening up of this script to greater scrutiny, via on-line reporting, has the potential to further reinforce this myth and providing a bigger mirror for image reflection while at the same time posing certain dangers. Thus this increased openness to scrutiny provides an opportunity for greater social grooming of the self through increased exposure. At the same time it provides an opportunity for self-reflection and surveillance as well as increasing the opportunity for surveillance by others. This can enhance self-esteem but only if the feedback received, from the self as well as from others, is positive. The danger is that this feedback might not be positive and one of the problems of on-line auditing is that feedback is, by implication if not directly, invited in a much more immediate manner and by a much wider range of stakeholders, thereby increasing the likelihood of critical feedback. Thus the reflection in the Lacanian mirror may not necessarily be the one which managers will wish to see. This makes the myth creating role of performance reporting of much greater significance to managers.

Myth Creation and Corporate Reporting

The myth creation role of corporate reporting has several aspects but one aspect is the creation of the myth of the unified whole. As Nietzsche (1956: 156) states: 'Only a horizon ringed about by myth can unify a culture'. One of the purposes of the corporate report therefore is the creation of the myth of the unified culture – in other word the common cultural bond of identity between the authors of the script and the audience (Crowther, Cooper and Carter, 2001). This is achieved by the creation of a symbolic order which is an autonomous order of reality independent of the things symbolised (Jenkins, 1979). The myth itself is a symbolic form (Brandist, 1997) which assumes a life of its own. As Cassirer (1955: 5–6) states the specificity of myth lies not in its content but rather in 'the intensity with which it is experienced, with which it is believed – as only something endowed with objective reality can be believed'.

Thus myth has the power to present a single viewpoint as directly expressive of the existence of the organisation, which consequently exists in the form presented in the annual report. The corporate report as myth therefore provides an authoritative discourse about the organisation, demanding acceptance (Bakhtin, 1981). Thus the corporate report replaces the organisation itself as the real through this power assumed from its myth creation role and the organisation becomes in the minds of both the readers and the authors (through the reflective quality of the readership) that which is presented through the corporate reporting mechanism. The concept of the corporate report can therefore be considered to have attained a life of its own through the resurrection of the myth of its origin and authenticity. It can therefore be considered to have attained hyper-reality through becoming more real than reality (Baudrillard, 1981). The promulgation of that reporting via the World Wide Web increases that sense of hyper-reality by making the myth omnipresent but runs the danger that the myth is subverted by the critiques of the shareholders. This is evident in the protest sites which exist associated with organisational activity (see Crowther, 2000a).[4]

In addition to the myth creation role of corporate reporting for the individual organisation, Campbell (1949) argues that all myths have an underlying commonality which transcends the individual myth. Thus as far as corporate reporting is concerned the common elements can be seen in the common format of such reporting, the common style and the use of common language – natural, accounting and non-linguistic – to provide a unified myth concerning corporate reporting as the authoritative discourse of organisational existence and activity.[5] Thus the history of organisations unfolds through this corporate reporting (Campbell, 1976) but unfolds in a manner which is common to all organisations and can therefore be depicted as universal and immutable. This unfolding of history can be seen from the development of corporate reports over time (McKinstry, 1996) but the mythical role of such reports ensures that, although the image of the organisation changes with the development of corporate reports (Preston, Wright and Young, 1996), the image of the organisation remains immutably fixed in the present.

The creation of the myth of organisational existence is an essential step along the road to the creation of the religion which binds the organisation together (Malinowski, 1962) and this religion becomes manifest in the rituals of organisational behaviour. One further purpose of myth creation in this context is the reinforcement of organisation boundaries, and hence the restatement of organisational existence. Corporate reporting can be considered as a myth creation mechanism for the redefinition and reinforcement of organisational boundaries which are in reality obsolete for performance determining purposes. External reporting serves the function of providing a statement to the external world that the organisation exists as a discrete entity and the production of the annual report actually is designed to fulfil this role. This statement is reinforced through the web presence of the statement of organisational existence and activity. Moreover the design of this reporting is carefully considered to make a statement not just that the organisation exists but also to create an image of that organisation. Thus over time such reporting has become more and more full of information, statements from the chairman and others, and pictures of organisational activities, designed to give to the reader the impression that this is an organisation to be interested in, with a dynamic present and an even more interesting future. In doing so the opportunity for the social grooming of the managers involved is increased.

Despite the assertions of Norris (1990), language creates reality which then becomes truth. Thus, as Barthes (1988) claims, meaning is not in the linguistic structure of a message but in the image created by the recipient of the message. Accounting by its nature creates an image of the organisation, the decision making within the organisation and the future of that organisation. This is achieved though the use of the language of accounting and the perceived certainty attached to that language. One of the purposes of such external reporting is to continually recreate the myth of organisational existence as certainty in the uncertain world. This certainty is of course a myth and one important function of accounting therefore is to act as a myth creation mechanism for the organisation as a statement of organisational existence as immutable.

One of the purposes of myth making is to remove temporality from the perception of the onlooker (Levi-Strauss, 1966), who in this case is an external consumer of the information supplied by the organisation. Removing temporality has the effect of conflating the past and present into the present and to make this present contiguous with the future. In doing so the uncertainty of images made through accounting, from one period to the next, is disguised within the omnipresent organisational myth based upon the eternal present. Rationality and predictability through using accounting information within the metanarrative myth of organisational immutability therefore seems reasonable within any discourse of organisational reporting. This removal of temporality has the concomitant effect of focusing upon spatiality. As far as spatiality is concerned the organisation seeks to create the myth of itself as omnipresent through the attention given to both the local and the global aspects of organisational existence. This is achieved through the use of appropriate text and image. For example, Severn Trent is by definition territorially bounded to the central part of the UK but produces a map in its 1994/95 annual report indicating its existence throughout the UK. Additionally it signals its global presence through text such as:

> In addition Severn Trent Water International is working with the appropriate
> authorities to deliver water and waste services in Swaziland, Puerto Rico,
> Mauritius and India.

Equally, J. Sainsbury in its 1994 annual report produces a map which shows
its presence not just in the UK but also in North America, thereby demonstrating
its global presence. The company also focuses upon the local and states: 'The
highlight of the year was the opening of our new store in Beckton in East
London'. Similarly, United Biscuits in 1995 states:

> In 1995 we became the first UK multinational to convene a Europe-wide
> employee consultative council. We broke new ground in Eastern China, where
> we started construction of a new factory and extended distribution and sales.
> We invested in major factory upgrades in Poland and Australia.

On the other hand Unilever in 1995 signals its special omnipresence not by
means of a picture or map but by a large heading on one page of its annual
report describing the company as '*the multi-local multinational*'.

Thus the myth of organisational existence is created by this means and
this existence is continually recreated as atemporal and omnipresent, but also
extremely local. In this manner synchronicity and diachronicity are conflated
and subsumed within the myth. Likewise, the past is removed in favour of the
eternal present and better future as the organisation signals its existence and
importance through this mythical role of corporate reporting. The use of the
World Wide Web for reporting reinforces this elimination of the past in favour
of the present and future because the reporting sites are designed to eliminate
the archiving facility, important for accountability (Derrida, 1996), and so
only the present is shown, continually changing. This is one mechanism by
which managers can reduce the critical gaze of stakeholder accountability
and reintroduce their own agenda of self worth.

This myth of organisation importance is naturally of concern to the authors
of the text. If the organisation is important then, by implication, those managing
the organisation, i.e. the authors of the script, must also be important. As
Barthes (1988) claims, meaning is not in the linguistic structure of a message
but in the image created by the recipient of the message. The form of corporate
reporting is designed, almost inevitably, to create an image of the importance
and permanence of the organisation and hence of those managing that
organisation. This therefore explains the increased dominance, not of

accounting information, but of messages from members of the dominant coalition managing the organisation and particularly the chairman, managing director and increasingly other powerful members of the management team. This message is designed to indicate the need for the organisation to exist as a discrete entity, defined through the reinforcement of the organisational boundary and reinforced through the production of appropriately constructed corporate reports. At the same time such reports demonstrate just how necessary those members of the dominant coalition are to maintenance of the organisation and to its future. The language of the statements from these people tends therefore to be used as a device for corrupting thought (Orwell, 1970) through being used as an instrument to prevent thought about the various alternative realities of the organisation's existence, in terms of the multiple representations of the organisation which are apparent through the use of the technology of accounting.

In binary opposition to myth as far as corporate reporting is concerned is ritual. For an individual, ritual is an essential part of personality integration – a process of becoming whole (Perls, 1975). Rituals therefore are steps along the way to completion of the whole (Beit-Hallahmi and Argyle, 1997). So, for organisations too, there are rituals steps to be completed along the way to wholeness. In the case of the organisation, however, the integration needed is not that of parts of the organisation but that of the various people involved in the organisation into a unified whole.

One of the purposes of such ritual behaviour is to remove spaciality from the discourse of organisational activity and to focus attention upon the temporal dimension. Thus organisational existence is legitimated in this manner as a temporal sequence proceeding from one rite of organisational existence to the next in a smooth flow of routinised ritual activity. Thus in the corporate reporting managers both signal that the organisation is moving forwards to better times, in the manner previously outlined, but also signal themselves as the instigators of this progress. This is achieved through the language of the report which clearly sends the message that they are the decision makers for the organisation. At the same time it signals that their knowledge enables them to make the best decisions on behalf of the other stakeholders, who merely accept the received wisdom of the managers. In annual reporting this is easily achieved by statements such as the following:

> Our circumstances have demanded a changed approach and the first pages of this annual report outline the actions we have taken. The first signs are encouraging ...

I am grateful for the time, support and involvement they (the non-executive directors) have committed and I share their unequivocal backing for the management team and the new way forward (United Biscuits, Annual Report, 1995).

This has been a difficult year in many of our markets, but a year in which we have made considerable progress in repositioning the group. As we anticipated, the oversupply of fresh produce, which was a key influence on our performance last year, persisted throughout the financial year. Recession and increasing competition in our major markets also made trading difficult for our European food processing businesses. Whilst our results reflect these problems, there has been a strong underlying improvement in the position of the group, based on our programme of strengthening management, reducing costs, acquiring complementary businesses and disposing of operations which do not fall within the areas covered by our long term strategic goals (The Albert Fisher Group plc, Annual Report and Financial Statements, 1993).

These extracts from the paper versions of annual reports are mirrored exactly upon corporate web sites but with the addition of further pictures and comments to reinforce the desired images. Of greater significance is that in the eternal present of such sites the information shown is not permanently in the public domain and information to show improved performance can be substituted at will. Thus on-line reporting not only enables instant auditing of performance but also actually demands such instant auditing as the audit trail of past performance is transitory and subject to rapid removal. The managerial drive for individuation requires that all information shows the organisation, and hence the managers themselves, continually in the best possible light.

Conclusion

It has been argued, on the basis of psychoanalytic theory, that the managers of an organisation have a motivation, which may well be unconscious, for the creation of a semiotic of performance which enhances their perceived status. In Freudian terms this is based upon their insecurity and their need to continually seek reaffirmation of their value in their constant drive towards individuation. In Lacanian terms this is manifest in their need to see their own worth as individuals through their representation in the mirror of organisational existence. It has been further argued that the organisational coalitions which have evolved, together with individual behaviour patterns, produce a tendency towards institutionalised behaviour, and this is evidenced in the organisation rituals outlined. This is because these organisational routines and rituals provide a validation of the present through its connection to the past, and the sanctity of that past which is manifest in annual reporting, while the online reporting legitimates itself through its existence in the eternal present.

A psychoanalytic perspective upon corporate reporting, particularly within the context of the motivations of the authors of the script is of considerable value in developing an understanding of such reporting. Thus it has been argued in this paper that this provides a motivation for managerial behaviour as manifest in their activities as authors of the corporate reporting script. When accountability was manifest only through the auditing of the activities of the organisation on an annual basis, through the vehicle of the corporate report then accountability was to a limited number of stakeholders and to a limited extent. On-line reporting has made auditing and accountability become more immediate and to a grater range of stakeholders. This has created the opportunity for stakeholders to have a greater involvement in the activity of organisations and has thereby increased the accountability of managers. At the same time however it has increased the scope for managers to engage in social grooming and to seek individuation through such reporting, and its audit, while making such auditing both instant and transient.

Notes

1　Self-respect is of course merely a mirror of the respect of others – see Lacan (1988).
2　This is because they have, through their positions within organisations, power to affect the behaviour of others which is not available to the average person. This power is what makes possible the psychotic behaviour described by Sievers (1994).
3　This is an extension of the conspicuous consumption thesis (Veblen, 1899) whereby the consumption of the respect of others gives one status in proportion to the importance of others because of the ascribed cultural capital (Bourdieu, 1984) thereby acquired. Thus the more important the person who gives respect the greater one's self esteem is bolstered.
4　A particularly good example is the site http://www.mcSpotlight.org.
5　It is recognised, of course, that legislation and GAAP requires a considerable element of this commonality, but it is argued that this is subsumed within the image creation requirements of corporate reporting.

References

Bakhtin, M.M. (1981), *The Dialogic Imagination*, trans. M. Holquist and C. Emerson, Austin: University of Texas Press.

Barthes, R. (1988), *The Semiotic Challenge*, Oxford: Basil Blackwell.

Baudrillard, J. (1981), *For a Critique of the Political Economy of Signs*, St Louis: Telos.

Baudrillard, J. (1993), *Symbolic Exchange and Death*, trans. I.H. Grant, London: Sage.

Baudrillard, J. (1999), *Fatal Strategies*, trans. P. Beitchman and W.G.J. Niesluchowski, London: Pluto Press.

Beit-Hallahmi, B. and Argyle, M. (1997), *The Psychology of Religious Behaviour, Belief and Experience*, London: Routledge.

Bettelheim, B. (1976), *The Uses of Enchantment*, London: Penguin.

Bettelheim, B. (1984), *Freud and Man's Sou,* New York: Vintage.

Bourdieu, P. (1984), *Distinction: A social critique of the judgement of taste*, trans. R. Nice; London: Routledge and Kegan Paul.

Brandist, C. (1997), 'Bakhtin, Cassirer and Symbolic Forms', *Radical Philosophy*, 85, pp. 20–27.

Briers, M. and Hirst, M. (1990), 'The Role of Budgetary Information in Performance Evaluation', *Accounting, Organizations and Society*, Vol. 15, No. 4, pp. 373–98.

Campbell, J. (1949), *The Hero with a Thousand Faces*, Princeton, NJ: Princeton University Press.

Cassirer, E. (1955), *The Philosophy of Symbolic Forms Vol 2: Myth*, trans. R. Manheim, New Haven, CT: Yale University Press.

Child, J. (1974), 'Managerial and Organisational Factors Associated with Company Performance – Part 1', *Journal of Management Studies*, 11, pp. 3–189.

Child, J. (1975), 'Managerial and Organisational Factors Associated with Company Performance – Part 2', *Journal of Management Studies*, 12, pp. 12–27.

Cooper, S., Crowther, D., Davies, M. and Davis, E.W. (2001), *Shareholder or Stakeholder Value? The Development of Indicators for the Control and Measurement of Performance*, London: CIMA.

Crowther, D. (2000a), 'Corporate Reporting, Stakeholders and the Internet: Mapping the new corporate landscape', *Urban Studies*, Vol. 37, No. 10, pp. 1837–48.

Crowther, D. (2000b), 'The Dialectics of Corporate Value Measurement', in G. Arnold and M. Davies (eds), *Value Based Management*, London: Wileys, pp. 105–31.

Crowther, D. (2001a), *A Social Critique of Corporate Reporting*, Aldershot: Ashgate.

Crowther, D. (2001b), 'Psychoanalysis and Auditing', in S. Clegg (ed.), *Paradoxical New Directions in Management and Organization Theory*, Amsterdam: Benjamins.

Crowther, D., Cooper, S. and Carter, C. (2001), 'Regulation – The Movie: A semiotic study of the periodic review of UK regulated industry', *Journal of Organizational Change Management*, Vol. 14, No. 3, pp. 225–38.

Derrida, J. (1996), *Archive Fever: A Freudian Impression*, trans. E. Prenowitz, Chicago: University of Chicago Press.

Emmanuel, C.R., Otley, D.T. and Merchant, K. (1985), *Accounting for Management Control*, London: Chapman and Hall.

Freud, S. (1975), *The Psychopathology of Everday Life*, trans. A. Tyson, Harmondsworth: Pelican.

Freud, S. (1976), *Jokes and their Relation to the Unconscious*, trans. A. Richards, Harmondsworth: Pelican.

Freud, S. (1977), *On Sexuality*, trans. A. Richards, Harmondsworth: Pelican.

Freud, S. (1984), *On Metapsychology*, trans. A. Richards, Harmondsworth: Penguin.

Fromm, E. (1957), *The Art of Loving*, London: Unwin.

Fromm, E. (1974), *The Anatomy of Human Destructiveness*, London: Penguin.

Fromm, E. (1980), *Beyond the Chains of Illusion*, London: Abacus.

Habermas, J. (1971), *Knowledge and Human Interests*, trans. J.J. Shapiro, Boston, MA: Beacon Press.

Harris, M. (1979), *Cultural Materialism*, New York: Random House.

Janis, I.L. (1972), *Victims of Groupthink*, Boston: Houghton Miffin.

Jenkins, A. (1979), *The Social Theory of Claude Levi-Strauss*, London: Macmillan.

Klein, M. (1932), *The Psychoanalysis of Children*, London: Hogarth.

Lacan, J. (1977), *Ecrits: A selection*, trans. A. Sheridan, London: Tavistock.

Lacan, J. (1988), *The Seminars of Jacques Lacan Book II: The Ego in Freud's theory and in the technique of psychoanalysis 1954–1955*, trans. S. Tomaselli, New York: Cambridge University Press.

Lacan, J. (1991), *The Seminars of Jacques Lacan Book I: Freud's papers on technique 1953–1954*, trans. J. Forrester, New York: W.W. Norton and Co.

Laing, R.D. (1961), *Self and Others*, London: Tavistock.

Lawrence, W.G. (1995), 'The Seductiveness of Totalitarian States of Mind', *Journal of Health Care Chaplaincy*, October, pp. 11–22.

Levi-Strauss, C. (1966), *The Savage Mind*, London: Weidenfeld and Nicolson.

Malinowski, B. (1962), 'Myth as a Dramatic Development of Dogma', in I. Strenski (ed.) (1992), *Malinowski and the Work of Myth*, Princeton, NJ: Princeton University Press.

Marcuse, H. (1956), *Eros and Civilisation*, London: Routledge and Kegan Paul.

Maslow, A.H. (1954), *Motivation and Personality*, New York: Harper and Row.

May, R. (1991), *The Cry for Myth*, New York: W.W. Norton and Co.

McKinstry, S. (1996), 'Designing the Annual Reports of Burton plc from 1930 to 1994', *Accounting, Organizations and Society*, Vol. 21, No. 1, pp. 89–111.

Mitroff, I.I. (1983), *Stakeholders of the Organisational Mind*, San Francisco: Jossey-Bass.

Nietzsche, F. (1956), *The Birth of Tragedy*, New York: Doubleday.

Norris, C. (1990), 'Lost in the Funhouse: Baudrillard and the politics of postmodernism', in R. Boyne and A. Rattansi (eds), *Postmodernism and Society*, Basingstoke: Macmillan, pp. 119–53.

Orwell, G. (1970), *Collected Essays, Journalism and Letters Vol 4*, Harmondsworth: Penguin.

Perls, F.S. (1975), 'Theory and Technique of Personality Integration', in J.O. Stevens (ed)., *Gestalt Is*, Moab, Utah: Real People Press.

Preston, A.M., Wright, C. and Young, J.J. (1996), 'Imag[in]ing Annual Reports', *Accounting, Organizations and Society*, Vol. 21, No. 1, pp. 113–37.

Rappaport, A. (1986), *Creating Shareholder Value*, New York: The Free Press.

Rappaport, A. (1992), 'CFO's and Strategists: Forging a common framework', *Harvard Business Review*, May/June, pp. 84–91.

Sievers, Bm (1994), *Work Death and Life Itself. Essays on Management and Organization*, Berlin: de Gruyter.

Veblen, T. (1899), *The Theory of the Leisure Classes*, New York: New American Library.

Chapter Twelve

Shifts in the Balance of Scottish Democracy: From the Far Side of the Historical Circumference Towards a New Information Union

Paul Griffin

Introduction

This chapter provides an account of the development and history of governmental reform within Scotland during the postwar era. It provides a detailed account of the evolution of the postwar Scottish political environment. It observes the political tensions evident in postwar Scotland from the perspective of technocratic administration (in the form of the Scottish Office[1]), at odds with political culture. It establishes the conditions under which the expression of a democracy denied a measure of its full political ambition operates – in doing so it explores the issue of the 'democratic deficit' and the alterations in Scotland's relationship with Europe which present themselves with the advent of new information communication technologies. These are themes which gather pace and political momentum within Scottish civil society during this time scale, and gather an equal measure of pace as the chapter develops.

Moreover, we consider the changing nature of Scottish society from its previously peripheral position to, and its relations with, the European Union (EU). This set of political and economic conditions has emerged from a number of circumstances. Firstly, a declining Scottish faith in the ability of the United Kingdom to generate wealth, or to ensure the survival of the welfare state system in Scotland. The failure to create the conditions for a vibrant economy, or to offset lack of success by a welfare state, established a duality of opposition from within Scottish political culture. The application of monetarist economic policies under the Thatcher (and latterly that of the Major) administration was not well received in Scotland.[2] The government would not acknowledge these differences in its Scottish-based political agenda, or for that matter within its social policy framework for Scotland.

This duality was combined with another: the disaffection of two classes. Both the middle classes and the working classes were effectively undermined by Thatcherist economic policies. The Scottish middle class had a set of vested interests to protect, many of whom were disproportionately employed within a public sector coming under increasing attack (Paterson, 1994).[3] The working classes of course felt the full force of de-industrialisation and the restructuring of the economy. This was especially so during the early 1980s when the full force of such conditions began to be realised. It is this context that gives rise to a reconsideration of the United Kingdom project within Scottish political culture. It is increasingly called into question in terms of the benefits and advantages that it once offered.

A Europe of the regions, a strengthening of Scotland's position within the EU by aligning itself with more sympathetic European policies aimed at including the more peripheral areas of Europe (Harvie, 1992), seemed to offer a new set of opportunities. This can be usefully contrasted with the relative postwar decline of the UK. Effectively there has been a major shift in the polarities of Scottish political geography from a strong Scotland-UK dynamic, to one much more closely aligned with the European Union.[4] This shift has been made possible through a series of interactions between politics and technology. For example, the plans that have been established to commit Europe to a joint 'Information Society' initiative.[5] These have moved Europe towards a set of guiding principles that stress an overall information based strategy.

These policies establish the foundations for a revival of the Scottish economy and a repositioning of its political interface with Europe. This revolves around the establishment of a set of electronic connections between Scotland and the EU. For example, the European Union structural funding project has established a set of policy lines that offer the possibility of a new inclusive vision for a united and informatised Europe. Its economic ambitions offer a new potential for member states and regions to revitalise their economies through e-commerce and enterprise.[6] This is to be achieved via the production of an energised European wide educational base via research project funding, and increasing the distribution of knowledge and learning via electronic information access (Antirroiko, 2001).

> The European structural funds support and complement important policy
> objectives [in the Scottish Parliament] ... in particular [they are] in line with

European and UK priorities, in complementing our policy objectives in enterprise and work related training ... structural funds also support new technologies and the development of the information society ... the allocation for the Scottish operational programme amounts to some £480 million (between) 2000 to 2006 (Minister for Finance in the Scottish Parliament, Mr Jack McConnell, 28 October 1999, Scottish Parliament Official Parliament @ www.scottish.parliament.uk/ official_report/session99-00/or30202.htm).

These strategic policies have touched upon a traditional association with specifically Scottish cultural-political sentiments.[7] This attaches credence to their position within Scotland, and in turn forges a new association for her identification with Europe. For example, the European Commission's (1996) 'Action Plan' (*Europe's Way to the Information Society*, COM.1996) proposed a number of social security and social policy programmes and initiatives.[8] The distribution of such programmes is disseminated increasingly through information architecture. This has a resonance within Scottish culture that extends such policies beyond their more obvious functional appeal.

In this way information technologies have repositioned the Scottish political system. They have reconfigured the role of a nation without a state (McCrone, 1992) within the impact of an expanding Europe of the regions at one level, and as a supranational entity in its own right. The formerly narrow political distribution of small countries such as Scotland take on a new perspective when seen through the lens of an expanding European Union.

For instance, as the European Union grows and evolves it will seek out a more finalised model of state.[9] Whatever its constitutional framework, it is increasingly likely that the macro decisions, and the macro policies will be taken at this level.[10]

The role of the EU therefore has both social and constitutional concerns. Socially, these involve the patterns of power that have developed in opposition to those of English politics during the early 1980s. This is epitomised by the campaign for a Scottish parliament which gathered serious pace since that time, and is now characterised by the historical Scottish moment of devolved governance from 1999 onwards.

These social features are evident in a number of ways that are written into the fabric of Scottish political culture. An understanding of them is necessary as way of introduction to the wider issues that we will encounter in this chapter. There are then a set of principles that have a position within the Scottish-Anglo-European axes. All are represented in table form below (see Figure 12.1).

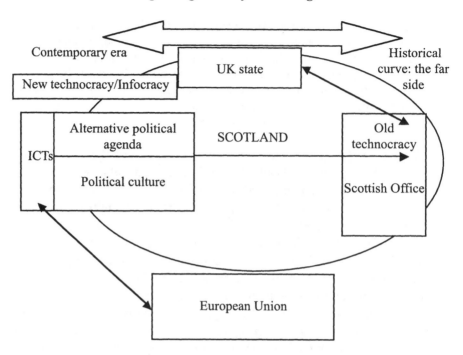

Figure 12.1 The historical curve of Scottish postwar politics

From the far side of the historical circumference towards a new information union, Figure 12.1 provides a graphic demonstration of how Scotland has been granted a new set of potential power relations within the European dimension. It offers a model of the changing set of relations between Scotland, the UK and the EU. The central area is the historical circumference referred to above. This is a design on the unfolding history that this chapter details. It offers a configuration of politics which starts at the outset of the postwar era and ends at the start of the twenty-first century. The uniting themes are that the United Kingdom is remaking the Union through information technologies, offsetting the political technology of the Scottish parliament in the process.

The trajectory of Scottish politics should be observed in a left to right fashion. Starting with the demise of the Scottish Office and technocratic administration, challenged by the alternative political agenda and an opposing political culture. New designs upon Scottish politics are observed in the form of the new technocracy. In this sense, we can also observe the creation of a new and powerful information union.

The recomposition of devolution is explored in terms of the pursuit of United Kingdom centrist ambitions. Our thesis here is that the UK project is being reasserted via informatisation. As such, it considers the strategic implications of the centralising strategy.[11]

This chapter charts what is essentially the historical movement towards these developments. It defines the historical moment within Scottish political culture in a manner akin to a circumference. Put simply, this refers to the hypothesis that the United Kingdom is being remade through information technologies, that it is being rewired through a new means of union. These are necessary for a number of reasons. In the first instance voting patterns have shown a movement away from the strong unionist affiliations of the early postwar era. Secondly, the position offered by ICTs affords a further diffusion from the centre. However, there exist the possibilities of control technologies to reverse such trends.

Formerly strong Scottish inclinations to attach the country onto a powerful English neighbour are less evident than before.[12] However, the abilities afforded by ICTs to break down national barriers, are capable also of reconstituting them also. This is the nature of the rewiring of the UK project. However, in order to comprehend the reasoning behind this we must examine the far side of the historical circumference. This is the aim of this chapter. It presents an account of the changing nature of Scottish political culture, and provides us with a perspective on the present, which is located in the recent past. This is a necessary precondition for an exploration of the developing historical moment. It sets down the influential themes.

We must address some of the subcurrents that have developed within Scottish politics during the postwar period. The necessary associations are made clearer via an understanding of the connections between these currents and their methods of communication, in particular the role of political journalism.

Furthermore, it will make the appropriate links between the demands for political reform, evidential in terms of the demands made for the extension of Scottish democracy evident from the 1960s onwards (Paterson, 1994), and the role that new technologies play in linking up the principle themes. For instance, the reaction against a rationalised technocratic society during the 1960s invoked by what Daniel Bell (1976, p. 365) described as a 'participation revolution' and the role now played by Information Communication Technologies (ICTs) can be regarded as a key linking moment. The demands made during the 1960s and 1970s for more extensive and more participative forms of democracy including those with a tele-democratic vision, such as Erich Fromm (1960)[13] with his radical political psychoanalysis within which an 'impaired' society can be remedied via a deliberative communicative democracy enabled by new technologies (Becker and Slaton, 2000) are evident today.[14]

For instance, the new Scottish parliament seeks to enlarge democratic participation via a set of key principles which aim to guide its working practices and to extend participation and accessibility and of creating new links between it and the institutions of government.[15] As such, the search for a new set of political arrangements for a new era are common currency within debates about the Scottish parliament and the forms and possibilities that might emerge from the new system.

Moreover, this chapter will examine the role of Scottish civil society in advancing the case for political change, and provide an account of the principle moments involved in the denial and extension of Scottish democracy. One of the of the main themes of twentieth-century Scottish politics is introduced, (the concept of a democratic deficit) and explored in detail, in terms of how political actors and Scottish civil society sought to overcome these deficiencies. This is in turn related to the shortcomings of traditional democratic outlets and mechanisms of representation, it is part of a broader movement which as Hassan and Warhurst (1999, p. 7) note, seeks to establish democratic initiatives and new methods of consultation between citizens and democratic structures:

> ... people (are becoming) increasingly aware of the limitations of representative democracy and look for new forms of participative democracy to reconnect politics and policy to people.

This is in turn related to the advent of new information communication technologies and the possibilities they afford for a further contemporary extension of democracy in Scotland. The focal point is the manner in which ICTs have been credited with a perceived ability to enhance democracy in the Parliament itself, and to facilitate greater inclusion, participation and access by Scottish civil society (CSG Report, 1998, p. 173; Gray and Smith, 1999). This has been a feature of the debate since 1991.[16]

The demands for democratic reform made throughout the previous decades is viewed as an ongoing evolving feature.[17] Scottish society, and Scottish political culture is involved in the process of resolving the remnants of past democratic deficiencies. However, new deficits emerge and present themselves within new conditions associated with change. We have already observed elsewhere (Griffin, 2001) the Scottish parliament's concerns at engaging with new technologies in a manner that is primarily economic in its focus. This ensures the development of a new form of democratic deficit, one that reflects a key note of the mid-1970s: the use of an economic surplus (in the form of North Sea Oil) without reciprocal political representation. This is mirrored by the development of ICTs which are economic, rather than political-democratic, in their focus and application.

In addition, within the political history of postwar Scotland, we can observe another associated theme .The discussion, and the theoretical account of what constitutes good and effective government is a keynote element of Scottish political culture during this era. Its contemporary element takes the substance of such themes and translates them into an ICT/modernisation set of agendas.

For example, the designs upon a modern innovative Scottish parliament focus their attention upon such ideas, particularly in terms of the issue of political and administrative 'transparency'. The new ICTs are it is claimed (Wilson, 1999) capable of bringing about a new interface between government and citizen. This definition of transparency[18] takes as its starting point the possibility of a resurrection between these connections. This is one principle measurement of what equates with good governance. This is an address to the defining political issue of postwar Scotland the 'democratic deficit'. Or, as Taylor and Burt (2001, p. 58) style this political (and social) feature: 'the phenomenon of citizen disengagement with conventional politics, or the democratic deficit'.

With this definition in place we can observe an extension of the concept to include an association with the present. We have observed in elsewhere the decline in citizen participation in elections (see Griffin, 2001, Table 1.1).

By this definition the democratic deficit has not been resolved, merely transformed into different political configurations. As such, the issue of modernising political institutions in order to produce economic efficiencies, rather than democratic order, is worthy of examination. It is this concern that we now address.

Democratic Deficit: Transformation or Resolution?

This feature gives us further insights into the origins behind the formation of the New Scottish Politics, and the role played by civil society in bringing about political and social change when the system was largely unresponsive to its demands (during the 1980s and early 1990s for instance), and those contemporary desires and designs aimed at encouraging the reversal of those who do not currently participate in the political system (CSG Report, ibid. p. 9). Additionally, there are more generalised international developments and shifts in the direction of postmodern politics, which interact within the Scottish dimension.[19] For example, the association is with the process of modernising government in accordance with new informatised government rationalities:

> While modernisation can be seen as a relatively linear process of differentiation, post-modernisation ... represents a shift towards de-differentiation or fragmentation. The pyramidal nature of public administration increasingly changes into an archipelago of network configurations (Frissen, 1998, p. 123).

This illustrates the changes within public administration, or government, which flow from the broader shifts in the political/economical (and technological) environment.[20] As such this chapter observes the changing nature of administration: from technocracy to more reflexive forms of governance.

Later in this chapter a registration of postwar politics in Scotland is developed which establishes the above connections and their historical context. In addition, there are other themes to consider. For instance, changes in political behaviour (particularly in terms of declining political participation – in its orthodox electoral turnout formulation – and a relative upward twist in direct political participation[21] and new postwar political philosophies and currents which are best characterised by 'grass-roots' politics (Kohler, 1998, p. 238; Paterson, 1994). With this in mind we can usefully illustrate the rising direct democratic innovations located in the past, but which appear today as an increasingly strident form of contemporary politics. Here is the connection between the appearance of a participation revolution, the reaction against technocracy and the emergence of sub-politics. However, in order to chart the encounter with these issues and their position in Scottish politics, it is necessary to examine the expansion of the state and its technocratic ambitions in postwar Scotland.

The Emergence of the Scottish Technocratic System

The condition of technocracy in its Scottish context is relative to the expansion of the Scottish Office.[22] The expansion of the state during the postwar period until 1979, gave rise to arguments which set out a strong case for increased state intervention in the day to day running of social-economic and political life in Scotland (Brown et al., 1996). These technocratic currents maintained that political problems and issues could be resolved through essentially technical methods of government and statecraft. This ruling model had political associations with science (both social and natural) and management-planning, and the expansion of the welfare state systems during the aftermath of the last war (Paterson, 1999). Moreover, the technocratic system fused within its ranks certain elements of Scottish civil society. Engaging 'expert' advice and skills, meant consultation and deliberation with the professional classes (drawn from civil society). This in turn assisted in attaching legitimacy to the system.[23]

An engagement with technocracy in Scotland should also take into account the British perspective regarding the utilisation of North Sea Oil in the 1970s In this sense, the responsibility for its revenue allocation was deemed to be not a matter for Scottish concern (Kellas, 1992). Thus the technocratic system, whilst maintaining a British technocratic remit, began to imply a downturn in political currency. This in turn called into question the legitimacy of the organisation itself. The Scottish Office increasingly became associated with British, rather than Scottish, interests. The symbolism of the new politics has centred around the use of a new set of legitimising practices and themes. The changing moniker of the Scottish Office (to the Scottish Executive) is noteworthy in this regard. With a new name, it is assumed that a new principle of organisation will be clarified.[24] These ideas help us understand some of the features behind 'transformational politics' (Schwerin, 1995).[25] The movement from a condition and context of technocracy to a more 'new institutionalist' approach should be further explored. We now turn towards an understanding of some of the reactions against technocracy and its composite ideological features.

Organisation and Power: the Relations between Technocracy and Elite Government

Here we can see something of the links which help us understand the lineage between past features of public administration, including ideas associated with technocracy, and political control.[26] Behind the principles which govern social organisation, there lies political organisation and the operation and use of power to achieve certain ends. So, the rationalisation of public administration goes hand in hand with the exercise of political power. There are those from both the left and the right of the political spectrum who see in such apparatus distinctly conservative political tendencies. From the left there are those such as Marcuse (1968) and Touraine who assert that technocracy is bound up within political-economy. Power, however defined, cannot be separated from this model of social relations (Touraine, 1974).[27]

The reaction against technocracy is to be found, argues Touraine, within the broad based countercultural movement of the late 1960s.[28]

However, the links between contemporary developments and the recent Scottish technocratic era should be clarified further, particularly in terms of their relation to forthcoming themes. This is now addressed immediately below. The themes that we are about to develop relate towards the forthcoming historical developments within Scottish postwar history. Again, the movement away from technocracy is the key to understanding its reassembly at the dawn of the twenty first century.

Scottish Reactions to Technocracy: the Origins of an Alternative Political Agenda

We can find evidence of the reaction towards technocratic administration within the realm of Scottish political history and culture. For instance, much of the campaign for a Scottish parliament from the 1960s onwards focussed upon very similar thoughts. The political aspirations of many, centred around the notion of democratising the state. As Paterson notes:

> From the 1960s onwards the campaign for home rule became entwined with a campaign to open up the system of consultation ... the state was ... too powerful and had to be democratised (Paterson, 1999, p. 34).

However, there are other elements which correspond with the themes of power, organisation, rationalisation and technocracy which we need to examine also. They will act as a means of uncovering what lies beneath the surface of power, technology and government. These will serve as a means of highlighting exploratory reactions against technocracy, and a more pronounced drive by citizens towards increasingly direct forms of democratic engagement. This is characterised by what is now termed as the new politics of participation.[29] In other words, contemporary use of the term has its roots within earlier political impulses and philosophies.

For instance, we can determine here some moments which are inclusive of the move away from technocracy, which Paterson cites as a result of a changing political environment during the late 1960s/early 1970s (ibid., p. 11). We can observe new forms of politics, and new ideals about the conduct, direction and purpose of politics, which begin to emerge as a reaction to these previously held models. For instance, within Scottish politics and its political undercurrents: 'There was another strand to reflection at this time, which raised questions about what politics is. This was the thinking that is now loosely referred to as 1960s radicalism' (Paterson, 1994, p. 8).

Tom Nairn (1981) presents evidence of similar currents of thought, particularly in terms of a reaction against postwar political crisis, orthodoxy, and a disaffection with the lack of a radical political agenda. Nairn suggests that the left-leaning intellectual political classes of the late sixties and early seventies, sought means whereby the workers might fuse with them, and thereby bring about a political reconstruction, a reordering of society. The student movement was to have been the catalyst for such developments, that somehow they were to provide the critical unrefined materials which could be translated into the idioms of political change:

> The student movement of the later 1960s was of course the chosen vehicle for this outlook – the place where for a moment philosophy appeared to have discovered its own mass movement, capable of directly modifying social structures (Nairn, 1981, p. 367).

This describes further elements which can be related to the development of an alternative political agenda. Let us now clarify this in greater detail, and make the appropriate linkages between the shape of this agenda and the directions it laid out for a new Scottish politics.

An Alternative Scottish Political Agenda

The concern with the pursuit of an alternative political agenda[30] within Scotland during the 1960s and 1970s (in the shape of the participation revolution) is evident also during the 1980s and early 1990s (McCrone, 1992), and stems from these preceding years. It provides another foundation for an exploration of the origins of the forms associated with the new politics. For example, contained within the: 'social environment of values which generated devolution' (Bonney, 1999). This quote illustrates the specifically Scottish social-political axis which, called into question (yet set against a wider backdrop of postwar Anglo-Scottish political divergence, within which the Union is called more and more into question) the tenets and practices of Thatcherism. The notion of a democratic deficit came to epitomise this moment, and within Scottish politics is a common feature of criticism during the era. This has a recent historical form, and is to be located within the attempts to resolve the legitimation problem afforded by consecutive 1980s English Conservative party parliamentary majorities, legitimate in England, and *constitutionally legitimate* in Scotland, but certainly not describable as government by consent. However, we should note other related areas of political life beyond the constitutional. An examination of Scottish civil society and its reactions, and the refracted forms of its expressions are worthwhile. It is to this that we now turn.

Culture against Technocracy, Scottish Civil Society and Political Journalism: the Development of an Alternative Political Agenda

As suggested above there developed a commonly-held notion that the government did not have a legitimate political mandate to govern in Scotland (Midwinter et al., 1991). The result was a broad-based movement determined to formulate a new political settlement in Scotland via a devolved parliament. A new political and social context emerged within Scottish civil society and Scottish political culture, fuelled in part by the media's interpretation of the existing political deficiencies (Paterson, 1994; Smith, 1994). By pointing out the limitations of the existing structures of government, and their inability to apply a legitimate democratic force, Scottish political journalism promulgated an alternative political agenda to that of Thatcherism (Hutchinson, 1987; Smith, 1994). Indeed, as Holliday (1992, pp. 448–60) notes, the factors which assisted Scotland in resisting/limiting Thatcherism were largely *cultural* as opposed to *institutional*.[31] It is argued here that the Scottish political environment was best defined and measured in terms of its 'political culture and opinion (including the media) than by formal institutions' (ibid., p. 459).

Moreover, the political boundaries of the existing institutional features are consistently called into question. There is a sustained scepticism regarding the democratic legitimacy of the Scottish Office, as Brown, McCrone and Paterson note (1996, p. 34) there emerges during the latter stages of the twentieth century increasing demands for more direct democratic forms of control over the policy and practice of the Scottish Office: 'the demands for concomitant democratic accountability over the Scottish office in the late twentieth century represent recognition of the limits that mere administrative devolution had reached'.[32]

A Register of Scottish Politics since the Postwar Era: the Evolution of Political Policy in Scotland and the Route Towards 'New Politics'

Scottish politics since the immediate postwar era can be divided into five phases which allow for a changing political architecture. These phases are inclusive of the period between 1945–99, and taken as a whole suggest the course of Scottish political culture during the era in question. They are the essence, as it were, of the defining political issues and agendas during the postwar years and can be represented in table form below (Table 12.1).

The table should be read from left to right. This traces the nature of the political transformations undergone within Scottish politics. It also makes the connection between the contrasting thematic principles of legitimacy that evolve over time. These move from a process associated with science and centralisation (this also encompasses the role of the expert in that such knowledge is withheld and non-devolved) towards more participatory democracy. The themes which unify these processes and political developments, and connect them with the present are science as a means of legitimation for the practice of government, and new forms of democratic participation, which Bell (1973, p. 12) describes as 'axial principle of the modern polity'.

The Scottish example of new forms of democratic participation is evident in a number of important ways. In the first instance, there are two referendums (1979 and 1997) during the period in question, and one large-scale petition (1949); both can be seen as evidence of such principles in action. However, before considering these an evolutionary history is necessary. The postwar era sees the decline both of empire (and thus much of the reasoning behind the Union) and of economic power. These two themes are linking points within the immediate stages of the following historical route towards the new politics of the late twentieth century.

The Immediate Postwar Era and Developments and Phases between 1944–55: Mass Participation and the Campaign for a New Politics

The first of these phases, from 1945–55, provides evidence of a degree of concern with the issue of postwar planning, the role of the welfare state (itself a reinvention of the role and scope of government) and state involvement in the economy, via nationalisation and various economic steering mechanisms, increases.[33] This was a UK wide issue and not exclusive in respect of Scottish politics *per se*, although we find that the Scottish Office's move from London to Edinburgh in 1939 arguably gave stronger focus to what its new political-geography might achieve for Scotland. According to Brown, McCrone and Paterson (1996) there was an emergent expectation that the site of the new administration might give further scope for Scottish centred political developments.

Moreover, Kellas (1992, p. 131) and Breuilly (1993, p. 320) both note the emergence of new forms of democratic action within Scottish civil society, and as such new forms of participation emerge that have a distinct relation to

Table 12.1   The Scottish postwar model of political-bureaucratic transition

Traditional principles of 'old' public administration: Scottish technocracy within United Kingdom.	Emergent principles of 'new' public management, entrepreneurial governance and new institutionalism. An EU synthesis.
Uniformity of provision: the administration (or equity principle). Citizen cast within a collective notion of social contract.	Targeted provision in search of economy, efficiency and effectiveness: the business principle within administration. Citizen as possessing individual interests.
Hierarchical structure in bureaucratic organisation: the top-down control principle (Weberian). State is provider of services. Nationalised industries.	Effector principles: network management, performance stressed over procedure. Public/private partnerships. State is regulator/purchaser.
Relative sovereignty of the nation state. Public service broadcasting.	Informatisation policies and the integrative principle. Transnational flows of communication and information.
Paternalistic relationships to clients, etc.: the professional principle. Determination of policy by technocratic elites.	Responsive relationships to customers and citizens: a reflexive principle. Determination of policy by consultation and accountability mechanisms. New Democratic Accountability (NDA) within the Scottish parliament.
← ——————— European Union synthesis ——————— →	
Macro policies determined by technocracy: economic, informatisation, political. Supra-national hierarchy.	Governance as related to social rights: European Social Chapter as confirmation of citizen based welfare rights. Subsidiarity principle.

Source: Griffin, 2001.

the contemporary era. In 1949 for instance (although they disagree upon the amount of signatures added to this particular petition: the former suggests perhaps two million, the latter over one million) a campaign was launched by the extra-parliamentary organisation the 'Scottish Convention' to secure what was then termed as 'Home Rule' for Scotland within the political framework of the United Kingdom (Devine, 1999, p. 565).[34]

These immediate postwar years are characterised by Western states as a whole committing themselves towards expansive bureaucracies, and in turn drawing legitimacy from social and economic management, i.e. technocratic administration.[35] Nevertheless, supposedly rational administrative designs concerning the economy did not stop Scotland from entering a period of economic decline. This became a significant issue both structurally and symbolically. This gradual subsidence of a previously industrialised economy gathered pace in the following era.

Affluence versus Decline: the Degeneration of the Scottish Economy (1955–64) and the Beginning of Political-economic Divergence

The key issue in this era was Scotland's relative economic decline vis-à-vis the less heavily industrialised southern points of the UK. Moreover, economic austerities were a component of the then Labour Chancellor of the Exchequer[36] before the advent of a Conservative government in 1959. By the late 1950s, as Michael Fry (1991, pp. 224–5) notes in support of this argument, during this era the sense and perceived impact of decline, at a European as well as at the UK level, was evident. Of the period under consideration he makes the following comments: 'Scotland fell behind the employment and living standards enjoyed by the rest of Britain. For a decade after 1955 she had the lowest growth rate in Europe'. Moreover, according to Kellas (1992, p. 132) this phase sees a wave of nationalism as levels of unemployment rose and standards of living, measured here in terms of housing, schools and public utilities, fell. Taken in conjunction with the Conservative election campaign of 1959, which placed much emphasis upon the supposed affluence of British society, the Scottish electorate sought to wrest more autonomy from Westminster (in order to increase the administrative capabilities of the Scottish Office) in periodic reminders which emphasised the negotiated nature of the Union (Brown et al., 1996). Additionally, Kellas (ibid.) notes the perceived influence of the then new IT medium of television, and in particular the engagement with commercial TV advertising, and Scottish society, during the 1950s, as influential:

The spread of television, particularly commercial television with its advertising appeals to this affluent society ... emphasised the contrast. Scots knew that much of the new affluence had passed them by.

Moreover, it is this moment in the contemporary political history of the Union which will first record the political divergence of Scotland and England in electoral terms, and therefore the starting point for an account of the developing democratic deficit: 'The first signs of the tension with England were evident in the late 1950s when the Unionist Party started its 40-year slide in the late 1950s' (Brown et al., 1996, p. 19).

The Authenticity of Government within the United Kingdom, Scottish Industrial Decline and the Emergence of an Economic-political Deficit: the Discovery of North Sea Oil

The problems experienced within the Scottish economy are characteristic of difficulties within the UK economy as a whole, disillusionment with the then Labour administration led to advances in the political standing of the Scottish National Party (SNP), who were able to capture former Labour supporters (Bogdanor, 1979; Miller, 1981). However, it is the failure of planning within public administration, in terms of its macro economic designs (such as the Central Scotland Plan of 1963) which characterises the era for Miller and Fry (1987, p. 224). Moreover, we should consider this within what is essentially an all encompassing postwar Scottish political theme. This is the issue of what precisely entails 'good' government, and how it might be realised. It is important because of its centrality to political life in Scotland, and its place as the prevailing set of political principles which continue today.[37]

However, aside from the issue of what entails suitable government there are other ideas worthy of exploration. For instance, as we have noted above, during the 1960s a radicalism emerged which invoked a hostility towards technocracy, scientific rationality and the presumed logic of its design and practice. Inclusive of this was a reaction against bureaucracy. In short, the vitality of the era brought forth a set of principles and actions which challenged the hierarchical assumptions and deliberations of technocratic administration.

With these notions in place it is possible to extend this question of the exercise of power, and in doing so to observe its contemporary existence in the struggle between the concept of citizens as an 'electorate', whereby decisions are made on their behalf, or alternatively, within the notion that citizens are the prime movers of political agency itself, via direct democracy.[38]

What was sought instead was a more participatory form of politics. This changing set of circumstances was initiated, in light of the changes sought by not only interest groups whose desires were of a more inclusive nature, from an understanding, a changing political mood, and that the political order was less governed by some political objectivity, and more by interest.[39]

However, the modification of Scottish politics began to be fuelled by a gathering intellectual currency. This was associated with a form of underdevelopment thesis given credence within Third World countries, but applied to Scottish economic and political affairs (Brown et al., 1996). This theme expresses the contention that the patterns of underdevelopment are strongly associated with external control of economic-political determination. This thesis gathered popular support with the generation of North Sea Oil in the 1970s and is worth exploring in more detail. It is to this we now turn. With particular emphasis upon the idea that economic wealth can generate political dissent.

The Generation of North Sea Oil: the Production of New Political Dissent and the Decline of the All-British Political System (1970–74)

As Scottish politics moved into the early 1970s a further set of circumstances emerged. These provided a contrast with the politics of the present. There was a Conservative government under Edward Heath which argued for Britain's membership of the European Economic Community (EEC). The issue was contentious in Scotland, and cut across party lines.[40] In addition, the concept of what a decade or so later would be termed the 'democratic deficit' was recognised in another related form.[41]

The continued electoral success of the SNP, which had reformed and re-energised itself during the era, was to play a significant part in the direction of political change (Scott, 1985). With the discovery of North Sea oil, the nationalists were able to capitalise on the potential use of the oil not only to revitalise the Scottish economy, but also to dispel any concerns that an independent Scotland would be able to survive in a competitive global economy. Levy (1990, p. 35) describes it as 'oil-fired nationalism'.[42]

To this end the nationalists firmly aligned their political programme to the development potential's associated with oil based economy (Brown et al., 1996, p. 20). However, as Tom Nairn (1981, p. 131) points out, there were a host of factors behind the drive for greater political autonomy during this moment in time, not least of which was:

The most critical, and the newest, is the incursion of the oil business ... this is busy creating a new material basis for political life in Scotland. The second is the decline of the all-British political system.

A tangible political reaction to such a decline is to be found in the Labour government of 1974. This will now be considered in greater detail.

Changing Democratic Access and the Referendum of 1979: 1974–79

The Labour Party responded to the nationalist impulses which saw a return of some 11 of the 71 Scottish Parliamentary seats in the (second) 1974 election,[43] (Devine, 2000, p. 586) and began its interpretation of the 1973 Royal Commission on the UK Constitution (otherwise known as the Kilbrandon Report; Cmnd 5460).[44] The appearance of the Kilbrandon Report is noteworthy in as much as although it rejected any form of federalism, its recommendations anticipated future political considerations, and ultimately the devolution settlement of 1997.[45]

Acting upon the Kilbrandon Report the Labour government of 1974–79 published a White Paper which attempted to address the future political arrangement's of the UK in November 1975 (*Our Changing Democracy*, Cmnd 6348). The guidelines expressed by the Paper proposed that responsibility for the domestic affairs of Scotland (and Wales) should effectively be handed over to elected assemblies if and when established. In the case of Scotland such powers as were deemed appropriate[46] were to be revoked from the Scottish Office, and given to what would have been known as the 'Scottish Assembly'.

Moreover, the White Paper made explicit reference towards the extent and location of the presiding sovereignty (Kellas, 1976, p. 63) any relinquishment of Westminster's ultimate sovereignty would move the UK towards an unacceptable degree of federalism it was argued.

Increased financial autonomy (specifically demands for a share of the oil revenues for a future Scottish government) was likened to the effective existence of a separate Scottish state and was thus rejected by the White Paper as politically inconsistent with the concept of the UK (ibid.). The Labour administration which existed between 1974 and 1979, managed to accommodate the proposals contained within the Report and legislated for a Scottish Assembly during October 1974. However, opposition to devolution both within and outwith the Labour Party was evident (Lynch, 1991, p. 445). For instance, the government had a slim majority, and faced hostility from both Scottish local government, and the Conservatives, whose leadership under Margaret Thatcher was now (unlike the Heath government whose 'Declaration of Perth' in 1968, had welcomed some form of 'home rule') firmly opposed to constitutional change.

Nevertheless, the Bill was passed through Westminster and became the Scotland Act of 1978. However, a number of important amendments were made. The most significant of these was that a referendum was to be established to secure the establishment of a Scottish parliament. Furthermore, there existed a requirement that at least 40 per cent of the electorate should vote in favour before the assembly could be established.

The referendum is an important moment within Scottish political history, in that it confirmed the concept of referenda within UK politics (after its initial introduction in the referendum on Britain's continued membership within the European Economic Community in 1975: see Perman, 1980, p. 54). Moreover, it is seen by many (Brown, 2000, p. 543; Paterson, 1994, p. 7) as setting the defining Scottish political agenda for the following two decades. In addition, within the wider context of political participation (or non-participation) it established what might be regarded as an *anti-democratic maxim* within UK politics in that it ensured that the: 'final judgement of the result would take account of those who did not vote' (Baur, 1980, p. 89).

However, on 1 March 1979 the referendum was held in Scotland, and while securing a narrow majority of votes in favour, the assembly did not reach the reach the 40 per cent mandate.[47]

The resulting failure of the referendum was a spur to those within Scottish civil society who still sought the establishment of a directly elected assembly. As such the Campaign for a Scottish Assembly was launched, a 'Claim of Right for Scotland' (1989) was drawn up, within which the argument for an Assembly/Parliament was set inside a historical context which located the then emerging 'democratic deficit' in terms of consistent historical Anglo-Scottish political relations.[48]

Moreover, the 'Claim of Right' set forth a set of normative political principles to which the future proposed parliament might adhere, and which it was argued, were lacking within British democracy *per se*. These alert us not only to the overarching theme of the new politics, but also to the values which the now established Scottish parliament expresses as part of its civil and political foundations (CSG, 1998).

Indeed, they point to some of the notions later to be found within both the Consultative Steering Group's report (*Shaping Scotland's Parliament*) and the *Modernising Government* White Paper of 1999 (@ http://www.cabinet-office.gov.uk/moderngov/1999/whitepaper/.htm), which in turn addresses the feature of revitalising British democracy.[49] As such, the chief concerns of the claim are to resolve what it observed to be a series of fundamental flaws in the way that Scotland was governed. For instance, the lack of administrative and democratic accountability of the Scottish Office, is an argument which came to the fore in the 1980s. Its political geography, once considered a way of strengthening its Scottish representation, is now called into question.[50]

Two months after the referendum the Conservatives under Margaret Thatcher came to power, thus marking out new political territory for the UK as a whole, and Scotland in particular. However, the issue of referenda as a democratic method goes beyond the historical Anglo-Scottish dimension; it fits into some elements of the contemporary. Scottish parliament's design as we shall see later.[51] However, the route towards a new political settlement traversed through other terrain. This crossed the boundaries of both the UK and the EU, as we shall now see.

Scottish Political Culture and Political Identity, Scotland the Union and the EU: the Reconstitution of a Political Project in the 1980s

The 1980s are marked by a number of significant political events. The Thatcher administration broke quite markedly with the hitherto established postwar political, social and economic consensus, and in particular the concept of the welfare state.

The Conservatives revitalised belief in laissez-faire economics and in the primacy of market logic above all else, brought them into conflict with important aspects of Scottish society. Scotland retained a 'broadly social-democratic consensus. But the new government of Margaret Thatcher was radically right wing' (Paterson, 1994, p. 169). New political tensions began to emerge revolving around the axis of welfare provision, the nature of community set against Conservative arguments about the primacy of the individual (as opposed to 'society') and the quality of human relationships based upon social community, and collective identities which were being challenged (Millar, 1999).

In addition, there was a series of debates surrounding the place of Scottish civil society in political and social decision-making, and the role of the European Union as a new centre of economic and political authority (Sillars, 1989). Divisions over the role of the European Union were also prominent during the 1980s particularly within the context of Scottish support for a welfare state under attack from a right wing government. Moreover, Scottish political culture (and political identity) seemed to have realigned itself once more with a grand political project, in doing so it distanced itself further from its once rooted English connections.[52]

In the 1983 General Election a Conservative majority was returned in England. With it came an increasing advocacy of 'new public management' and other radical points of departure from the postwar consensus. The Scottish decline of Conservatism was reflected in a decrease of seats from 22 to 21. As Marr (1992) notes, Thatcherism gave rise to a new wave of nationalism in Scotland. The momentum of such a political-national identity continued into the following election in 1987. After the 1987 General Election a Conservative government was returned to overall UK office, albeit with a decreased Scottish representation/minority.[53]

Yet despite its lack of a Scottish electoral mandate, the government of 1987 was more radically inclined towards Scotland than had previously been the case. When the Conservatives began to channel their political energies away from macroeconomic policies, and began a move into the social arenas of education and health, they began to confront resistance not only from established policy communities whom saw it in their interests to resist radical change, but from civil society at large.[54] During the 1980s the course and form of the new politics becomes perhaps clearer. There emerges in Scotland during this time a reaction to the new right policies and ideologies of the Thatcher administration. It is linked to a number of issues including the increased articulation of an alternative political agenda. This assisted in the evolution of public opinion in Scotland and ensured that it was disseminated via a number of agencies within Scottish political and cultural life including, for instance, political journalism.

It offered an alternative sense of national identity in Scotland and helped to establish an 'emerging Scottish frame of reference [which] fixed a new dimension in politics' (McCrone, 1992, p. 173). What we find then emerging during this era is a coincidence of national identity and political sentiment, as various political and cultural groupings in Scotland appear to formulate a collective antagonism and political resistance towards the new right, and Mrs Thatcher in particular (MacInnes, 1992). The formation of the Scottish Constitutional Convention, and other factions within Scottish civil society, drew from such political impulses, and helped sustain their initiative.

The Finality of the British Project? A New Commitment to Devolution, the Transformation of Scottish Politics and the 1990s

The 1990s are synonymous with further shifts in the relationship between Scottish civil society and the British state. The original political formula was predicated upon a relatively stable constitutional base. Self governance of Scottish institutions such as law, education and so on was an integral component of these formulae. Prior to 1979 constitutional issues were not, by and large, an overarching feature of Anglo-Scottish political relations.

The relative autonomy of Scottish political existence was the defining feature during the high point of the Union (Paterson, 1994).

However, the advent of three terms of Conservative government coupled with their near relentless desire to dissolve what they saw as state dependency, and to increase privatisation (theirs too was a programme of modernisation, but looked towards liberalisation of the economy as catalyst) was not only politically unpopular in Scotland, it called into question the Union itself in a much more challenging manner than before (Devine, 1999, p. 606).[55] However, as these debates evolve into the 1990s, we can observe new political arrangements and programmes which further the concept of New Politics and provide further explanations as to its development and practices.

The Union and the Contemporary Development of New Political Innovations/Technologies

The Conservatives were re-elected to office in 1992. Their rejection of devolution was consistent policy, even after the downfall of Thatcher in 1990 (MacWhirter, 1992). However, the John Major administration detailed plans towards making the bureaucracy in Scotland more democratically accountable by reorganising the existing system, and a re-evaluation of how Scotland might be dealt with at Westminster. This was termed 'taking stock of the Union' by the government, and included three particular components. These are interesting not only because they form a new Conservative approach to the governance of Scotland, but also because they offer a response not only to the ideological difficulties posed by Thatcherism in Scotland, and to the 'democratic deficit' of which explicit mention is made. They also make reference to the existence of changing political circumstances and the need for more democratic accountability, the recognition of Scotland's political distinctiveness, and Scotland's status as a nation in its own right (Lang, 1994).

Within these three themes we have the final Scottish-based political motifs of the Conservative government. Lang's blueprint for a future Scotland is inadvertently suggestive of the changes which were to be engineered under the forthcoming Labour administration. In 1995 Bernard Crick and David Millar prepared a publication for the John Wheatley Centre (now the Centre for Scottish Public Policy). The document outlined proposals for a new Scottish Parliament. In doing so it launched a set of guiding principles both structural and normative in their approach.[56] Much of its focus is on ensuring that the new parliament takes every opportunity to be an innovative political institution. One which will redefine Scottish politics amidst a new vision of progress and governance as opposed to government (Hassan, 1998).[57]

As such, there is an implicit recognition that a new political system should resolve some of the features/problems associated with traditional representative government including for example; lack of citizen involvement, the relative decline of trust in perceptions of representative competence, degrees of political judgement, and the extent to which political elite's respond to citizen participation. In addition, and perhaps most importantly of all, the opportunity to participate in decision making processes outwith periodical elections (Parry and Moyser, 1994; Rennger, 1999). This became a recognised point of departure for the new Labour administration which came to power in 1997.

New Labour: New Reformation or New Regulation?

Set within the Labour Party's election to power in 1997 there have been major constitutional reforms in the shape of Scottish and Welsh devolution, the possibility of a stable Northern Ireland Assembly, and further political change in the shape of proportional representation in elections to the Scottish parliament. These changes, these redesigns upon the UK state, are part of a wider pressure for constitutional transformation within Britain. As expressed earlier in the chapter, these themes are related to transformational politics. This set of principles include a focus on the *machinery* and *practice* of government in the UK and a relative shift in its political culture(s) which include, for example, 'democratic decentralisation, introducing proportional representation, altering procedures, incorporating rights, it is about the transformation of a political culture' (Osmond, 1998, p. 1).

The new government launched its 'Modernising Government' programme and its synonymous White Paper.[58] The proposals contained and outlined within the White Paper were clarified by a two part referendum which laid down both the electorates desire for a Scottish parliament, and its ability to raise the varying rate of tax. There was considerable support for both features, with 74.3 per cent voting in favour of its establishment and a further 63 per cent who recommended that it have limited powers of taxation (McCarthy and Newlands, 1999, p. 4). In many respects the referendum result suggested the revival of a centre-left political spectrum within Scottish politics. This entailed the twinning of two political forms which once ordained the democratic system in the UK. These are contained within the notion of an Enlightenment based vision of progressive politics, and the rationality of democratic office. For example, as Lindsay Paterson (1999, p. 38) notes in this regard: '... the argument which won during the 1997 referendum was about making Scottish government responsive to civic Scotland. That is ultimately where all the talk of the "New Politics" emanates'.

Similarly, again central to our discussion, is Paterson's further observation which points towards the issues between ICTs, the participation revolution of the 1960s, and the use of ICTs as an extension of democratic practice:

> The theme of good government has taken account of a wide number of themes
> ... It has encompassed new currents of political thought from feminism to the
> revolution in information technology, so that the scope for increased participation
> has increased (ibid., p. 2).

Paterson touches on two related schemas which this chapter will explore; that is to what extent should a 'new politics of information' (Bellamy et al., 1995, p. 80) impact upon established political systems? Or within the dimensions of a new political settlement, to what extent might this new politics create new sites of political contest and areas for negotiation between government and civil society? Will for example, the new information politics extend outwith the UK parameters, into instead those provided by the new European information society initiatives? The combination of new democratic forms and the available technology threatens to extend the boundaries of democracy in new ways. The European Union offers precisely this opportunity for a small relatively marginalised nation such as Scotland.[59]

Conclusion

The new political arrangements of twenty-first century Scottish politics offer intriguing prospects for a democratic future. The extension of electronic democratisation promises to transform the dimensions of politics. But in what specific directions? The possibilities of the EU are counterbalanced by the organisational principles of a new information union between Scottish public administration and its UK parallel. In this manner the circumference of Scottish politics lacks a decisive destiny. It may move towards the EU, or a reintegration into the UK system may be the end result. On the other hand there are other possibilities along a continuum of electronic democracy.

Herein lies a political fault line. It resides in the technical opportunities, which are now available, for a potential radicalisation of the core relations at the centre of the political establishment (Budge, 1996). Other principle democratic initiatives which promote the use of ICTs to extend democracy do so in an altogether different form. Effectively they wish to disregard political institutions, and focus on the idealism of democracy which they charge as being elitist and self serving. These groupings and coalitions have ambitions to produce a politically self empowered class which employs power through rule by referendum, or plebiscitary democracy (Hacker, 2000; Hagen, 2000). As Keane (2000) suggests, these new social movements/groups show a high degree of concern and interest with the production, distribution and legitimation of knowledge and meaning than previous movements whose interests were predominantly defined along class lines, the as yet unrecognised economic interests of classes, and specific 'scientific' ways of transferring ownership of the means of production (Therborn, 1980). Both these formulas occupy common ground in that they observe the latent possibilities afforded by the new ICTs to reposition the hierarchical nature of institutional politics with a more lateral version.

Finally, this chapter offers a graphic summary of the overall themes encountered can be represented figuratively (see Figure 12.2). The representation illustrates the transitional features of Scottish democracy. It has moved from democratic deficit to a transitional condition. The top left hand corner shows the relations between Scottish civil society and the pre devolutionary system of government. Power flows in one direction, or is limited in sympathetic exchange mechanisms. As such the evolution of public opinion moves the culture into the direction of sub-politics. With the introduction of the parliament the areas of sub politics are partly integrated into the parliamentary system.

Civil society is given leeway to interact within the devolutionary settlement. However, to compensate for the proliferation of alternative political technologies (including radical demands for more autonomy and more direct versions of democracy such as the S28A campaign) the *infocracy* develops

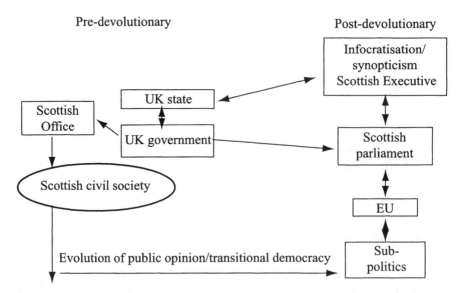

Figure 12.2 The Scottish political system and its units and sub-units

alongside. The synopticism between the devolved areas of the UK state can be said to be a reaction to the relative loss of state autonomy experienced as a result of sub and macro-national pressures.[60] Hence the need for a new politics of integration via political computing and the regulation of alternative communication networks and circuits via the Regulation of Investigatory Powers Act (2000).

Notes

1   The Scottish Office occupies an important role within any understanding of politics north of the border. Its position is important for the following reasons. Firstly, it is an administrative body that effectively symbolises what is arguably the high point of the technocratic era, the twentieth century. This is the age of the expert and of a belief in scientific advancement through rationality. Established in 1939 the new organisation advanced its position largely after the last war. It did so in relation to its effective delivery of the new postwar welfare state. As such, it created the conditions for its legitimacy, and indeed the legitimacy of administrative politics within the Scottish frame of reference. However, with a decline in the technocratic context (aided by attacks from both the 'New Left' and the 'New Right') its position became increasingly questionable. Furthermore, it had an in-built tension which resonated throughout the latter part of twentieth century politics in Scotland. For instance the Westminster parliamentary system observed a right of decision over the choice of Scottish Secretary of State (effectively a type of proconsular position: Kellas, 1992). Therefore, despite long associations with Scottish interests, and close working relations with much of

Scottish civil society, the election of a radical Conservative party under Margaret Thatcher in 1979 broke the correlation between democracy and technocracy. In other words, a previous synthesis between political control and advocacy of Scottish interests declined rapidly. As the right wing agenda of the government pressed on with policies for which there was no popular Scottish mandate, the logic of neutrality previously applied to the Scottish Office, gradually dissolved (Brown et al., 1996; McCrone, 1992).

2   This is evidential in relation to the percentage of votes cast for the Thatcher government in Scotland during her tenure. For instance, during the 1979 election the Conservatives commanded 31.4 per cent of the total Scottish vote (translated into 22 seats under the Westminster system). By 1983 this had fallen to 28.4 per cent (translated into 21 seats). At the 1987 election the figure had fallen to 24.0 per cent (10 seats). There is a slight upturn during the 1992 general election when the Conservative share of the Scottish vote rises to 25.7 per cent (making 11 seats). But by 1997 the Conservative share had fallen to 17.5 per cent (this translated into zero seats) (Brown et al., 1998). Mrs Thatcher had left during 1991, so the latter election figures reflect a loss of confidence with Conservative party policies as a whole rather than her stewardship of Scottish affairs.

3   The state sector within Scotland employed a higher relative number of workers than both England and Wales. Although the financial and service sectors have both grown since the early eighties, this period is more accurately defined as public sector (Kendrick, 1986).

4   For instance, the former peripheral nature of Scotland in relation to the European Union has developed to a condition of centrality. The realisation from within Scottish politics is that the position of Europe has superseded that of the United Kingdom in terms of its future scale and relations of influence. This is what could be termed as the 'political economy of accesssion' (Mayhew, 1998, p. 200). In this sense the balance of advantage in terms of transition to expanded markets and so on has shifted towards the EU. With its integrative policies and subsidies, it is seen as more advantageous. In addition, there is the constitutional and cultural climate of the EU. This provides a further set of positive considerations for a small nation such as Scotland. The EU grants a stable political base within which to pursue the conditions of subsidiarity (subsidiarity implies that the process of decision making occurs at the lowest position within the democratic scheme of things), that has appeal to a Scotland long used to the application of a centralised state (Brown et al., 1996). The cultural position is accompanied by the revival of European sentiments. These can be related to the progressive modernisation of European politics, especially when contrasted with the narrow definitions of Europe supplied by the English media (and the traditional Scottish antagonism to their largely insular accounts of alternative political-cultural scenarios) (Brown et al., 1996; McCrone, 1992; Paterson, 2000).

5   See, for instance, Council of Ministers, 1994, or the Bangemann Report (less commonly referred to as *Europe and the Global Information Society: Recommendations to the European Council*) @ www.ispo.cec.be/infosoc/backg/bangemann.html.

6   E-commerce in the EU has grown from £6bn in 1999, to a figure approaching £120bn by 2003 (European Survey of Information Society, www.ispo.cec.be/esis/).

7   For instance, within Scottish culture, education has a specific value system which sets it apart from its English counterpart. The Act of Union in 1707 established a trinity of distinctions which have continued to enforce a sense of Scottish detachment. They consist of a separate legal system (through which the machinery of state operates and legitimises itself) (Poggi, 1990). As such, a detached legal system has traditionally operated as a constraining institution over external British imposition. Furthermore, the religious values of a strongly Protestant state were enshrined through a series of compromises within the

Act that effectively safeguarded religious difference and values (Paterson, 1994). However, the educational process in Scotland helped in establishing a pattern of independent thinking. This went beyond its functionalist conditions, and focused energies onto what Davie (1961) termed as Scotland's 'democratic intellect'. In this sense education set up barriers, to varying degrees of success, to defend its unique system. It also served as a means of consolidating a society very much premised around the values of laissez-faire economics, yet aware that market provision and competition was not necessarily compatible with educational-democratic virtue (Paterson, 1994).

8   These include 'improving the business environment; enhancing Europe's knowledge base by investing in research, education and learning; working for more integrated policy with a view to social and security issues; and meeting the global challenge by promoting the information society on a global scale' (Antirroko, 2000, p. 32).

9   This may prove to be of either the French technocratic model, whereby decision making is increasingly centralised and formalised, or that of the German federal system epitomised by the *Lander* framework. This is a system that operates checks and balances upon the growth of central power (Siedentop, 2001).

10 These policies are part of the progressive movement towards a full union of European states. Macro policies, such as a joint European defence force, the single currency and surrounding monetary concerns, will be developed along such lines. This calls into question the Westminster parliament's control over these outstanding affairs, and the centrality of their relationship within Scotland.

11 This includes an account of integrated infrastructures and the standardisation of information systems at the UK level. And also examines nformatisation as the dominant technology of the information age. This focuses on the issues that are raised throughout Chapter Two, namely, the route towards devolution at the level of the United Kingdom and political developments therein, and the relative decline of the nation state. To this end the strengthening of bureaucracy via political computing is a tool with which to offset the political technologies of devolved governance, and the supranational gravities of the EU. As such, it is a project aimed at countering the effects of meta-governance, and reconfirming the power of the centre. Within Zuurmond's infocracy the informatisation process renders bureaucracy effectively invisible. Formalisation and standardisation are removed from the surface and displaced into the information architecture itself. The information union uses the maxim of increased service delivery and cost effectiveness to the tax payer-citizen to further the project. These informatised relations regenerate the possibilities of the nation state, they renew the primacy of space and territory and give a new dimension to those elements of political geography placed under threat by globalisation and post-modernisation, de-territorialisation and virtualisation.

12 The decline of the Unionist party vote in Scotland has collapsed since the 1955 General Election. At this moment it collected some 50.4 per cent of the vote. However, by 1987 this figure had halved in total to some 24 per cent. By 1997 the Conservative and Unionist party vote in Scotland had fallen to 17.5 per cent returning them no Scottish seats at Westminster at all (McCrone, 1992; Brown et al., 1996).

13 There is a relevance here. It resides in the contrasting political philosophy of the technocrats, their desire to control, and with those alienated by the conditions they associated with such processes. For instance, Fromm found the communications quotient to be at the heart of the modern condition. Like his Frankfurt School contemporaries he produced an analysis of alienation. The connecting theme is that these thoughts were to be found at the heart of the reaction, forthcoming in this chapter, against technocracy, by others influenced by

such ideas. Fromm develops a theory of psychological identity that locates freedom with community. This has additional relevance in the following footnote, which in turn observes the communicative aspect of the individual and his her place in a new model of society. This is associated with communitarianism, and the techno-communitarianism that is evident in New Labour policies.

14 For instance, the dimension of political thought which styles itself as 'Third Way', a way effectively of managing the transition and tensions between the economic liberalism of the New Right which characterised the 1980s and the Old Left, with its commitment to more direct forms of state intervention which in turn characterised previous decades. This is the prevailing Western political philosophy of the immediate twenty-first century, and as we will see in chapter three, makes much of its commitment towards developing and reinventing government, by using new technology to implement new political relations (see the 1998 Internet discussion of the Third Way @ http://www.netnexus.org/debates/3way/Default.htm) and offering to its citizens a 'new politics for the new century' (Blair, 1999). This new politics centres around these concerns, and is accompanied by a commitment towards 'modernising politics and government' (http://www.dlcppi.org/ppi/3way/3way.htm) and using new technology not only to modernise public administration, but to resurrect a form of what Webster (1999, p. 230) describes as 'techno-communitarianism'. This offers a concern to redress the concentration during later postwar years on the primacy of the individual within political philosophy. Rawls (1999, p. 457) describes this as best exemplified by 'the notion of private society' whereby individuals pursue private ends or ends which are deemed non complementary. The premise of techno-communitarianism is, according to Webster (op. cit., p. 227): 'Communication is supposed to promote the idea of greater social intelligibility, which in turn is supposed to enhance the general concorde among peoples. Every social problem is formulated in terms of a new communications equation, and every solution is considered in terms of a communications fix'. As Robson and Webster (1998) also note, the re-conceptualisation of 'community' around the linked notions of ICTs and communication, are a Third Way response to the atomised society prevalent after the extensive era of neo-liberalism.

15 In Chapter Five we examine the crisis of representative democracy, and the ways which ICT might revitalise democratic practice and procedural efficiency. In this instance other themes relevant to our thesis are introduced, namely, the possibility of extending and deepening democratic practice, making it more inclusive of civil society, and of creating new links between it and the institutions of government.

16 For example, in the work of Crick and Millar (1991) which set out to provide a draft model of information based arrangements for a future parliament. The logic behind such ideas was to offer an information service which would, it was argued: '[be] an important part of fulfilling the Scottish Constitutional Convention's aim to encourage an open, accessible and democratically accountable government and a participatory democracy which will bring Parliament and people closer together in determining what is best for Scotland' (Crick and Millar, 1995, p. 29).

17 I use Nisbet's (1969) work here to define the overall logic of change. This will become evident at a later moment in this chapter. However, Nisbet himself drew theoretical strength from Auguste Comte who, with his theory of 'statics' and 'dynamics' was able to suggest the deeper structural elements of social-political change and evolution. Comte argued that there was a false dichotomy posited by some theorists between the order-change axis. In this important sense order is 'order in change; and change is simply the incessant realisation of a higher level of order' (ibid., p. 167).

18 Whereby the operations of government are open to citizen inspection, for example.

19 We should take these into account when making reference to a 'new politics'. Postmodernism as a term represents a mass of political and cultural configurations. However, to isolate a few of them illustrates the relative points of political departure between modern and post-modern. The formation of a new world order within which there exists an increasingly internationalised system of economic and political conformity is but one dimension. For example, we have the idea that the classical modern concept of the nation state as considered within a Westphalian model, (whereby the relatively sovereign, territorially discreet, political community was in charge of its own destiny, and oversaw both a comprehensive fiscal, legal and monetary system is perhaps politically, economically, culturally and ecologically out of date) (Held, 1999, p. 87; Kearney, 1997; Giddens, 1999; Paterson, 1994).

20 These broader shifts are concerned with the channels of influence surrounding globalisation. For instance, the gradual erosion of nation state boundaries and sovereign powers. These ideas also argue for a more transnational economy. The associative point however is that of ICTs. The ability of the technologies to extend time and place, to move beyond regulation and the reduction of the economy to the national interest, is said to be a feature of the spread and influence of ICTs. However, as some authors note (Hirst and Thompson, 1996), the whole remit of globalisation is a brake on social and economic policy making. It serves as a useful tool with which governments can adopt to deny responsibility for their actions (or lack of them).

21 There is additional evidence suggests that citizens are not withdrawing into an increasingly privatised microenvironment, but rather that their participation and involvement is being channelled in different ways; through voluntary organisations for instance (Burt and Taylor, 2001). As such, the political parties themselves are arguably being dis-intermediated in their traditional role as interlocutors between citizen and government, a host of civil factions are taking their place; NGOs for example (Walker, 2001, @ www.lse.ac.uk).

22 The Scottish Office was the administrative arm of the UK state in Scotland. It has been replaced by the Scottish Executive which now operates at the behest of both Westminster and Edinburgh.

23 To this end these boundaries became more fused and unified than before (Brown et al., 1996). Legitimacy was established upon expertise and its symbolic trappings. In addition, as Habermas notes (Habermas, 1971, p. 81) much of the legitimacy of these postwar models of public administration came from Weber's ideal-typical conception of rationality and its relationship with bureaucracy. Weber's concept is pertinent in as much as social and political administrative organisation is premised upon the ideal of a functioning rational bureaucracy, established to secure the efficiency of government. These ideas can in turn be related to the appropriate frameworks necessary for legal authority and as a way of providing 'growing precision and explicitness in the principles governing social organisation' (Albrow, 1970, p. 43).

24 This approach is a component of the theoretical field of relations within governance. It is known as the 'new institutionalist' approach has its origins within micro-level approaches, themselves associated with the perspectives and emergence of the human relations movement in the social sciences. From this perspective informal structures are an important part of administrative reality and are a link between formal legal administrations and the complexity of the real world. In informal structures the issue is one of group culture and of contacts that are not incorporated into formal organisational structures, but are constituted by the individual opinions of the staff, it is the squaring of interests, rather than the following of legal rules. New institutionalism is characterised by cooperative work at both the

horizontal as well as the vertical level (Clegg, 1990). Institutional theory has its roots in the sociological approaches developed by Berger and Luckman . They argue that where organisational structures tend to become similar, this is not the result of ecologies (this perspective maintains that organisations are akin to population species with distinct ecologies or environments) what conditions sustain and also inhibit particular forms of organisational existence etc., it also goes against market pressures ideas, rather organisations are the result of the ways in which the infusion of values are reproduced/produced by people engaging in constructing institutional reality out of the cultural fabric that is available to them. This is developed as a theme in later chapters, particularly Chapter Seven. Here we examine the displacement of centralised power; new institutionalism and meta-governance and the contemporary origins of the participation debate. Political participation as a form of meta-governance, sub-politics and the Scottish parliament are all features of the governance-new institutionalist axis.

25 'Transformational politics' is a new field within political science that concerns itself with offering a vision of future political forms: a new politics. It develops transitional strategies which aim to move a system away from one set of points towards another preferred process(es).

26 Similarly, scientific-rationality and kudos has long been associated with modernist twentieth century attempts at political reformation, and those ideologies supportive of plans to 'reinvent government'. Many of these have centred upon the notion of 'efficiency' whether measured or defined in an economic or technical-administrative fashion. Some have focussed upon radical changes within the personnel of public administration as a means of executing the appropriate shifts, whilst others have sought technical solutions to perceived problems (Kavanagh, 1990, p. 7). For example, Kavanagh draws our attention to the feature of historical continuity present within these debates at the end of the nineteenth, and at periodic moments within the twentieth (ibid.). He notes: 'At the beginning of the twentieth century ... critics demanded "National Efficiency", and in the 1960s "Modernization" or "Remodernization". The thematic similarities between demands made by opinion formers in these two cases is remarkable and in both cases transcended party lines. For example, the main complaints of both were addressed to Britain's economic weakness, international decline, and the alleged amateurism and lack of expertise among administrative and economic elites'.

27 The foundations of this feature, its functional abilities, are in turn situated around the development of the new 'science' of statistical technique, or 'political statistics' (Foucault, 1990, p. 77) which the state assumes for itself (during the seventeenth and eighteenth centuries), and which takes the form of technological calculus, and other modes of effectively operationalising government and its actions (Foucault, 1991, p. 99). Moreover, the 'police' of a state, within which these characteristics of seventeenth and eighteenth century power and administration are established (this historical moment also witnesses the birth of the concept of the nation state: 'a bounded area over which is exercised political power' (Webster, 1996, p. 58)) – are (according to Foucault, 1990) best understood as a governmental technology. Its aim is to ensure the organisational intervention of the state in those domains which it considers to be in its sphere of interest. In effect it is a technology which operates, within Hood's conception of the apparatus of state, as a form of detecting tool (Hood, 1983), with which it gauges the strength of its own operations, and those of other states, via political intelligence (Foucault, op. cit.).

28 Similarly, although drawing his ideas from earlier political moments, but still with contemporary validity, there is the work of Robert Michels which asserts that: 'The technical

specialisation that inevitably results from all extensive organisation renders necessary what is called expert leadership. Consequently the power of determination comes to be considered one of the specific attributes of leadership, and is gradually withdrawn from the masses to be concentrated in the hands of the leaders alone ... organisation implies the tendency to oligarchy' (Michels, 1915, p. 31). As such, what Michels is highlighting is the relationship between political power and organisational structure, the defining variable being in this instance what his counterpart Weber termed the 'law of the small number, the universal principle that politics is dominated by small groups' (Beetham, 1985, p. 105). Similarly, Max Weber (1978) points towards the paradoxical nature of democracy and rational-bureaucracy.

29 There is increasing evidence for a decline in citizen participation in conventional political engagement (Dalton et al., 2000; Taylor and Burt, 2001). Is there any evidence to suggest however that political parties are losing their role in the formation of democratic governance (Smith, 1998)? The question then arises then as to whether new social movements or interest groups are taking the place of political parties, or whether citizens are simply choosing to disengage from politics per se: a retreat into privatisation. However, the perceived decline in the democratic link between citizens and parties can be located back to the early 1960s and the work of Almond and Verba (1963). The authors suggested that political parties as vessels of political participation were diminishing in their authority, questioning Duverger's (1974) contention that mass parties signified the dominant means of political organisation and political participation (Scarrow, 2000). However, if political parties are being dis-intermediated, then there is room to suggest that their place and position has been undermined by the 'participation revolution' of the 1960s and the additional components of sub-politics. These moments saw the rise of alternative political demands and forms of action. In addition, the concept of class de-alignment and class affiliation with political parties has, it is argued, weakened their role as mediators between citizen and state (Nash, 2000). In addition, the perception held by some citizens that political parties pursue partisan group interests rather than the 'public' interest, has weakened the proportion of those who identify with political parties (Smith, 1998). The contemporary context of the participatory citizen can be regarded as a 'producer of social surplus' (Maes, 1998, p. 115). This notion develops the idea that the citizen has a series of network relations that can be developed for his/her own benefit (in place of the gaps left for instance by public sector reform) and for the overall good of the community.

30 This is in best understood within a number of associated variables. Firstly, the democratic deficit gave rise to an exploration of alternatives. The demise of Conservatism as a distinctly Scottish party of the middle classes also proved to be a feature. This meant that Unionism was unable to keep hold of its Scottishness. Mackenzie (1978, p. 109), offers the following relevant definition: 'A discussion of political identity is ... primarily a discussion of the conditions in which it is possible to realise "common purpose"'. It is a valuable definition in that it realises the limitations upon the common purpose of Scottish politics: a politics, or a set of loosely identified ideas, thwarted by unresponsive institutions. The vision of an alternative possesses strength under such occasions and, even if lacking coherence, points to what it is *not* as its defining goal.

31 The derivation of new politics has been highlighted in Chapter One in relation to the contrasting principles of ideals against institution. The blueprint for a new set of ideals and institutions is carried by a series of documents that promote a fusion of both: see CSG Report, 1998, for instance. It sets out an idealist dimension in terms of a vision of new political reason, and the template for a new system.

32 In other words, there existed within Scotland a set of political and economic tensions which emerged as a general feature of the postwar economic and military decline of the UK as a whole, the collapse of the postwar consensus, political divergence as manifested by political behaviour, and as a more precise effect of the Thatcher administrations pursuit of monetarist macro economic policies and their perceived assault on a more public sector dependant Scottish society (McCrone, 1994).

33 As Blair (1991, p. 1) notes, whilst outlining contemporary New Labour political philosophy and the concept of the 'Third Way': 'The Labour government elected in 1945 was shaped by the legacy of wartime conditions of prewar depression and poverty ... it proceeded to nationalise industry, manage demand, direct economic activity and expand health and social services'. Blair is making the historical connections between previous Labour administrations and their contemporaries in government today.

34 There was a reaction, or response, to the mass petition formulated by the Scottish Covenant in the form of the Balfour Commission on Scottish Affairs (1952–54) which, according to James Kellas (1992, p. 310), made some 'minor administrative changes' in relation to the latent expressions and possibility of intent which the petition signified.

35 'Legitimacy came from the fundamental belief in science and planning' (Paterson, 1994, p. 16). As Marcuse's basic thesis notes (1968), technology and science are functional in that their union operates to legitimise political power. Similarly, as Held notes, in these respects there are some interesting ideological associations at play in that the state's expansive approach leads to: 'A fusion of science, technology and industry, [and] to the emergence of a new form of ideology: ideology is ... based on a technocratic justification of the existing social order' (Held, 1988, p. 80). Within the realms of these theories we find an address from the state which utilises scientific 'logic' to legitimate its knowledge. With the expansion of scientific enquiry, and technocratic administration, go increases in the amount and degree of 'control', as it were, over society. It is, as Lyotard (1994, p. 46) contends, a discourse of power that is used to 'constitute a legitimation'. In other words, science can be observed as a set of discourses which attempt to further the powers of controlling political and social energies (Poster, 1990, p. 33).

36 Sir Stafford Cripps.

37 'The theme of good government is important because it eventually won the day for the supporters of a Scottish parliament ... endorsed in the 1997 referendum' (Paterson, 1998, p. 2).

38 There is evidence that there is a motion in the direction of such a model (Rennger, 1999, p. 6). It takes the form of a growing tendency towards the increasing use of what Fishkin (1991) describes as the plebiscitary model. This model is characterised by the use of referenda as a means of producing overall majoritarian decisions. ICTs, central components of the devolved nature of power in Scotland, now include opportunities to extend the sites of such power, and in doing so represent points of possible political tension between advocates of representative government, and direct democratic exponents (Moore, 1999, p. 55).

39 As he describes it: 'The conception of a rational organisation of society stands confounded. Rationality, as means – as a set of techniques for efficient allocation of resources – has been twisted beyond the recognition of its forebears; rationality as an end, finds itself confronted by the cantankerousness of politics, the politics of interest and the politics of passion'.

40 According to Miller (1981) there was a fear that: 'entry into Europe threatened Scotland with the prospect of becoming a periphery within a periphery'. Relative hostility towards

the then EEC was (in comparison to England) a current within Scottish politics, in the 1975 referendum on continuing membership of the Community, electoral results showed that Scotland was less clearly committed to the idea (Paterson, 1998, p. 146).

41 The Secretary of State for Scotland (Gordon Campbell) was the first Secretary of the twentieth century to take up office without a conforming Scottish democratic mandate: 'Labour had a clear lead in Scots votes and a majority of Scots MPs ... in short there was no real precedent for the imposed secretaryship of Gordon Campbell ... his very existence testified to the power of external influences' (Miller, 1981, p. 17). This was a theme which was to gather increasing political momentum some 10 years or so later.

42 For instance, as Kellas (1992, p. 63) notes it was the rise of nationalism in Scotland, expressed via the electoral success of the SNP, which had been the prime-mover in terms of placing devolved constitutional matters onto the political agenda: 'The SNP had risen to 30 per cent of the vote and 11 MPs in October 1974. The focus of the political debate in Scotland was on the run-down nature of the economy and its potential salvation through the discovery of North Sea oil'. Similarly, as Jack Brand (1978, p. 58) also notes with reference to the Labour administration: 'The success of the SNP in February [1974] convinced the National Executive of the party that more account must be taken of the demand for devolution'.

43 There were two elections in 1974. The Labour Party could not command a significant majority and was forced to go to the country again. The second poll produced the necessary mandate.

44 This had been established under a previous Labour administration during 1968 and its initial (three year) remit was to: 'Examine the present functions of the central legislature and government in relation to the several countries, nations and regions of the United Kingdom, and to consider whether any changes are desirable' (Fry, 1987, p. 234).

45 For instance as, Lindsay Paterson (1998, p. 17) notes: 'The publication of the Kilbrandon Report in 1973 was a key moment in the whole three decades ... the key legacy was from its scheme of legislative devolution ... On that was based not only the Labour governments reaction in the 1970s, but the 1997 Labour government's proposals ... endorsed in the referendum of 1997'.

46 The power of raising monies however, one of the essential 'tools of government' (Hood, 1983, p. 5) in that it enables a degree of autonomy and responsibility within the government-society interface, was to be a restricted power held by Westminster.

47 'While 62.8 per cent of the Scottish people turned out, and a clear majority (51.6 per cent) of those who voted cast a Yes preference, the pro-Assembly votes amounted to 32.9 per cent of the registered Scottish electorate, thereby falling foul of the peculiar 40 per cent device' (McLean, 1999).

48 These sought to locate contemporary political grievances in a framework of constitutional design stretching back to the 'Revolutionary Settlement' of 1689–90 (and the political vacuum left by the flight of James VII to France and the ascension to power in England of William of Orange (Lynch, 1991, p. 300)) and the 1842 Claim of Right presented to Westminster in relation to the religious schisms of the established church in Scotland (ibid., p. 401). The relevant links here are those which Brown (2000, p. 543) describes as being consistent with '[the] critique of an unrepresentative and unaccountable Westminster government which creates an illusion of democracy'.

49 For example, as Burns (1999, p. 47) expresses these ideas: 'The vision of the Constitutional Convention was based upon the idea that Scotland (and the rest of the UK) needed to enter a new political era. Scotland was seen as potentially pioneering a new modernising role, in terms of updating the UK constitution'.

50 'The Scottish Office can be distinguished from a Whitehall Department only in the sense that it is not physically located in Whitehall' ('A Claim of Right for Scotland', quoted in Paterson, 1998, p. 162).

51 For example, the 1999 report undertaken on behalf of the Consultative Steering Group on the Scottish parliament by the Scottish Office (now the Scottish Executive) and the Centre for the study of Telematics and Governance at Glasgow Caledonian University, noted the use of referendums as a mechanism with which to 'enhance democratic legitimacy'. As such, they recommended that they might be utilised as a means of increasing civic participation in policy decision making (see SP info.@.scottish.parliament.uk). These referendums were to be established in conjunction with democratic 'initiatives'; these are referendums supplied and supported by petitions submitted to an executive body. These are, as Budge (1996, p. 4) notes the 'nearest approach to direct democracy in the modern world'.

52 'No longer is England admired as the source of progressive ideas: that role has been taken over by Europe ... to call yourself 'European' in late twentieth century Scotland has something of the same modernising connotation as 'British' did in the eighteenth century and the middle of the twentieth' (Brown et al., 1996, p. 23).

53 Twenty-four per cent of the overall Scottish vote (Paterson, 1998, p. 143).

54 These concerted efforts are noted by (Holliday, 1992, p. 455) who makes particular mention of the role of the then Scottish Secretary (and advocate of Thatcherism) Michael Forsyth: 'It is true that Scottish local government, Scottish teaching unions, and the Scottish media have often been critical of Forsyth, but effective resistance to his policies has mainly been mass rather than elite'.

55 It has been argued that during this time the Scottish middle classes began a process of gradual political detachment from the concept of the British state and Britishness as a political and cultural construction (McCrone, 1992). The erosion of their power base, as epitomised by their predominant position within the public sector (and Conservative hostility towards it) caused them to reconsider the unionist pact, and its relative advantages. For example: '[the] institutions that held the Union together now become reasons for breaking it, if their autonomy is being eroded. Coupled with economic stagnation this could create a decay of legitimacy, in the sense that most Scottish voters would have stopped believing that their interests could be met through the UK state ... the importance given to constitutional change rose sharply after ... the 1992 ... general election' (Paterson, 1994, p. 178).

56 These prescriptions were to influence later policy based discussions, and indeed many of the established conditions of the parliament itself. For example: 'A new parliament needs new ideas and adequate resources in three respects: (a) effective procedures relevant to modern Scottish conditions and opinion; (b) an efficient organisation and administration; and (c) a modern information service to both members and public' (Crick and Millar, 1995, p. 1).

57 As such, it sought to offer forth rules of procedure which: '[Struck] a balance between the need to carry on responsible government ... and the rights of the electorate not merely as expressed through their elected MSPs, but by some new devices ... to allow the public to express their opinions directly' (Crick and Millar, 1995, p. 1).

58 'Scotland's Parliament' (later to become law as 'The Scotland Act, 1998', www.scottish.parliament.uk/whats_happening/docs/scoact-00.htm).

59 However, the desire to allow citizens to channel their political preferences (and for action to be forthcoming as a result) does not take fully into account the extent to which such

aims might now meet, within what is essentially a newly realisable citizen-government-technological interface. For instance, technology now allows for the radical expansion of citizen access to the political machinery the ability to 'short-circuit the representative process' (Moore, 1999, p. 55). This might take the form of a variation on the theme of direct democracy in one of the following ways. For instance, citizen-initiated democracy, or the recall or referendum model.

60 In the past, opposition to the established power base came from organised labour and the possibilities afforded by dialectical class struggle to re-organise the state within the given parameters, or confines of, a mode of industrial production (Poulantzas, 1976, p. 74). However, within postmodern politics (whereby within one relevant interpretation of this form) power is situated in a variety of sites, including computer science (Lyotard, 1994) opportunities now exist to reconfigure political arrangements via variations on the themes associated with direct democracy, and the new mode of information, within which politics and economics are increasingly electronically formed and mediated (Poster, 1990). It is the possibility of this new set of methods that now offers itself as a site of potential resistance towards the centrifugal political establishment. The new information technologies, as part of this new politics of information, increase dramatically the power of civil society, relative to the state, as a result of the diffusion of information based resources. This is but one reading, and a contentious one at that given other theorists accounts of the growth of computerised state power in relation to the expansive panopticist and surveillance powers of the electronic state (Poster, 1984).

References

Albrow, M. (1970), *Bureaucracy*, London: Macmillan.

Almond, G.A. and Verba, S. (1963), *The Civic Culture*, Princeton: Princeton University Press.

Anttiroiko, A.V. (2000), 'Towards the European Information Society', *Communications of the ACM*, Vol. 44, No.1.

Bangemann Report (*Europe and the Global Information Society: Recommendations to the European Council*), www.ispo.cec.be/infosoc/backg/bangemann.html.

Baur, C. (1984), 'The Election Conundrum', in D. McCrone (ed.), *The Scottish Government Yearbook 1984*, Edinburgh: Unit for the Study of Government in Scotland at the University of Edinburgh.

Becker, T. and Slaton, C.D. (2000), *The Future of Teledemocracy*, Westport, CT and London: Praeger Publishing.

Beetham, D. (1985), *Max Weber and the Theory of Modern Politics*, Oxford: Blackwell.

Bell, D. (1980), *The Coming of Post-Industrial Society*, Harmondsworth: Penguin Books.

Bellamy, C., Horrocks, I. and Webb, J. (1995), 'Community Information Systems: Strengthening local democracy?', in W.B.H.J. van de Donk, I.Th.M Snellen and P.W. Tops (eds), *Orwell in Athens: A perspective on informatisation and democracy*, Amsterdam: IOS Press.

Berger, P.L. and Luckmann, T. (1969), *The Social Construction of Reality*, London: The Penguin Press.

Blair T. (1999), 'The Third Way: New politics for the new century', *New Left*, Fabian Society Pamphlet 588, pp. 1–20.

Bogdanor, V.(1979), *Devolution*, Oxford: Oxford University Press.

Bonney, N.L. (1998), 'Scotland's Parliament: Some social policy and research implications', inpublished research paper.

Brand, J. (1978), *The National Movement in Scotland*, London: Routledge and Kegan Paul.

Breuilly, J. (1993), *Nationalism and the State*, Manchester: Manchester University Press.

Brown, A. (2000), 'Designing the Scottish Parliament', *Parliamentary Affairs*, Vol. 53, pp. 542–56

Brown, A., McCrone, D. and Paterson, L. (1996), *Politics and Society in Scotland*, London: Macmillan.

Brown, A., McCrone, D., Paterson, L. and Surridge, P. (1998), *The Scottish Electorate: the 1997 General Election and Beyond*, Basingstoke and London: Macmillan Press Ltd.

Budge, I. (1996), *The New Challenge of Direct Democracy*, Cambridge: Polity Press.

Burns, A. (1999), 'How the Parliament will work', in G. Hassan (ed.), *A Guide to the Scottish Parliament: The shape of things to come*, Edinburgh: Centre for Scottish Public Policy/The Stationery Office.

Clegg, S.R. (1990), *Modern Organisations: Organisation studies in the postmodern world*, London: Sage.

Consultative Steering Group (1998), *Shaping Scotland's Parliament: Report of the Consultative Steering Group on the Scottish Parliament*, The Scottish Office, December.

Council of Ministers (1994), *Europe's Way to the Information Society. An Action Plan*, Brussels: European Commission.

Crick, B. and Millar, D. (1995), *How to Make the Parliament of Scotland a Model for Democracy*, Edinburgh: John Wheatley Centre.

Dalton, R.J. and Wattenberg, M.P. (eds) (2000), *Parties without Partisans: Political change in advanced industrial democracies*, Oxford: Oxford University Press.

Davie, G.E. (1961), *The Democratic Intellect: Scotland and her universities in the nineteenth century*, Edinburgh: Edinburgh University Press.

Devine, T. (1999), *The Scottish Nation 1700–2000*, London: Allen Lane, The Penguin Press.

Du Preez, P. (1980), *The Politics of Identity: Identity and the human image*, Oxford: Blackwell Publishers.

Easton, D. (1964), *A Systems Analysis of Political Life*, Chicago: Phoenix Press.

European Survey of Information Society, www.ispo.cec.be/esis/.

Fishkin, J. (1991), *Democracy and Deliberation: New directions for democratic reforms*, New Haven, NJ: Yale University Press.

Foucault, M. (1990), *Michel Foucault: Power/Knowledge*, ed. C. Gordon, Brighton: Harvester.

Foucault, M. (1991), 'Governmentality', in G. Burchell, C. Gordon and P. Miller (eds), *The Foucault Effect. Studies in Governmentality, with two lectures by and an interview with Michel Foucault*, Chicago: University of Chicago Press.

Frissen, P.H.A. (1998), 'Public Administration in Cyberspace: A postmodern perspective', in I.Th.M Snellen and W.B.H.J. van de Donk (eds), *Public Administration in an Information Age: A handbook*, Amsterdam: IOS Press.

Fromm, E. (1960), *The Fear of Freedom*, London: Routledge Kegan Paul Ltd.

Fry, M. (1987), *Patronage and Principe: A Political History of Modern Scotland*, Aberdeen: Aberdeen University Press.

Giddens, A. (1998), *The Third Way: The renewal of social democracy*, Cambridge: Polity Press.

Gray, P. and Smith, C. (1999), 'The Scottish Parliament: Re-shaping parliamentary democracy in the information age', in S. Coleman, J. Taylor and W.B.H.J. van de Donk (eds), *Parliament in the Age of the Internet*, Oxford: Oxford University Press in association with the Hansard Society for Parliamentary Government.

Habermas, J. (1971), *Towards a Rational Society: Student Protest, Science and Politics*, London: Heinemann.

Hacker, K.L. (2000), 'The White House Computer-mediate Communication (CMC) System and Political Interactivity', in K.L. Hacker and J. van Dijk (eds), *Digital Democracy: Issues of theory and practice*, London: Sage Publications.

Hagen, M. (2000), 'Digital Democracy and Political Systems', in K.L. Hacker and J. van Dijk (eds), *Digital Democracy: Issues of theory and practice*, London: Sage Publications.

Harvie, C. (1992), 'In Time of the Breaking of Nations', *Scottish Affairs*, No. 1, Autumn.

Hassan, G. and Warhurst, C. (eds) (1999), 'Tomorrow's Scotland', *A Modernisers' Guide to Scotland: A different future*, The Big Issue/Centre for Scottish Public Policy.

Held, D. (1998), *Models of Democracy*, 2nd edn, Cambridge: Polity Press.

Hirst, P. and Thompson, G. (1996), *Globalisation in Question*, Cambridge: Polity Press.

Holliday, I. (1992), 'Scottish Limits to Thatcherism', *The Political Quarterly*, Vol. 63, No. 4, October–December.

Hood, C.H. (1983), *The Tools of Government*, London and Basingstoke: The MacMillan Press Ltd.

Hutchison, D. (1987), 'The Press in Scotland: Articulating a national identity?', in D. McCrone (ed.), *The Scottish Government Yearbook 1987*, Edinburgh: Unit for the Study of Government in Scotland, Department of Politics, Edinburgh University.

Kavanagh, D. (1990), *British Politics: Continuities and change*, Oxford: Oxford University Press.

Keane, J. (2000), 'Structural Transformations of the Public Sphere', in K.L. Hacker and J. van Dijk (eds), *Digital Democracy: Issues of theory and practice*, London: Sage Publications.

Kearney, R. (1997), *Post-Nationalist Ireland: Politics, culture, philosophy*, London: Routledge.

Kellas, J.G. (1976), 'Reactions to the Devolution White Paper', in M.G. Clarke and H.M. Drucker (eds), *Our Changing Scotland: A yearbook of Scottish government, 1976–77*, Edinburgh: Edinburgh University Press.

Kellas, J.G. (1992), *The Scottish Political System*, 4th edn, Cambridge: Cambridge University Press.

Kendrick, S. (1986), 'Occupational Change in Modern Scotland', in D. McCrone (ed.), *Scottish Government Yearbook 1986*, Edinburgh: Unit for the Study of Government in Scotland, Department of Politics, Edinburgh University.

The Kilbrandon Report, Cmnd 5460, London: HMSO.

Kohler, M. (1998), 'From the National to the Cosmopolitan Public Sphere', in D. Archibugi, D. Held and M. Kohler (eds), *Re-imagining Political Community: Studies in cosmopolitan democracy*, Cambridge: Polity Press in association with Blackwell Publishers Ltd.

Lang, I. (1998), 'Taking Stock of Taking Stock', in L. Paterson (ed.), *A Diverse Assembly: The debate on a Scottish parliament*, Edinburgh: Edinburgh University Press.

Levy, R. (1990), *Scottish Nationalism at the Crossroads*, Edinburgh: Scottish Academic Press.

Lynch, M. (1991), *Scotland: A new history*, London: Century Ltd.

Lyotard, J.F. (1994), *The Postmodern Condition: A report on knowledge*, foreword by Fredric Jameson, *Theory and History of Literature*, Vol. 10, Manchester: Manchester University Press.

MacInnes, J. (1992), 'The Press in Scotland', *Scottish Affairs*, No. 1, Autumn.

Mackenzie, W.J.M. (1978), *Political Identity*, Manchester: Manchester University Press.

MacWhirter, N. (1992), 'The Political Year in Westminster: October 1990–July 1991'. in D. McCrone and L. Paterson (eds), *The Scottish Government Yearbook 1992*, Edinburgh: Unit for the Study of Government in Scotland, Department of Politics, Edinburgh University.

Maes, R. (1998), 'Political and Administrative Innovations as a Social Project: The Belgian case', in A. Hondeghem (ed.), *Ethics and Accountability in a Context of Governance and the New Public Management*, Amsterdam: IOS Press.

Marcuse, H. (1968), *One Dimensional Man*, London: Routledge and Kegan Paul.

Marr, A. (1992), *The Battle for Scotland*, London: Penguin Books.

Mayhew, A .(1998), *Recreating Europe: The European Union's policy towards Central and Eastern Europe*, Cambridge: Cambridge University Press.

McCarthy, J. and Newlands, D. (1999), *Governing Scotland: Problems and prospects: The economic impact of the Scottish parliament*, Aldershot: Ashgate Publishing Ltd.

McConnell, J. (1991), *Scottish Parliament Official Report*, www.scottish.parliament. uk/official_report/session99-00/or30202.htm.

McCrone, D. (1992), *Understanding Scotland: The sociology of a stateless nation*, London: Routledge.

Michels, R. (1959), *Political Parties*, New York: Dover Publications.

Midwinter, A., Keating, M. and Mitchell, J. (1991), *Politics and Public Policy in Scotland*, London: Macmillan Education Ltd.

Miller, W. (1981), *The End of British Politics? Scots and English Political Behaviour in the Seventies*, Oxford: Clarendon Press.

Moore, R.K. (1999), 'Democracy and Cyberspace', in B.N. Hague and B.D. Loader (eds), *Digital Democracy: Discourse and decision-making in the information age*, London and New York: Routledge.

Nairn, T. (1981), *The Break-up of Britain*, London: Verso Books.

Nash, K. (ed.) (2000), *Readings in Contemporary Political Sociology*, Cambridge, MA: Blackwell Publishers.

Nisbet, R.A. (1969), *Social Change and History: Aspects of the Western theory of development*, London: Oxford University Press.

Osmond, J. (1998), 'Reforming the Lords and Changing Britain', *Redesigning the State*, Fabian Society Pamphlet 587.

Parry, G. and Moyser, G. (1994), 'More Participation, More Democracy?', in D. Beetham (ed.), *Defining and Measuring Democracy*, Vol. 36, Sage Modern Politics Series, London: Sage.

Paterson, L. (1994), *The Autonomy of Modern Scotland*, Edinburgh: Edinburgh University Press.

Paterson, L. (1999), 'Why Should we Respect Civic Scotland?', in G. Hassan and C. Warhurst (eds), *A Moderniser's Guide to Scotland: A different future*, The Big Issue/Centre for Scottish Public Policy.

Perman, R. (1980), 'The Devolution Referendum Campaign of 1979', in N. Drucker, H.M. Drucker and P. Harris (eds), *The Scottish Government Yearbook 1980*, Edinburgh: Unit for the Study of Government in Scotland, Department of Politics, Edinburgh University.

Poggi, G. (1990), *The State: Its nature, development and prospects*, Cambridge: Polity Press.

Poster, M. (1984), *Foucault, Marxism and History; Mode of Production versus Mode of Information*, Cambridge: Polity Press.

Poster, M. (1990), *The Mode of Information: Poststructuralism and Social Context*, Cambridge: Polity Press.

Poulantzas, N. (1976), *Political Power and Social Classes*, London: New Left Books.

Rawls, J. (1999), *A Theory of Justice*, revised edition, Oxford: Oxford University Press.

Rennger, N. (1999), *E-Governance: Democracy, Technology and the Public Realm*, Scottish Council Foundation.

Scarrow, S.E. (2000), 'Parties without Members? Party Organisation in a Changing Electoral Environment', in R.J. Dalton and M.P. Wattenberg (eds), *Parties without Partisans: Political Change in Advanced Industrial Societies*, Oxford: Oxford University Press.

Schwerin, E.W. (1995), *Mediation, Citizen Empowerment, and Transformational Politics*, Praeger Series in Transformational Politics and Political Science Westport, CT and London: Praeger.

Scott, P.H. (1985), 'In Bed With an Elephant: The Scottish experience', *Saltire Pamphlets*, New Series, No. 7, The Saltire Society, Edinburgh.

Siedentop, L. (2001), 'This is a New Kind of Europe', *Sunday Times, 3* June.

Smith, M. (1994), *Paper Lions: The Scottish press and national identity*, Edinburgh: Polygon Press.

Smith, C. (1998), 'Political Parties in the Information Age: From "mass party" to leadership organisation?', in I.Th.M Snellen and W.B.H.J. van de Donk (eds), *Public Administration in an Information Age: A handbook*, Amsterdam: IOS Press.

Taylor, J.A. and Burt, E. (2001), 'Not-For-Profits in the Democratic Polity', *Communications of the ACM*, Vol. 44, No. 1, January.

Therborn, G. (1980), *Science, Class and Society*, London: New Left Books.

The Scotland Act, 1998, www.scottish.parliament.uk/whats_happening/docs/scoact-00.htm.

The Third Way, Internet discussion, http://www.netnexus.org/debates/3way/Default.htm.

Touraine, A. (1974), *The Post-industrial Society*, London: Wildwood House.

Weber, M. (1978a), *Economy And Society: An Outline of Interpretive Sociology*, eds G. Roth and C. Wittich, Berkeley: University of California Press.

Webster, F. and Robins, K. (1999), *Times of the Technoculture: From the information society to the virtual life*, London and New York: Routledge.

White Paper (1975), *Our Changing Democracy*, Cmnd 6348, London: HMSO.

White Paper (1999), *Modernising Government*, http://www.cabinet-office.gov.uk/moderngov/1999/whitepaper/.htm.

Wright, K. (1997), *The People Say Yes: The making of Scotland's parliament*, Glendaruel: Argyll Publishing.

Chapter Thirteen

Changing the Contours through Information Technology: the Open Management of Transport

Julian Hine, Jeff Turner and Margaret Grieco

This chapter considers the role new information technology can play in providing a demand responsive public transport and communications system which better meets the information and transport needs of the socially excluded enabling them to extend their participation in the 'open management' of public services. The chapter is written in the context of widely observed public service failures and in a context where the Cabinet Office itself is investigating the relationship between public transport and social exclusion and the role that information technology can play in remedying current deficiencies. The direct voicing of public service consumers or the government's clients through transparent local monitoring and feed back systems is now beginning to receive policy attention. This chapter provides an indication of the interface between clients' voices, technical systems and policy progress in the transport sector of the United Kingdom.

Introduction: a Policy Issue with a Limited Budget

'Transport and social exclusion/inclusion' is rapidly emerging as a major policy issue and has become a highly visible item of the 'joined up government' agenda of New Labour Britain. This visibility, however, has operated more strongly at the level of rhetoric or language than in the commissioning of substantial research into the relationship between transport and social exclusion or in the commissioning of on the ground projects designed to improve the transport circumstances of the disadvantaged. As a process, the relationship between transport and social exclusion is little understood by local authorities who are struggling to target resources e.g. subsidised travel. For example, public transport service provision is not explicitly mapped and planned in terms of servicing identified areas or zones of deprivation: bus routes frequently bypass the areas of greatest deprivation and social exclusion methodologies which chart the relationship between these two attributes are thin on the ground. As an academic area, the field is fragmented and the rush to generate an analytic literature which matches the policy priority of social exclusion in relation to transport has been haphazard in its ground clearing and generated an unnecessarily weak literature. Indeed, the recent DETR study on social exclusion and public transport (DETR 2000; http://www.mobility-unit.detr. gov.uk/socialex/) adds little to the understanding of the debate: it is essentially a qualitative piece of work with a loose methodology, revisits existing literatures and concepts and can give little guidance to local authorities and national planning authorities engaged in the practice and policies of social transport provision.

In order to engage with the relationship between social exclusion and transport in a manner useful to local authorities, there is need to begin to chart the structural dimensions of the relationship. The exclusion of the needs of low-income populations in transport policy and the exclusion of deprived localities from expenditure and service in the transport sector is structural. In much the same way that transport planners have been gender biased, they are also social exclusion-biased. They concentrate on certain work journeys to certain locations (city centres), they view some transport problems (congestion) more seriously than others (lack of access to health services and fresh food).

'Social exclusion' requires formal inclusion in transport planning strategies for transport services and operations. There is an expectation that local authorities and related local agencies move rapidly on the transport and social exclusion agenda without a suitable policy budget, framework, literature or operational tools being available. The two transport and social exclusion studies funded currently by government have been conducted below a collective budget of £200,000. A new round of studies have been commissioned but no substantial resources have yet been invested in the investigation of the precise relationship between transport and social exclusion.

The weakness of policy activity in the transport and social exclusion area is best demonstrated perhaps by viewing the methodology used for constructing the government's own indices of local deprivation (http://www.regeneration. detr.gov.uk/rs/03100/index.htm). The accessibility data incorporated in these indices is not related to either public transport service levels nor to car or vehicle ownership statistics: it is a straight 'as the crow flies' measure of geographical distance from some very basic services such as primary school and general practitioners' surgeries. Presently, parents in Bermondsey in South

London are holding their children out of secondary school and attempting to form a local school of their own because the secondary school facilities available to these parents and children is eight miles away, involves two bus changes and a journey of one-and-a-half hours in either direction (http://www.simonhughesmp.org.uk/article8.html). The present indices of local deprivation would not capture this severe failure of public service availability. Poverty or social exclusion is not simply a matter of household income, it is also strongly related to the quality of public service availability.

Worryingly, the studies which have been conducted have had no remit to investigate the extent to which the new information technologies can be utilised to overcome the accessibility and mobility disadvantages of the socially excluded. The use of information technology by parents in Bermondsey could assist in the viable and sustainable provision of a local 'charter' school: technology could provide an alternative to 'journey' and provide the skilling through e-technology necessary for the future employment of youth (Turner et al., 2000). Substitution of physical journeys by electronic journeys requires consideration within an overall transport framework – for employment, for education, for health, for household financial managements and social welfare provision.

Transport circumstances are not only a reflection of social exclusion but they operate to compound and contribute to further social exclusion (Grieco, 1995). Deprivation in physical communication infrastructure can be mirrored by deprivation in telecommunication structure if policy intervention is not undertaken: transport and social exclusion ought properly to be viewed within the overall framework of communication and social exclusion. In this short paper, and in opposition to the recently published DETR report on transport and social exclusion (DETR 2000; http://www.mobility-unit.detr.gov.uk/socialex/), we argue that the information requirements of the socially excluded in respect of transport is greater than that of socially advantaged and that the areas of transport information and 'intelligent' transport provision (Hine et al., 2000) need to be incorporated in government attempts to address the 'digital divide'.

In discussing transport and social exclusion, there has been relatively little discussion to date of the extent to which new information technologies can enable the 'excluded' to participate in decision-making and planning of public transport services. Exclusion has not only been about the exclusion from the use of services but also from the governance of those services. A larger part for the socially excluded in the planning and governance of public transport services will enable a better fit between the needs of the socially excluded in respect of transport whether these be health, employment, or education related.

Why 'Social Exclusion'?

The term 'social exclusion' has been developed and utilised by New Labour to signify the restricted participation in a range of 'normal' social functions experienced by substantial numbers of citizens. The term 'social exclusion' has been used to focus attention on the role played by social processes and institutional structures in excluding individuals and communities from full participation in civic life. Whilst direct or formal exclusion is relatively straightforward to identify and the removal of formal barriers is relatively transparent and rapidly accomplishable through law, the removal of indirect or social exclusion is more difficult to accomplish.

The processes and institutions through which social exclusion is effected are more 'sticky' to address and correct. Whilst social exclusion is measurable and evident from outcomes, identifying the processes which produce the outcomes is a more difficult task. The discussion of social exclusion has recognised the compound nature of the problem with social exclusion being understood in terms of the clusters of characteristics which chart together: low educational attainment, high unemployments, residence in high crime environments, child poverty. Inside of this complex policy area, and most particularly in the relationship of transport to social exclusion, there has been a degree of professional naivety about the lived circumstances of the socially excluded.

Transport as a profession and perspective has had an engineering focus which has failed to identify the user needs of deprived communities and to incorporate feed back mechanisms and the integration of the excluded into governance structures which would keep services on track. Social policy as a profession and perspective has been time/space naive: analyses of the scheduling difficulties experienced by low income individuals and communities in a social and national context where there has been a substantial lessening of accessibility to primary services without adequate improvements in low income mobility have been very few on the ground.

The Need for New 'Transport And Social Exclusion' Methodologies and Operational Tools

For many local policy makers, the social exclusion discussion is a new and confusing one. The auditing capabilities of new technology enable a rapid charting of 'social exclusion' in terms of the indices of local deprivation, indices which as we have already seen are not fine tuned in terms of transport functions, but the mechanisms by which such measured social exclusion can be corrected are not clear.

There is a past literature on transport disadvantage but in the main it is fragmented and very limited in respect of gender, ethnicity, older person, disabled and single parent household needs and provision. Recently, under the auspices of the DETR, Professor Kerry Hamilton of the University of East London undertook the important and necessary task of integrating the available UK and international materials available on gender and transport into an on-line facility within the scope of the DETR funded Gender Audit of Transport Provision (Hamilton, 2000; http://www.women-and-transport.net; http://www.mobility-unit.detr.gov.uk/gender/). The outcome of this exercise is that local planners can quickly scan the literature in their search for improvements in transport practices which can reduce social exclusion, at least in respect of gender. Professor Hamilton's work has built a base upon which further activities of the DETR in respect of gender and transport can build (see the latest gender and transport checklist – http://www.mobility-unit.detr.gov.uk/check/index.htm).

A similar exercise could usefully be performed in respect of the range of social exclusion categories. Jeff Turner has developed a Transport and Social Exclusion Toolkit on the University of Manchester transport web site (http://www.art.man.ac.uk/transres/socexclu0.htm); Margaret Grieco, Julian Hine and colleagues have used geocities.com to build a Transport and Society on-line network to begin the on-line structuring of a social exclusion and transport literature (http://www.geocities.com/transport_and_society); Nottingham University has started an on-line transport and social exclusion bibliography (http://www.nottingham.ac.uk/sbe/planbiblios/bibs/sustrav/refs/10a.html). Each of these resources has usefulness in a field where the policy pressure for action is intense but where the fundamental ground clearing on terms and the realities they chart has only just begun, however, the need for substantial resources to be invested in a literature and best practice toolkit that local authorities, transport operators and community organisations can make use of in the real planning context is critical – the gender audit provides the evidence for the utility of such an approach.

The three on-line resources on transport and social exclusion identified here, taken together, represent an emergent data base on transport and social exclusion, including its relationship to employment, providing both a mapping of existing knowledge and a resource for best practice – there remains, however, a major task for a larger policy agency to undertake in expanding and maintaining these on-line resources – the role played by the World Bank in knowledge management in the field of social issues and the developing world provides an appropriate example (http://www.worldbank.org). Such 'knowledge management' sites are not constrained simply to be locations of 'expert' knowledge but can provide locations for grass root perspectives on and feedback about transport and social exclusion initiatives, experiments and policies.

Patterns of compound disadvantage require new methodologies for measurement and the adoption of front of the field information technologies for their resolution. In Germany an individual can punch in their post code to a national travel information system and the post code of their destination and obtain a travel and scheduling map for the whole of their desired journey. For low income citizens with limited search budgets and highly constrained circumstances for experimentation with journeys, a similar system available at a public library or in a shopping mall or at a community centre (perhaps with the assistance of the BT Community Connect programme) could be used for guiding their journeys to work, to hospitals, to training locations. Presently, in Nottingham, travel plans are prepared and printed out for work seekers in a small, face to face counselling experiment. Practically, such facilities could readily be made available directly on-line to large numbers of work seekers or visitors to and patients of health establishments. The German experiment proves the possibility: in the absence of an integrated transport and social exclusion on-line facility the prospect of on-line travel guidance and its implications for the reduction of social exclusion may remain disguised from the British transport planner and transport using public.

Social Exclusion: Clusters and Scatters

Much of the focus on social exclusion and transport has been at the areal or zonal level – indeed, the indices of local deprivation are precisely an areal or zonal measure. There is, however, a dimension of social exclusion and transport which requires the policy maker, planner and researcher to think beyond the areal or neighbourhood perspective. The socially excluded are not only clustered together in areas or zones where transport is particularly bad or particularly inappropriate but are also scattered as a consequence of life circumstance.

Think, for example, about older persons living in relatively affluent areas or zones who have no kin and who have limited mobility and income. Such older persons not only have limited direct accessibility to services and facilities but also have limited indirect accessibility (Grieco, 1995) – low income households often compensate for the lack of income to buy services by making use of relational resources (friends, kin) to assist in meeting their survival needs. Work undertaken in Liverpool (Grieco, 1995) revealed a high incidence of the borrowing of time between households with neighbours assisting one another in shopping and child care tasks. The socially isolated, whether by disability, age, marital circumstance, ethnicity, can not easily obtain assistance in accessing resources – illness may mean that key shopping can not be done or medication obtained or escorts obtained for making journeys through dangerous spaces.

By identifying the difference between direct and indirect accessibility it becomes clear that different categories of the socially excluded will have different transport needs. Servicing the transport needs of the socially excluded who are clustered in a particular neighbourhood, zone or area is a different prospect to servicing the transport needs of the socially excluded who are also socially isolated in terms of their immediate neighbourhood.

Where the socially excluded are clustered a better fit between bus routes, bus times and vehicle types and measured areas of deprivation can accomplish much. Where the socially excluded are scattered or dispersed, new information technologies can play an important part in lessening the negative impacts of their reduced physical accessibilities by providing on-line services such as home working, home banking, shopping and the ordering of medication to be delivered and also in improving their mobility by the utilisation of information technology to provide transport on demand.

New information technologies can readily collect together information on persons with low mobility wishing to make similar journeys, provide a booking system or intelligent reservation system which permits the pick up and drop off at home and organise this in a way which is cost effective at the community level. Passengers moving towards buses was a irremovable feature of a past technical ages, buses routing around the needs of low mobility passengers is an existing capability of the new information age.

The same technologies which could be used to accommodate the needs of the least mobile can be used in ensuring that work seekers receive appropriate transport support to maintain and sustain their space in the workplace. Routing 'intelligent reservation' vehicles so as to enable youth to arrive at work on time would be a useful addition to the new deal. In reflecting on the difficulties experienced by those on low income and those with restricted mobility in accessing civic resources, it is important to reflect on the extent to which this is the outcome of modern urban design – design which in the attempt to cut costs through increases in scale placed critical services outside of local neighbourhoods. Employment was one of the casualties of the pressure to upscale: new technologies with their distributed characteristics enable activities that previously could only have been accomplished in large scale premises to be undertaken once again within the local domain. Rethinking the fit between scale, travel and communications in the age of congestion must certainly be on the agenda.

There is then a difference between mass and responsive transport provisions, however, ICT technology can cut across old boundaries even in respect of the interface between mass and responsive transport systems. For example, mass transport has very clear peaks and troughs within the duration of a day: removing vehicles which are operating at under capacity in the mass system during the troughs would enable such vehicles to be used as full load vehicles in a responsive mode. The use of such vehicles for unsocial work shift journeys provides one example of a viable 'transport and social exclusion' tool.

Thinking of transport in terms of achieving a real time match between available fleets of vehicles and the travel purposes of the socially excluded through the capabilities of the new information technologies provided a very different perspective on what is possible within existing budget constraints. Responsive transport is very important in the context of crisis journeys. Crisis might be a job interview event or a sickness event or some other non routine journey which has to be made. Learning the journey path in circumstances of crisis is expensive and risky – the hospital appointment is missed or the job lost. The new information technologies open up the prospect of the integration of public, private and voluntary sector transport resources in providing assistance to citizen's in crisis transport circumstances.

The new information technologies are well suited for installation in the domestic environment: networked terminals, web access through the domestic television set, web capability mobile telephones. This information capability in the domestic environment opens up new scheduling capabilities and can restore local information in the neighborhood environment (Grieco, 2000). A new relationship between accessibility, mobility and the previously socially excluded is possible.

A New Relationship between Accessibility, Mobility and the Socially Excluded? The Employment Implications

There are important employment implications of the new information communication technologies both of themselves and in their annexation to transport technology and transport organisation. In this short section, we wish to provide a number of pointers to the potential for developments which improve the employment circumstances of the socially excluded.

Firstly, the e-form (electronic communication) enables the setting up of electronic employment exchanges. These have the potential to simplify and reduce the search and transaction costs encountered by the work seekers both in the local neighbourhood and in the wider geographical area. This has important consequences for travel to search for employment patterns.

Secondly, the e-form can enable even the homeless to have a base at which they can be reliably contacted. This can enable those who have experienced the most fragmented social profiles to develop and project reliability characteristics which assure employers and enable employers who wish to make a contribution to reducing social exclusion to make contact with the work seekers. This has the capability of removing or lowering the need for the expensive middle class professional worker in servicing the socially excluded.

Thirdly, the e-form can enable those with restricted income to more easily pool their transport resources in the journey to employment. There are good reasons why government agencies should be exploring the potential for pooled transport in general, most particularly the choking of British cities by congestion levels. The pooling of transport requires a well organised information environment.

Fourthly, there is a need to scope the opportunities for telework and community business in socially excluded neighbourhoods. Reducing journeys reduces travel costs and travel costs with real benefits for low income household budgets. The distributed character of the new information technologies enables the relocation of e-business and e-work activity to both the inner city and the remote location. This new potential for altered work organisation can be utilised to assist single mothers participate in economic activity – through new technology available in the home, single mothers could obtain increments of work in a manner which fits their child care schedules.

The new technologies can be used to reduce the time poverty of women with dependent children by reducing their search and journey times in accessing key economic resources.

We have already talked of the way in which intelligent reservation systems could be used to assist the socially excluded make employment journeys within the framework of a public transport system. These five areas of potential improvement are all worthy of serious policy consideration by both local and national government agencies. Taken together they would enable the previously socially excluded to play their own part in the open management of a public service.

Conclusion: Social Inclusion as Direct Participation in Governance of Neighbourhood Functioning

Our argument is that the characteristics of 'socially excluded' are generated out of exclusion from participation. Exclusion from services is a consequence of the exclusion from participation. Not only is service provision and service functioning in need of improvement but the redesign of governance is required. Exclusion is about participation or the lack of participation the inclusion of 'social exclusion' in transport strategies therefore needs to be more widely adopted than it currently is.

Following the arguments presented here the reduction of social exclusion through transport mechanisms is likely to occur on a revenue rather than a capital investment basis (the provision of information services, scheduling and booking systems rather than the development of physical infrastructure): present government policy precludes revenue assistance to the various local agencies in their quest for the reduction of social exclusion. Technology could allow residents to become more effective, active advocates for their area. It would allow them perhaps not to have to negotiate or understand the sheer fragmentation in responsibility and delivery that characterises transport policy. It could allow them to 'watch' the work of variety of agencies and demand coordination from those agencies. It could allow them to more easily monitor performance of agencies and benchmark their own experience against that of other areas. It could also allow the agencies or professional 'advocates' themselves to be better coordinated. But whether it does depends on a change in government policy – to better join the citizen to governance through the use of new technology. The levels of public service failure experienced within the UK public infrastructure and the resulting levels of electorate frustration as evidenced by recent events in Kidderminster (where a non-politician displaced a junior labour minister in a safe labour seat on the single issue of hospital closure) suggest that the 'open management' approach of incorporating client feedback into operations through new information technology may be about to have its day. In such organisations, leadership becomes distributed – it is a movement away from the old focused and secluded leadership structures.

References and Background Reading

Carter, C. and Grieco, M. (2000), 'New Deals, No Wheels: Social exclusion, tele-options and electronic ontology', *Urban Studies*, Vol. 37, No. 10, pp. 1735–48.

Grieco, M. (1995), 'Time Pressures and Low Income Families: the implication for "social" transport policy in Europe', *Community Development Journal*, Vol. 30, No. 4.

Grieco, M. (2000), 'Intelligent Urban Development: The emergence of wired government and administration', *Urban Studies*, Vol. 37, No. 10, pp. 1719–22.

Hine, J., Swan, D., Scott, J., Binnie, D. and Sharp, J. (2000), 'Using Technology to Overcome the Tyranny of Space: Information provision and wayfinding', *Urban Studies*, Vol. 37, No. 10, pp. 1757–70.

Turner, J., Holmes, L. and Hodgson, F. (2000), 'Intelligent Urban Development: An introduction to a participatory approach', *Urban Studies*, Vol. 37, No. 10, pp. 1723–34.

On-line References

East Midlands Development Agency; http://www.emda.org.uk/cgi-bin/search.cgi.

Education provision in Bermondsey; http://www.simonhughesmp.org.uk/article8.html.

Index of local deprivation; http://www.regeneration.detr.gov.uk/98ild/index.htm.

Indices of deprivation 2000; http://www.regeneration.detr.gov.uk/rs/03100/index.htm.

Social exclusion in Scotland; http://www.scotland.gov.uk/library/documents1/socexcl.htm.

Summary of DETR report on Transport and Social Exclusion; http://www.mobility-unit.detr.gov.uk/socialex.

The Roskild symposium; http//www.unesco.org/most/besseng.htm.

Chapter Fourteen

The Distribution of Telecom Technology Across the Indonesian Border

Alfons van Marrewijk

This chapter focuses on the globalisation of the telecom sector in which Western telecom operators have taken minority participation in telecom operators in emerging telecom markets. In this process knowledge and technology is distributed to improve the operational quality of the local operators and to increase revenues. How does this process of technology distribution takes place in the daily cross-cultural contact between Western and local operators? This chapter discusses the cross-cultural experiences of Dutch telecom operator KPN with the distribution of knowledge and technology to an Indonesian operator. The daily life of KPN employees in Indonesia is perceived from an organisation-anthropological perspective. Therefore, a model that is based upon the work of Chanlat (1994) and the network theory of Latour (1994) is discussed. The model developed is applied to describe the transfer of knowledge and technology by the Dutch KPN expatriates in Jakarta. The strategies of the KPN employees to distribute knowledge and technology can be divided in three categories: the rejection of the local culture, the 'going native' strategy and the strategy of maintain personal networks in both the local and expatriate culture. The success of the distribution of knowledge and technology is highly depended of the cultural strategy used.

Distribution of Technology and Cultural Cooperation in the Telecom Sector[1]

No industry has gone through such a fundamental change as the tele-communication sector in the last decade. The national governments have agreed upon in the World Trade Organisation (WTO) to liberalise the telecom market. They have committed in the General Agreement on Trade in Services (GATS) to restructure their national telecom markets according to specified time schedules. As a consequence, each government faces the difficult task of dismantling the power of the local, state owned, operator and opening up the home market for new and foreign competitors (Mansell, 1994). Furthermore, technological inventions have resulted in a technological convergence of information structure, telecom infrastructure, and access media and services (Estabrooks, 1995). Telecommunication has thus become the driver of a global economy and telecom operators are supporter as well as subject of this process. In conclusion, the new liberalised telecom policies, technological innovations and a growing awareness that telecommunication is an important aspect of the international trade system have caused fundamental changes in the telecom sector.

In reaction to these fundamental changes American, European and Asian telecom operators have transformed their organisation from governmental monopolists into commercial service providers. The operators in developed countries, in many cases, started much earlier in their process of restructuring then those in developing countries (Smith and Staple, 1994). These, mostly Western, operators have had a competitive advantage and have expanded beyond their traditional national markets in periphery markets (van Marrewijk, 2000). They have taken minority shares in telecom operators in emerging markets and created dynamic networks of cross-border strategic alliances. In this process of internationalisation they have transformed Western technology, management practises and organisational structures to local telecom operators to improve the quality of local telecom operators and thus get a positive refund of their investments. The Director of International Telecommunication Union therefore, warned of a new form of imperialism in the developing countries (*De Volkskrant*, 3 October 1995).

The distribution of technology and organisation cultural practises of Western to non-Western telecom operators can result in a domination of Western operators (Scott-Stevens, 1986). Hannerz (1992) understands the autonomy and boundedness of organisation culture as a matter of degree affected by a structure of asymmetrical, centre-periphery relationships. Cultures are not all territorially bounded. Cultural flow is internally diverse and has its own diverse ways of organising (Hannerz, 1992: 263). The end result of these cultural processes, however, is not a homogenisation of culture (Featherstone, 1990; Hannerz, 1992; Friedman, 1994; Touraine, 2000). Hannerz (1992) calls it the creolisation of culture, a creative interplay between the centre and the periphery. Cultural elements, organisational forms, technology and knowledge flows from the centre to the periphery. The cultural flow creates a greater affinity between cultures of centre and periphery giving the latter possibilities of entering the global market (Hannerz, 1992; Lash and Urry, 1994). But does the cultural flow create a greater affinity in the cooperation of operators in developing and developed countries?

Fung (1995) explains how three strategies in the handling of cultural diversity are related to the corporate orientation, culture and its objectives. With the first strategy, the *ethnocentric* strategy, the management tries to impose the headquarters' world-view upon locals in foreign subsidiaries while the organisational culture of the home country organisation is imposed upon other local offices. In such a situation the Western management is regarded as superior and universally applicable. The second strategy, the *polycentric* strategy, is one that assumes that the host-country perspective is the most suitable for local business. The organisational culture is constructed and reconstructed in a search for a balance between the local and the home country demands. Fung (1995) also calls this strategy the *local ethnocentric* strategy. The third strategy, the *geocentric* strategy, tries to find a balance between global coordination and local adaptation to create synergy. This division into three strategies can also be found in Adler (1986), Adler and Ghadar (1993) and Schneider and Barsoux (1997: 211). Can these strategies also be found in the cooperation of operators in developing and developed countries?

This chapter therefore explores the question of how the processes of technology distribution manifest itself in the daily cross-cultural contact between Western and local operators? To explore the cooperation of a Western and a local telecom operator, the case of Dutch telecom operator KPN and the Indonesian operator PT Telkom is discussed in this chapter. These two organisations have a long colonial relationship and an intensive cross-cultural cooperation (van Marrewijk, 2000). The distribution of technology is best studied when focusing on daily life behaviour of employees. Employees have a strong capacity to absorb information, to order this information and, to cope with new situations. Employees organise chaos, new developments that cause insecurity to a comprehensive level, in order to control their situation. People know how to reduce this complexity to usable proportions. Therefore, a closer inspection on the subject of study, the human being, is needed.

Human Beings Back in Cross-cultural Studies

We must remember that the objects of study in cross-cultural cooperation are human beings. Human beings that cannot easily be squeezed into simplistic models and schemes. Human beings that can act, speak, think, have desires and drives, exist in space and time and are simultaneously the object and subject of science (Chanlat, 1994). People construct their social reality through their actions and in turn, this social reality prescribes the behaviour of the people. Human beings are always constructing, deconstructing and reconstructing their reality from both old and new experiences. Through this process culture is reproduced. Strategic behaviour of people can transform social reality because culture is constantly being reproduced. Giddens (1990) calls the reflective ordering and reordering of social relations that exert influence on the actions of individuals: 'the reflexive monitoring of action'. In their daily activities people reflect on their interactions because *all human beings routinely keep in touch with the ground of what they do as an integral element of doing it* (Giddens, 1990: 37). In traditional cultures each new generation honours the past and reproduces a larger part of the cultural patrimony of the last generation because of a relatively unchanged context. Giddens (1990) states that in modern society the daily routines of individuals have much less connection with the traditions of the past. As a result, the reflexivity of new knowledge, which is absorbed and applied by groups or individuals, is faster. Social practices are constantly being reordered by means of incoming information. Because reproduction is based on information, reflexivity in modern society is even faster than it was before. Modern society is created on reflexive knowledge and generates expert systems in which individuals have to trust. These expert systems such as financial and technical systems organise the daily reality of individuals. The daily reality of human beings therefore needs more attention in the study on cross-cultural cooperation.

To understand the logic of the daily life behaviour of human beings it is necessary to focus on the routine of every day life. In *The Logic of Practice*, Bourdieu (1990) focuses on the *habitus*. The *habitus* uses schemes of past experiences to produce individual and collective actions. People are capable of generating thoughts, perceptions, actions and expressions that are not limited in number and are relatively unpredictable. However, people are also limited in the production because of the schemes of past experiences. The *habitus* therefore tends to produce unlimited actions determined by the schemes which, at the same time, are limited by the schemes. Bourdieu calls these *regulated improvisations* (1990: 55). These regulated improvisations allow a relationship between the individual schemes and the collective common sense. Individual history models the individual schemes. The harmonisation of experiences takes place by the individuals receiving reinforcement from individual or collective activities such as ceremonies. The harmony of practical sense and objectified meaning produces a commonsense world.

Strauss and Quinn (1994) use Bourdieu's concept of regulated improvisations to emphasise the role of social actors and to introduce the concept of individual schemes in studying the relationship between individuals and their cultural environment in modern societies. They conclude that current anthropological theories do not have a strong tradition in explaining the relationship of individuals with their cultural environment. While Bourdieu (1990) stresses the habits of people, Strauss and Quinn (1994) focus on variation and changes in the habits of people. They stress upon the role of motivations and emotions in the construction of schemes. The cultural schemes are learnt by experiences that remain in the memory and mediate the behaviour and actions of an individual. These schemes consist of loose networks of associations, which have been learnt by previous experiences. The outcomes of these networks of associations are not fixed but can vary in their prescription for human behaviour. In this way, individual actions are not directly determined by the social-cultural environment but mediated by learnt schemes. Tennekes (1995) also points out that the structures are simultaneously sources as well as restrictions of actions. He distinguishes three sources of and conditions for action: culture, society and personality. Through their actions people generate culture, society and personality at the same time. Tennekes (1995: 25) stresses the dialectics of action and structure in which people generate structures by means of actions that can lead to new independent structures. Cultural analyses therefore, have to focus on the meanings of the context given by the actors.

When applying these theoretical insights to the study of cross-cultural cooperation in the telecom sector we learn the need for open systems models of cross-cultural management, which view the entire situation as a dynamic, interdependent system. The world of daily human life has to be discovered by actors in an intensive relation with their context (Strauss and Quinn, 1994). Therefore, it is necessary to see the daily world through the eyes of the studied subjects, to come to a *verstehen* of the constructed social reality in the phenomenological tradition. To obtain detailed information on the behaviour of employees the daily life in an organisation has to be studied. Latour (1988, 1994 and 1997) studied the daily world of scientists in laboratories, offices and construction places. He concluded that in the daily practice of technicians, administration workers, managers and business developers it is impossible to study the social and technical artefacts separately because they are strongly intertwined. In their daily practices employees connect social and technical artefacts to different levels in and outside the organisation.

Bate (1997: 1161) emphasised that 'insight always comes from the inside'. Behaviour of employees in organisations cannot be understood without our knowing the context in which they are situated and cross-cultural management cannot be studied separately from organisational cultures. Kunda (1992), for example, gives a beautiful picture of the daily life of employees in an American software company. Other scientists also noted the importance of observing daily life rituals of employees in order to obtain a detailed and more accurate picture of the organisational culture and to understand the culture through the eyes of the employees (van Maanen, 1984; Orr, 1986; Warnier, 1995). How could the cross-cultural cooperation in the telecom sector be studied from an anthropological perspective?

Anthropological Model to Unravel Cultural Complexity in Organisations

The anthropological perspective on organisations distinguishes itself from other organisational perspectives as a method of fieldwork activity (the 'doing'), as a paradigm (the 'thinking') and as a narrative style (the 'writing') (Bate, 1997: 1151). The major invention of anthropologist is the 'doing' of ethnographic fieldwork by means of participant observation. Bate states that there is a very fussy methodology in doing ethnographic research and criticises the 'mystique' attitude of some anthropologists. The 'thinking' of anthropologists concerns looking critically at organisations and perceiving the organisation as a cultural phenomenon. An organisation is seen as a modern 'tribe' with its own cultural values and norms that prescribe the behaviour of employees. Finally, the 'writing' of ethnographies by anthropologists distinguish organisational anthropology from other organisational studies in that it can be narrative, poetic, fictional, autobiographical and post-modern (Bate, 1997). A true anthropology of organisations focuses on human behaviour and at the same time explores all the relationships within the environment that run through organisation life at different levels.

> The complexity of the problems that confront us both on national and an international scale, the importance of cultural elements, the emphasis on individual aspirations ... all of these influences have, in effect led us to propose models of management that will henceforth be based on a true anthropology of organisations (Chanlat, 1994: 160).

Alvesson and Berg (1992) therefore, stress the need to separate these different levels involved with organisational studies. They distinguish six levels of culture: 1) national cultures; 2) regional and industrial cultures; 3) company culture; 4) professional culture; 5) department culture; and 6) worker culture. In order to grasp human reality within organisations Chanlat (1994) distinguishes five closely linked levels of organisational reality: 1) the first level is the individual level, in which Chanlat sees human reality as a subtle interaction of the biological, the psychic and the social. At this level individuals construct and deconstruct their own reality and cope with conflicts, tensions, uncertainties and ambiguities. 2) At the second level, the interactional level, the identity of the individual is formed in interaction with others. The interactions, both formal and informal, can appear between two different individuals or two different groups. 3) The third level, the organisation level, focuses on the organisational cultures. 4) The fourth level, the society level, concerns national cultures. These national cultures have involved due to geography, history, political and economic forces, language and religion. 5) The fifth level, the world level, deals with transnational ideologies such as religion, globalisation and liberalisation.

It is now possible to create a conceptual framework which can be used to explore the complex telecom sector. Chanlat's framework is used to approach the telecom industry starting at world level and to study it level by level in order to unravel its cultural complexity. Each level of this multilevel model is analytically independent and contains elements that are linked to each other in relatively stable relations. Each of the levels is contingent in nature and the relationships between the levels could go in any direction (Chanlat, 1994: 174). This multilevel model helps in the exploration and unravelling of the telecom industry as van Marrewijk (1996) did with the cross-cultural relations of three Dutch development organisations and their Bolivian counterparts in the Bolivian development sector. In this study, there appeared to be the relationships between the different levels of analysis. How can these links be studied? The links of cross-cultural cooperation are connected to all levels of the model.

To study cross-cultural cooperation the 'symmetric anthropology' of Latour (1994) is used. Latour (1994) concludes that 'traditional' anthropology is not suitable for studying modern cultural complexity because of the distinction that has been applied in a 'natural' and a 'social' world. The aim of symmetric anthropology is, according to Latour, to study the natural and social from a holistic perspective. This separation is based on the idea that nature has always existed as it is while society has been created by people. Latour (1994) states that nature and natural artefacts are created by human beings and he criticises the scientists who construct nature and at the same time 'discover' it. Latour

(1994) calls these products of the interaction of nature and society hybrids. He propounds that the more modern science tries to separate the two different zones of nature and society, the larger the production of hybrids will be. The 'symmetric anthropology' investigates these hybrids by treating them as networks, which like a railway never goes beyond the local as long as one stays on the rail. In this way, large organisations can be studied.

> The organisation of an American company is not like the Kafka organisation. It is a basket-work of networks that is embodied by order notes and organisation flows, local procedures and specific arrangements that can stretch over a continent just on the condition that it does not cover the whole continent. One can follow networks in an organisation without ever a change of level or without ever discovering a deconstructed rationality (Latour, 1994: 171).

The anthropologist follows networks within the organisation and by doing so he does not go beyond the local level. The hybrids can be unravelled by means of following the local network of connections because macro actors are constructed with micro actors. Latour therefore, proposes to follow the construction and production of hybrids. If this is done it will become clear that at a specific point the 'quasi object' has the character of a natural artefact and at another point it assumes the character of a societal artefact and at other times it has the character of a social relationship.

This theoretical perspective of Latour can be used as a methodology to study cross-cultural cooperation in the telecom sector. The network of the actor is approached from the actors' perspective and follows the actions and daily activities. The connections are made by free associations and are not restricted by presuppositions of its reality. Latour calls the mapping of heterogeneous associations 'sociologica' (Latour, 1988: 261). The connections in the actor's network are always 'logical' from the actor's perspective even when different levels within or outside an organisation are being passed. The theoretical framework constructed to study the cross-cultural cooperation in the telecom sector is thus a combination of Chanlat's multilevel model and the sociologica of Latour (see Figure 14.1).

The Case of the Dutch and Indonesian Telecom Operators

By exploring the world and society level of the telecom sector it is learnt that the Netherlands is one of the major investors in Indonesia. With a total value

Field of study

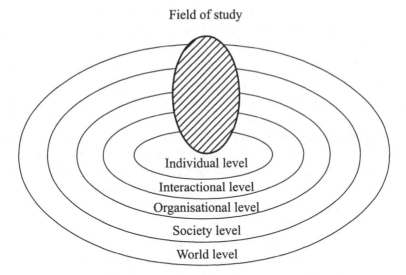

Individual level

Interactional level

Organisational level

Society level

World level

Figure 14.1 Multi-level model for the exploration of cultural complexity in the Indonesian telecom sector

of US$ 6.8 billion it occupies the sixth place, with investments in sectors such as the chemical sector, the food industry and the electronic manufacturing and the telecommunications sector (Smith, 1994). Fifty per cent of the joint ventures were initiated after 1984, which confirmed the establishment of a renewed business relationship between the Netherlands and Indonesia. Furthermore, the restructuring of the Indonesian and Dutch market are different in pace and nature. The Dutch government was among the first in Europe to reform its national operator PTT Telecom in the early 1990s (Mansell, Davies and Hulsink, 1995). Gradually the market was opened for competitors and in 1997 full competition was possible. The Indonesian government was more behind in this process.

Indonesia's population of nearly 200 million people and its rapid economic growth that lasted till the autumn of 1997 spurred an enormous demand for telecom services. The fixed-line penetration of nearly 1 per cent was in 1993 one of the lowest telephone densities in Southeast Asia (PT Data Consult Inc., 1995). The Indonesian government planned to raise the penetration to 5 per cent but the Indonesian telecom sector was not able to meet this objective. Furthermore, the General Agreement on Trade in Services, signed by Indonesian government, forced a liberalisation of the Indonesian telecom market. In June 1994, the Indonesian telecom industry was opened to direct foreign equity investment through the establishment of a joint venture. Foreign investment licenses were granted for an initial period of 30 years and private companies could obtain operating licenses in revenue sharing agreements under the ultimate control of PT Telkom in *Kerjasama Operasi* (joint operating schemes). Five private consortia were selected to install and operate fixed-lines in five selected regions: Sumatra, West-Java, Central Java, Kalimantan and East Indonesia. Each consortium is made up of an experienced foreign operator such as Telstra, Singapore Telecom, NTT, US West, Cable & Wireless and an Indonesian company. Each consortium has to install a minimum number of fixed-lines and will operate all local lines in the assigned region for 15 years, including those originally installed by PT Telkom. PT Telkom will retain full operational control over the remaining two commercially important regions of Jakarta and East Java. The government still controls the two primary operators PT Indosat and PT Telkom.

The exploration of society and organisational level shows the long-term personal and institutional relationship between KPN and the Indonesian telecom sector which helped the KPN management to establish business relations (van Marrewijk, 2000). In 1993, PT Telkom sought for information on mobile communications systems. In response, KPN sent an expert to Jakarta to help PT Telkom with the construction of a small GSM network. The network was set up to beat Singaporean competitors on the islands of Bintam and Batam two small Islands located just south of Singapore. Indonesians have a negative image of Singaporeans thus an Indonesian mobile operator on the Indonesian islands would make good publicity in Indonesia. The Dutch expert played an important role in the success of the initiative of PT Telkom. This stimulated the acquisition by KPN of a 17 per cent share in the mobile operator Telkomsel owned by PT Telkom. To improve the market position and the profitability of Telkomsel, KPN committed to distribute knowledge on technology and management practices.

At the interactional and individual level, the distribution of knowledge on technology and management practises met with distinct national and business cultures. Cultural differences between Dutch and Indonesian telecom organisations obstructed the cooperation between Dutch KPN employees and Indonesian employees. Western researchers mention six topics when referring to Indonesian business culture (e.g. Hofstede, 1982; Zijlstra, 1994; Mann, 1996; Brandt, 1997): 1) the perception of time; 2) the language; 3) personal connections; 4) the ethnic diversity; 5) the religious diversity; and 6) the Indonesian management practices. Employees of KPN in Indonesia have found three strategies to deal with these differences in business culture in order to successfully transfer technology to the Indonesian PT Telkom employees in the mobile operator Telkomsel: 1) the rejection of the local culture; 2) the 'going native' strategy; and 3) the strategy of maintaining personal networks in both the local and the expatriate culture.

The Absorption into the Dutch Expatriate Community in Jakarta

A large part of the Dutch KPN expatriates have used ethnocentric strategies in the daily cross-cultural practises of technology distribution between KPN and Telkomsel. These Dutch employees do not have any in-depth experience in Indonesia or for that matter of any other country besides their own. In the preparation there is no time for developing intercultural knowledge or learning Bahasa Indonesia. And in their private life they are totally involved in the Dutch expatriate circuit through sports, spouses and social events.

Playing sports together creates informal relations among the KPN expatriates and provides the occasion for news and stories to be exchanged and personal relations to be developed. Many of the expatriates consider sports as a necessary activity. All of the expatriates have a car and a driver and only walk inside air-conditioned buildings. Dutch expatriates who are used to biking, skating, or running feel restricted because of the heavy traffic and pollution in Jakarta. The expatriates therefore play tennis with his KPN colleagues at the hot Chilandak tennis court or join the volleyball group in the gym of the Dutch. Every Saturday some of the KPN expatriates play soccer in one of the teams of FC Knudde. A variety of Dutch people play in the teams; students, small business entrepreneurs, but also general managers and executives.

A larger part of the expatriates' private network is built through the personal contacts of their spouses who meet with other Dutch mothers and helps the children with computer lessons at the Netherlands International School, a school with more than 180 children and 17 Dutch teachers. This voluntary work helps them to establish new contacts with other people. Apart from 1) the mothers of school-going children at the Dutch school, there are three other groups of Dutch expatriate partners: 2) spouses without children; 3) women with older children studying or living in the Netherlands; and 4) Indonesian women. The situation for the spouses of KPN expatriates in Indonesia is not easy from an emotional point of view. They are expected to be strong and support their partners. Emotions such as boredom, homesickness and jealousy destabilise their relationships and are not discussed with other expatriates' partners. Partners keep busy with housekeeping, raising children, voluntary work, visiting each other, playing bridge, playing tennis, swimming and shopping.

When a KPN expatriate is new in Jakarta it is very difficult not to get totally involved in the Dutch circuit and, for expatriates living in the Dutch circle it is difficult to establish contacts within the Indonesian society because of the Indonesians' negative image of the Dutch expatriate circle. In 1996, in a multi cultural management workshop, managers of PT Telkom formulated a general image of the Dutch. The results of this workshop showed a rather negative image of the Dutch; too direct, blunt, sarcastic, want a direct yes or no, aggressive, not to be trusted, unfriendly, too absorbed with memories of the past, do not care about local politics, 'do it my way' thinking, don't want to understand Indonesians. The difficulties faced in trying to establish relations with Indonesians and in learning the language coupled with the awareness that the residence in Jakarta is temporary makes it thus easier and more attractive for expatriates to invest in Dutch networks. Because of the many contacts, expatriates and their wives are frequently invited to parties on weekends. Almost every Friday and Saturday there is a party. With more than 2,500 Dutch expatriates in Jakarta contacts are easier made with Dutch than with Indonesians. According to this group of KPN expatriates assimilation into Indonesian society is just an illusion:

> We live here together with other Dutch expatriates in the same neighbourhood. We live in a golden cage. People ask me if I like living in Indonesia. Then I say yes, but life is not so much different from the Netherlands. Only here I have a white house with a swimming pool (Interview with KPN expatriate).

It is thus explainable that regulated schemes of Dutch expatriates are completely based upon Dutch values and norms. An example to show this. A Dutch KPN manager was not satisfied with the quality of his financial department. He did not want to control the work of the department in detail or tell them exactly what they have to do but would rather that they manage the objectives and exercise self-responsibility. Thinking that the quality of the work would improve if a part of the work was to be transferred to an external professional office Leo then decided to dismiss the Indonesian manager and two of the Indonesian employees on the count of redundancy. He took full responsibility of the dismissal and even gave the employees the news himself instead of leaving it to the Indonesian HRM manager. Furthermore, in his earlier experience as manager in the Netherlands he had learned that bad news should be addressed directly at the start of the conversation. He therefore invited all of the affected employees one by one into his office and told them that they were to be retrenched carefully explaining the reasons for the decision and offering them support in finding another job in one of the KPN joint ventures in Indonesia. He felt genuinely sorry for them and did not enjoy being the harbinger of bad news.

The Indonesian employees at the KPN Jakarta office were shocked. For them the message came as a complete surprise. The dismissal disturbed the harmony of the office however, shouting, showing anger, being rude and direct conflict are seen as undesirable social behaviour and are thus avoided at all costs since they can endanger harmony. The open nature of the dismissal conflicts with the Javanese concept of *rukun* or harmonious unity (Mulder, 1994: 38). The dismissed employees are also shocked by their superiors' behaviour. In their perception Leo and the General Manager are responsible for the social welfare of their employees (Hofstede, 1982; Mann, 1996; Brandt, 1997). The dismissal means the terrible 'loss of face' or *'malu'* of the Indonesian employees. All other members of the Jakarta office, family, business networks and friends interpret the dismissal as a painful failure. The dismissal does not only mean a loss of work but a loss of social status and networks. To cause *malu* or bring someone into deep shame is a sensitive issue in Indonesia. The dismissed employees do not show emotions of anger and grief at the office but at home or in private meetings at the office or behind closed doors. Only half an hour after the dismissals, the news has already spread through the staff of the joint ventures. The news of the dismissals is the only subject of discussion in the department for days but underlying emotions are not outwardly shown. Because of the emotional aspects of *malu* Indonesians consider dismissal as dangerous not only for the employee but also for the company. The dismissed employee can injure the manager or can take him to court. The tangible repercussions of having caused someone a 'loss of face' are not always immediately observed. The dismissed employee can go to the newspapers, might be related to your business partner, with high-ranking persons or even with the family of the president. These networks can be used to take revenge and obstruct further business activities.

This example shows the ethnocentric strategies used by a great deal of the Dutch expatriates to deal with Indonesian business culture. This strategy corresponds to the *ethnocentric* strategy as discussed by Fung (1995), in which the expatriates try to impose the headquarters' world-view upon locals in foreign subsidiaries. The culture of the home country organisation is imposed upon other local offices. In such a situation the Western management is regarded as superior and universally applicable. That is the case for this group of KPN expatriates. Those who want to escape this dominant Dutch expatriate culture have to make a conscious choice to do so.

Totally Wrapped up in Indonesian Culture

Some of the KPN employees have fallen in love with the Indonesian culture. They learn the language, get to know Indonesian friends and explore the countryside. Some even adapt their life-style to the local culture. Soon after their arrival in Jakarta they experienced the difficulty of exploring Indonesian culture while participating in the Dutch expatriate circle. It is very difficult to establish personal relations in both the Dutch expatriate society and the Indonesian society at the same time.

> If I come to a party of one of my KPN colleagues they will ask me more than ten times if I am coming to play tennis, play hockey, soccer etc. Before you notice your complete week is filled up with the Dutch circle. But we have made as much Indonesian friends as possible. You have to choose if you are living here. Where do you belong? (Interview with KPN employee).

These employees do not want to hide in the Dutch expatriate circle and choose to explore the Indonesian culture rather than the Dutch expatriate culture.

> It is difficult for me to live in two worlds at the same time. I live either in the Dutch world or in the world where I am working at that moment. That can be London, Czech Republic or Indonesia. But then I take the frame of reference of the host country. I understand how Dutch think, do and live, but it is not my world. I find it difficult to concentrate on that. I am completely focused on the Indonesian society, try to learn the language, develop cultural sensitivities, read Indonesian newspapers and keep at a distance from the Dutch expatriate society (Interview with KPN employee).

Dutch expatriates who already have personal relations with Indonesia or male employees who have come without partners to Indonesia are most likely to adopt this strategy. Employees, who have been born in Indonesia, have Indonesian parents or grandparents or, already have an Indonesian spouse who has family and friends in Jakarta spend part of their time with these relations and are therefore part of the Indonesian society. Some of the single employees are not particularly interested in participation in the Dutch circle but search for friends among Indonesians. The isolation from Dutch expatriate society is not always a matter of free choice but also a matter of personal interests and situation.

> Many of the Dutch say I am more Indonesian than Dutch. The people here at the office know that. It is not that I cut myself off completely from the Dutch

expatriate culture. For me it is very logical – I am not with NIS, and many of the parties there are only couples. They can invite me for dinner but then I come alone. I can take an Indonesian friend, but she speaks English. The conversation has to be in English and that is not comfortable for the hosts. How do we have to treat an Indonesian guest? ... they are not used to that. I have a good relationship with all of the Dutch at the office, I know them all (Interview with KPN employee).

Because of their Indonesian networks and the knowledge of Bahasa Indonesia these employees get more information and pick up rumours more easily than the expatriates who employ the first strategy discussed. The problem for employees with this strategy however, is their loyalty towards their Indonesian networks and the exclusion from the Dutch circle. Information obtained from Indonesian sources is given on the basis of trust and the Dutch expatriate identifies with his Indonesian networks. The missing of personal networks within the Dutch circle prevents these Dutch expatriates from passing on valuable information to bridge the cultural gap between the Indonesian and Dutch management. This preoccupation with the Indonesian culture and identity has been an important factor for the success of the mobile operator Telkomsel. They have constructed a mobile infrastructure that covers the 27 provinces of Indonesia. The marketing of the mobile telephones were supported with commercials with a strong accent on the cultural diversity of Indonesia and nation wide coverage of the infrastructure. An old popular Indonesian folk song 'From Aceh to Merauke' served as a connection to the dream of one Indonesian nation. In each province, the daughter of the governor was asked to pose in traditional clothing for the cover of the telephone cards. The customers and government positively received this concept. The opening of a new branch office of the joint venture in Jakarta was also held in a completely Indonesian style. The Dutch General Manager of the office was even dressed in a traditional Batavia costume. This coaxed a compliment out of the Minister of MTPT who remarked on the positive support of some KPN employees in helping to strengthen the Indonesian identity of the joint venture.

This second strategy of 'going native' corresponds to the *polycentric* strategy as discussed by Fung (1995). A small group of KPN expatriates assume that the Indonesian perspective is the most suitable for the Business of Telkomsel. This strategy is in contrast with the ethnocentric strategy. Both strategies have proven not to be very successful in the cooperation between Dutch and Indonesian employees. And yet the cooperation between KPN with its Indonesian counterparts was earlier classified as successful. The key to successful cross-cultural cooperation is in fact based upon a small number of

KPN employees who managed to establish and maintain personal relations with both Dutch expatriate and Indonesian society.

The Narrow Path of the Cosmopolitans

The Dutch KPN expatriates who are mentioned as being successful in the distribution of their knowledge by colleagues maintain equilibrium in their relations with the Dutch expatriate culture and the Indonesian culture. It is these employees that have been able to establish personal relations with Indonesian telecom professionals, who are highly appreciated by the Indonesian counterparts and who are used to channel sensitive information from the Indonesian side to KPN. Among these expatriates are employees with and without families, people with and without Indonesian backgrounds, internationally experienced and inexperienced employees and young and old. Apart from maintaining equilibrium, the similarities of successful expatriates are found in: 1) interpersonal skills; 2) showing respect to other people; 3) flexibility; 4) cultural curiosity; 5) cultural empathy; and 6) cross-cultural contacts.

1) Interpersonal skills in entering into relationships with people and building trust are aspects of utmost importance to a successful expatriate in Indonesia. There is a need for people orientated managers for foreign participation. According to KPN standards the best employees in Indonesia are employees with an excellent track record of technical or professional abilities. These employees, who are selected for their aggressive style, focus on tasks and their will to achieve the objectives set by the corporate headquarters are however, not the most successful employees in Indonesia. This clearly indicates that other criteria for selection must be found.
2) Successful Dutch KPN employees avoid arrogant behaviour and show respect to their Indonesian counterparts thus avoiding the earlier described emotional reaction of Indonesians. Arrogance and lack of respect have been shown to be two sensitive aspects in the relationship between Dutch expatriates and their Indonesian colleagues. While the need to show respect and not be arrogant may be the golden rule of international business familiar to all, it is the one most broken.
3) Successful Dutch KPN employees have the ability to tolerate and to cope with uncertainty. Although a majority of the expatriates show a flexible attitude towards their Indonesian colleagues, KPN has in fact been

traditionally a highly controlled organisation. The flexible implementation of the corporate objectives is therefore a point of attention in Indonesia.

4) Cultural curiosity is needed to respect ideas and the behaviour of others. Successful employees show interest in the Indonesian style of management and make an effort to learn the language. In general, successful Dutch KPN employees show interest in the Indonesian culture.

5) Cultural empathy helps the employee to understand the Indonesian culture. The management models and management practices of KPN in the Netherlands cannot be expected to work successfully in Indonesia.

> For Indonesians it is important that the room for the meeting is comfortable, that there is enough to eat and the atmosphere is harmonious, that the CEO is seated on the right chair etc. We Dutch fight each other during a meeting, we interrupt each other and we sometimes even curse. Our Indonesian counterparts think we want to kill each other. But that is the way we interact. Therefore, we decided not to fight during meetings but to do that after the meetings, if necessary outside. So now we say to each other; 'sshtt, don't say it now, listen'. That is the message we give each other: listen! (Interview with Dutch KPN employee).

6) Cross-cultural contacts help to establish a balance in the relation between Indonesian and Dutch expatriate culture. This helps the successful expatriate to bridge the gap between the Dutch and Indonesian employees and helps in the link up with the national headquarters in The Hague.

> My parents live in the Netherlands, like my sister and brother, but the rest of my family is living here; my grandpa, uncles and aunts are all living here. We have family businesses over here. I learn to know my nephews and nieces much better ... In my spare time I spend 10–20 per cent of my time with Dutch expatriates, 30 per cent with other International expatriates and 50 per cent with my family and other Indonesian friends (Interview with KPN employee).

This third strategy of KPN employees in Indonesia to deal with these differences in business culture has appeared to be the most successful for the transfer of technology to the Indonesian PT Telkom employees in the mobile operator Telkomsel. The organisational culture is constructed and reconstructed in a search for a balance between the local and the home country demands. Fung (1995) calls this strategy the *geocentric* strategy; a balance between global coordination and local adaptation to create synergy.

Conclusion: Technology Distribution across Cultures

This chapter has discussed the question of how the distribution of technology manifests in the daily cross-cultural cooperation between Dutch KPN and Indonesian PT Telkom. A multilevel model to unravel the cultural complexity in the Indonesian telecom sector was first discussed. Therefore, the levels of organisational reality of Chanlat (1995) were combined with the sociologica of Latour (1994). The suggested multilevel model first explored the context of the cooperation of Dutch KPN and Indonesian PT Telkom. It was learned that the liberalisation of the telecom market in the Netherlands was ahead of the process in Indonesia. Furthermore, the long-term relationship between KPN and PT Telkom had helped KPN to acquire a 17 per cent share in Telkomsel, the mobile operator of PT Telkom. KPN therefore, distributed technology and managerial practises in order to improve the quality of services and the profitability of Telkomsel.

KPN expatriates working in Indonesia have found three strategies in the daily cross-cultural practises of distributing technology and managerial practices: 1) the absorption into the Dutch expatriate community; 2) the 'going native' strategy; and 3) the strategy of maintaining personal networks in both the local and the expatriate culture. This classification is in accordance with the ethnocentric, polycentric and geocentric cross-cultural strategies as described by Fung (1995).

A large part of the Dutch KPN expatriates are easily absorbed in the large Dutch expatriate circle in Jakarta. As discussed before, the individual history models individual schemes of people (Bourdieu, 1990). The regulated improvisations of this group of KPN expatriates are based upon earlier experiences within the expatriate circle. The harmonisation of experiences takes place within the Dutch expatriate circle by means of sport, social activities and personal networks. In this way, the individual actions of KPN expatriates are mediated by means of the learned schemes (Strauss and Quinn, 1994). This process hampers the learning of Bahasa Indonesia, the contact with Indonesian colleagues, and an open attitude towards Indonesian culture.

Another, much smaller, group of KPN expatriates avoid the expatriate subculture. The regulated improvisations of these KPN expatriates are based upon experiences in the Indonesian society. The harmonisation of experiences takes place within the Indonesian society. This strategy of 'going native' has a disadvantage in that no information is relayed from the Indonesian employees to the Dutch management and vice versa. Hence, it is the KPN employees who keep the difficult balance of having networks in both cultures who appear to be the most successful in cross-cultural cooperation. The personal skills and qualities that appear necessary in order for employees to succeed in cross-cultural cooperation are: linguistic ability, ability to tolerate and cope with uncertainty, patience and respect, optimism, cultural empathy, tolerance, a positive outlook, an interest in culture, acceptance, cross-cultural education and cross-cultural contacts.

In this daily life rituals and routines focus on the habitus and the production of thought, meaning, actions and expressions (Bourdieu, 1990; Tennekes, 1995). This anthropological perspective on the distribution of technology focused on the daily cross-cultural cooperation of Dutch telecom employees in Indonesia. It has been shown that successful distribution of technology is highly depended on a very small group of cosmopolitans able to understand the Indonesian needs and to translate Western technology and management practices into the Indonesian context.

Note

1   Parts of this chapter have been published in Marrewijk, 1999.

References

Adler, N. (1986), *International Dimensions of Organizational Behavior*, Boston: Kent Publishers.

Adler, N. and Ghadar, F. (1993), 'A Strategic Phase Approach to International Human Resource Management', in D. Wong-Rieger and F. Rieger (eds), *International Management Research. Looking to the Future*, De Gruyter Studies in Organization 46, Berlin: Walter de Gruyter.

Alvesson, M. and Berg, P. (1992), *Organisational culture and Organizational Symbolism. An Overview*, Berlin: Walter de Gruyter.

Bate, S. (1997), 'Whatever Happened to Organizational Anthropology? A Review of the Field of Organizational Ethnography and Anthropological Studies', *Human Relations*, Vol. 50, No. 9, pp. 1147–71.

Bourdieu, P. (1990), *The Logic of Practice*, Stanford: Stanford University Press.

Brandt, T. (1997), *'Kunci Budaya'. Business in Indonesia. The Cultural Key to Success*, Bad Oldesloe: GoAsia Verlag.

Chanlat, J. (1994), 'Towards an Anthropology of Organizations', in J. Hassard and M. Parker (eds), *Towards a New Theory of Organizations*, London: Routledge.

Estabrooks, M. (1995), *Electronic Technology, Corporate Strategy and World Transformation*, Westport, CT: Quorum Books.

Featherstone, M. (ed.) (1990), *Global Culture. Nationalism, Globalization and Modernity*, London: Sage Publications.

Friedman, J. (1994), *Cultural Identity and Global Process*, London: Sage Publications.

Fung, R. (1995), *Organizational Strategies for Cross-Cultural Cooperation. Management of Personnel in International Joint Ventures in Hong Kong and China*, unpublished thesis, Erasmus University of Rotterdam, Eburon, Delft.

Giddens, A. (1990), *The Consequences of Modernity*, Cambridge: Polity Press.

Hannerz, U. (1992), *Cultural Complexity. Studies in the Social Organization of Meaning*, New York: Columbia University Press.

Hofstede, G. (1982), *Culturele problemen voor Nederlandse managers en deskundigen in Indonesië*, Amsterdam: Twijnstra Gudde Internationaal.

Koot, W. (1995), *De complexiteit van het alledaagse. Een antropologisch perspectief op organisaties*, Coutinho: Bussum.

Kunda, G. (1992), Engineering Culture. Control and Commitment in a High-Tech Corporation, Philadelphia: Temple University Press.

Lash, S. and Urry, J. (1994), *Economies of Signs and Space*, London: Sage Publications.

Latour, B. (1988), *Wetenschap in actie. Wetenschappers en technici in de maatschappij*, Amsterdam: Prometheus.

Latour, B. (1994), *Wij zijn nooit modern geweest. Pleidooi voor een symmetrische antropologie*, Amsterdam: Van Gennep.

Latour, B. (1997), *De Berlijnse Sleutel en andere lessen van een liefhebber van wetenschap en techniek*, Amsterdam: Van Gennep.

Maanen, J. van (1984), 'Cultural Organization: Fragments of a theory', in P. Frost (ed.), *Organizational Culture*, London: Sage Publications.

Mann, R.I. (1996), *The Culture of Business in Indonesia*, Indonesia: Gateway Books, PT Harvest International.

Mansell, R. (1994), 'A Networked Economy: Unmasking the "globalization" thesis', *Journal of Telematics and Informatics*, Vol. 11, No. 1, pp. 25–43.

Mansell, R., Davies, A. and Hulsink, W. (1995), *The New Telecommunications in the Netherlands. Strategy Developments in the Technology and Markets*, The Hague: Rathenau Institute.

Marrewijk, A.H. van (1996), 'The Paradox of Dependency: Cross-cultural relations of three Dutch development organizations and their Bolivian counterparts', in W. Koot, I. Sabbelis and S. Ybema (eds), *Contradictions in Context: Puzzling over Paradoxes in Contemporary Organizations*, Amsterdam: Vrije Universiteit Amsterdam Uitgeverij.

Marrewijk, A.H. van (1997), 'The Internationalization of Dutch PTT Telecom from a Cultural Perspective', *Telematics and Informatics. An International Journal of Telecommunications & Information Technology*, Vol. 14, No. 4, pp. 365–81.

Marrewijk, A.H. van (1999), *Internationalisation, Cooperation and Ethnicity in the Telecom Sector. An Ethnographic Study of the Cross-cultural Cooperation of PTT Telecom in Unisource, the Netherlands Antilles and Indonesia*, Delft: Eburon.

Marrewijk, A.H. van (2000), 'Landes and the Internationalisation of European Telecom Operators?', in D. Kooiman (ed.), *Het verschil tussen arm en rijk. De culturele factor*, Anthropologische bijdragen 11, VU, Amsterdam: Amsterdam University Press.

Mulder, N. (1994), *Inside Indonesian Society*, Bangkok: D.K. Today Co. Ltd.

Orr, J. (1986), *Talking about Machines. An Ethnography of a Modern Job*, Ithaca: Cornell University Press.

Schein, E.H. (1985), *Organizational Culture and Leadership*, San Francisco: Jossey-Bass.

Schneider, S.C. and Barsoux, J.L. (1997), *Managing Across Cultures*, London: Prentice Hall.

Scott-Stevens, S.R. (1986), *Foreign Consultants and Counterparts: Cross-cultural problems in the transfer of technical knowledge*, Michigan: UMI Dissertation Information Service.

Smith, C. (1994), 'The Expatriate Business Community in Indonesia', *Indonesian Netherlands Association Magazine*, Vol. 5, No. 6, pp. 16–18.

Smith, P.L. and Staple, G. (1994), *Telecommunications Sector Reform in Asia. Toward a New Pragmatism*, World Bank Discussion Papers, No. 232, Washington DC: The International Bank for Reconstruction and Development, The World Bank.

Strauss, C. and Quinn, N. (1994), 'A Cognitive/Cultural Anthropology', in R. Borofsky (ed.), *Assessing Cultural Anthropology*, New York: McGraw-Hill.

Swanborn, P.G. (1987), *Methoden van sociaal-wetenschappelijk onderzoek: nieuwe edetie*, Meppel: Boom.

Tennekes, J. (1995), *Organisatiecultuur: een antropologische visie*, Leuven/Apeldoorn: Garant.

Touraine, A. (2000), *Can We Live Together? Equality and Difference*, Cambridge: Polity Press.

Trice, M.T. and Beyer, J.M. (1993), *The Cultures of Work Organizations*, Englewood Cliffs, NJ: Prentice Hall.

Warnier, J.P. (1995), 'Around a Plantation: The ethnography of business in Cameroon', in D. Miller (ed.), *Worlds Apart. Modernity Through the Prism of the Local*, ASA Decennial Conference Series, London: Routledge.

Chapter Fifteen

Epilogue: a Juxtaposition of Virtual Discourse Communities and Organisational Life

Earon Kavanagh

In this chapter I present some considerations for understanding interactional processes that occur in the space of virtual discourse communities. In doing so I employ an overview of theoretical perspectives that inform a developing stance for understanding some of what shapes the text-based relational acts and coordinations that bring about shared meaning, organisational learning and renewal, a greater sense of community, and the engendering and resolution of conflict in virtual communities. It is my hope that my current research into on-line communities can lead to an understanding of their value in developing new relational approaches for organisation behavior and development, and what collaborative interventions might be developed from such stances and related insights.

Introduction: Organisations as Conversations

The Internet on-line community has become known as a 'place' of convergence for organising between individuals and larger group systems, serving as a virtual meeting ground for Naisbett's (1984) dialectic poles of 'high tech' and 'high touch'. The progeny of this juxta-positional relationship are possibilities that have actuality evolved into reality, and include the meeting of the expert and layperson, the educator and learner, the product/service provider and consumer, the helper and the seeker, the lonely and the would-be lover, and the peoples of the east and the west and the north and the south. Such derivatives are centered around information sharing and bring potential for a flattening of power relations as relationships are cultivated with potential for 'new information', and the heralding of news of difference (Bateson, 1972, 1979). The above information sharing accommodates an increase in the potential for 'power to' relations as opposed to 'power over' relations (see Hosking and Bass, 1999; O'Hanlon, 1994), a new era in accessing feedback from consumers and a postmodern repositioning of organisations of all kinds under the new electronic gaze of the public.

But coupled with the above possibilities there are also the complexities associated with understanding each other. Fortunately, unlike non-virtual organisations, the 'conversations' in on-line communities are conveyed in electronic text and have the ability to leave a trail which can be analyzed and learned from. This paper proposes that all organisations, like the virtual discourse community, are indeed discourse communities, and that the shaping of preferred realities (desired outcomes) and optimum organisational climates come down to relational acts and meaning. The essence of this theme is that functioning occurs via and within the categorising and implementation of a variety of conversations. In states of conversational flux and flow participation can oscillate between learning through observing and modeling, learning through contributing, and learning through leading.

Virtual Organisations and Conversational Complexity and Possibility

The grandfathers of 'appreciative inquiry', Cooperrider and Srivasta, state that 'groups are formed around common ideas that are expressed in and through some kind of shared language which makes communicative interaction possible' (1987: 129–69). Discursive communication, from inner vision to brainstorming and on to implementation, forms the basis of every organisation, and discourse communities exist everywhere in various forms. These are organised around conversations which are centered around the sharing of personal interests, projects, adventures, enterprises, unions, friendships, the politics of public life, gender, sexuality, romance, family and the workplace. Whenever two or more people get together to converse a group, or discourse community, is formed (see Berrien, 1980). From a social constructionist perspective, discourse is seen as performative action, in that it brings people and possibilities into being. To borrow a term from Bertalanffy (1980), active on-line communities are as 'open systems' in that they generally meet Hall and Fagan's (1980) definition for such as incorporating a lot of transfer, new energy coming in from the surrounding environment in the form of messages, questions, and discussion topics. Non-virtual organisations that are outcome driven are also seen by organisational theorists as open systems, and possess such similarities.

Despite their tertiary nature, being mediated by technology, the social realities that are created in virtual organisations can range from states of primary and secondary collaboration identified with close relationships and high functioning teams and workplaces (see Weinstein, 1997; Weisbord and Flower, 1987, 1995), to open conflict. Between these poles can exist moments of peak learning, curiosity, possibility and a range of other states; sometimes they have 'flow' – ideas get generated, people feel connected, there is a sense /glimpse, even experience, of possibility – possible desired futures, based on the present. The immediate social reality that emerges is mutually enjoyable and exciting, one that Tomm (1992) might term as derived from the *opening of conceptual space*, and O'Hanlon (1994) might describe as engendering *possibilities*. I will posit here that these characteristics are found in inclusive and collaborative dialogue. Within inclusive and collaborative dialogue there exists a conversational reality which I shall term 'generative', one that has 'flow' (see Csikszentmihalyi, 1991).

In the cyber-world we are experientially introduced to a new metaphor for lived experience. This metaphor is encompassed by the social constructionist premise that we create social realities via discursive interactions, that we cannot take in all of the information we are presented with, and therefore we cannot really 'know' without engaging with others and their ideas and perceptions (see Burr, 1995). Thus, arriving at mutually understood meaning in on-line discourse organisations becomes a key challenge, often inviting further exploration and negotiation, and calling for relational skills. The diverse array of people coming together on-line brings the pre-written textual identities of self (Bakhtin, 1986; Parker, 1989; Sampson, 1989) to that endeavor, embedded in what Shotter (1993), addresses as a 'multiplicity of interconnecting social and cultural narratives', the ultimate form of diversity. With the absence of vocal dynamics and other nonverbal communications cues so important to face-to-face interactions (Akhmanova, 1980; Bandler and Grinder, 1975, 1976; Dilts et al., 1980; Watzlawick, Bavelas, and Jackson, 1967) on-line communication, and therefore on-line organising, becomes a more complex endeavor (Balka, 1991; Miller and Gergen, 1998; Denzin, 1998; Utz, 2000).

Commenting on characteristics of electronic text, Lanham (1993) writes that 'any prose text, by the very nature of the denial/expression tensions that create and animate it, oscillates back and forth between literate self-denial and oral permissiveness' (p. 75). Greater complexity is invited by the volatile surface associated with electronic text, one that 'invites us to intensify rather than subdue this oscillation, make it more rather than less self-conscious'. In such an 'atmosphere', without nonverbal communication cues, with messages coming and going, will there be a recycling group process (e.g., forming, storming, norming and performing), as engendered by the work of behavioral scientists such as Kurt Lewin (1948) and W.R. Bion (1961)? Or are we entering a new era that has accelerated beyond group dynamics into discursively constructed social realities which, by implication, can be deconstructed, reconstructed, and change-experienced via engaging in change-generative conversation?

Honeycutt (1994) writes that such intensified oscillations as distinguished by Lanham (above) are not dissimilar to Bakhtin's notion of the tension provided by the internalised voices of others, constituting the 'already always inner monologue' by which we frequently filter our experiences for meaning and form our responses to others. This is now referred to as a postmodern phenomenon which Gergen (1991) has called the 'social saturation of the self'. Social saturation engenders a quality of lived experience which Baudrillard has termed 'hyperreality'. Hyperreality is the postmodern sense of the real that accounts for our loss of certainty in being able to distinguish clearly and hierarchically between reality and its representation, and in being able to distinguish clearly and hierarchically between the modes of its representation (from Fiske, 1996).

But in the domain of the on-line community, as with non-virtual reality, people are still faced with the need and desire to build relatedness, whether as a means to a separate desired outcome or as an end in itself. As Potter and Wetherell (1987) and Austin's earlier speech-act theory (1962) have pointed out, language is frequently used as a means to bring about different purposes or effects (to influence realities from the point of view of the speaker). In Gergen's view it is also employed to gain conversational influence for the privileging of 'speaking rights', 'voice' and to have the speaker's interpretation of events accepted as the truthful one (Gergen 1989, cited in Burr, 1995). Such appraisals represent a diverging away from the commonly held understanding that language is primarily used to represent experience. As Bakhtin has observed, 'an utterance is never just a reflection or an expression of something already existing outside that is given and final. It always creates something that never existed before' (1986: 119–20).

Communication in on-line communities can be seen as a series of inter-textual moves between speakers/writers and listeners/readers. Such relational acts move to create conversational influence toward desired social realities as generated by such texts, but within an environment that is devoid of interactional artifacts other than the 'verbal indicators' (Utz, 2000). Such indicators are often termed in internet jargon as 'emoticons', the internet-based textual signals used to convey states of emotional being and attitudinal intention. With the use of emoticons the speaker/writer takes responsibility for the effect of the textual move on the listener/reader, but one downfall is that 'mixed-messages' can be intentionally given by blending emoticons that are contra to the message being sent. Participation in the on-line discourse community calls for consistent attention to interpretations until mutual understanding is reached. Doesn't this sound a bit like negotiation and mediation?

Researchers such as Miller and Gergen (1998) found that on-line communities have little means of generating interpersonal responsibility, that the 'cast of characters' on-line is somewhat transient and lacked the subtle and richness of face-to-face interchange, particularly in terms of gesture, gaze, and tone of voice. Somewhat differently, I have found in my own research that such lack allows for greater exploration, and demands ongoing negotiation of meaning for the message receiver (listener/reader/other) to understand the perspective of the communicator (speaker/writer/self), an endeavor which builds greater levels of relatedness and community (Lincoln and Guba, 1985; Ury, Fisher and Patton, 1991). As in my own insights from research, Bakhtin (1973, cited Honeycutt, 1994) 'welcomes this vagueness of language as a means by which to create meaning dialogically'. Yet, as Senge (1990) writes, dialogue is much different than discussion in that it is holistic and opens up an entrance into shared meaning. As Bohm, Factor, and Garret (1991) observe, this requires much greater effort.

Virtual Discourse Communities as Dialogical Models for Organisational Inquiry?

Attaining shared meaning is challenging at best (both virtually and non-virtually). Organising in the post-industrial society entails the organising of diversity, which brings even greater complexity to the foreground. Such diversity in on-line organisation, as in other organisations, calls for the reconciliation of power differentials and other hierarchical distinctions, a reconciliation with, a recognition of, and a nurturing of the narrative local knowledge of organisational members. Phrased for non-virtual organisations, this can mean developing within one's leadership style the discursive practices (inner and outer) associated with *lending power to* instead of *wielding power over* employees (Hosking and Bass, 1999; Frame, Hess and Nelson, 1982). Vaill (1989) has addressed this in his discussion of 'power sharing' in organisations. Bushe (2001) has touched on the subject in his work on appreciative leadership. Weisbord and Flower (1995) address this as the need to reconcile and include the voices of diversity.

Some on-line discourse communities have not developed sufficient 'equilibrium' to handle the 'disturbances' of people coming and going, or other challenges from the environment (see Berrien, 1980). But as Hall and Fagan write, it is relationships that hold a system together while achieving its purpose, or as Beer (1985) terms it – 'adaptive connectivity'. The discourse community as a system is a set of objects (texts), each having attributes that elicit meanings and responses. The relationships that tie the system together (above and beyond the stated purpose) center around the quest for meaning and desired outcomes. Discursive skills required by consultants and therapists, and leaders and managers, are virtually the same as for participants in on-line communities, and include *reflexivity* – the ability to consider and reflect upon one's speaking interactions with others (Burr, 1995; Anderson, 1997). This idea has been addressed in part by Funches (1989) in her work on the use of *self* in organisational consulting. As Ackoff (1980: 455) has written, 'all data are the result of inferential processes', and inference is perhaps an over-functioning hyper-real activity in on-line communities. Problems to be solved through discourse (all human systems problems), to use Studer's definition (1980: 465), stem from the inference of 'things as they are and things as they ought to be'. From the position of the receiver/listener/reader, this usually translates to 'I don't understand you', 'I don't agree with you (or your action)', or 'where are we going from here' – 'shouldn't we be someplace else (that I'd like to go to)'?

Virtual Discourse Communities and Organisation – Some Research Tidbits

Staying with the concept of the virtual discourse community and following the thinking of Schein's patterns of organisation (1965), and distinctions rendered by Egan (1988), I propose that on-line communities, and therefore non-virtual organisations, exist as four categories of discourse: *formal, informal, social and self-organising*. Formal discourse tends to be primary – the basics in carrying out the everyday work of the organisation. Informal discourse tends to be secondary – commentary on the work and discursive patterns of the work (e.g., water-fountain talk, humorous stories from sales-calls, griping about bosses and changes). Social discourse tends to occur outside of the workplace in relationships that develop. In on-line communities participants might develop casual e-mail relationships outside of the main discussion 'space', and some of such interactions might be more social in their nature. Finally, self-organising discourse tends, like formal discourse, to be primary, but with an inward focus (see Egan, 1988). Egan calls for separating the business dimensions of an institution from the organisational dimensions; this means that the everyday (formal) discourses of carrying out a business or institutional mission are clearly distinct from those discourses which have to do with organisation and development. Self-organising discourse has a self-reflexive quality.

My own research interest in on-line communities revolves around the value of on-line communities as a vehicle for determining new theoretical positions on how social realities are determined intertextually among speakers and listeners in non-virtual organisational settings. As an example, one case study (in-progress) collected text data over a concentrated period of six months. The data was collected via observation of archived discussion texts of a group of over 200 innovation-minded family therapists. These therapists subscribed to various forms of 'systems' thinking, relational theory, and narrative and solution-focused consulting practices similar to the organisational development intervention known as 'appreciative inquiry' (Cooperrider and Srivasta, 1987; Bushe, 1995).

The above case study incorporates the use of ethnographic analysis methods (Spradley, 1979, 1980), and poses research questions such as: 'what are potentials for discovery in computer-mediated discussions of practitioners interested in new approaches to thinking about and delivering services and promoting a positive product for their consumers which meets the need-triad of "self-other-and context" as laid out in communications theory' (Satir, Banmen, Gerber, and Gomori, 1991)? What discoveries can be made from how these practitioners organise themselves, or resolve conflict? How can these discoveries be projected into other areas of virtual and non-virtual organisational social systems?

Some or all of these categories will be present in on-line communities, depending on the purpose/mission of the community and the relationships that develop. For example, in my case study of discussion texts of post-structural family therapists, the six months of data amounted to 1427 messages making up 29 discussions, from which four key areas emerged when subjected to a surface analysis:

1) clinical work discussions (a *formal category of discourse*);
2) theory discussions (a *formal category of discourse*);

3) 'generic' discussions pertaining life, family and community (not framed by speakers/writers as work-related, and therefore falling into the *informal category*);
4) discussions pertaining to organising of the on-line therapist community (an inward focus – a *self-organising category*).

It is interesting to note that of the 1,427 discussion messages comprising this case study the discussions pertaining to organising as a community represent the largest (self-organising discourse – 53 per cent), the second in quantity were the clinical discussions (formal discourse – 29 per cent), the third in quantity were the theoretical (formal discourse – 17 per cent), and the least in quantity were discussions on life, family, and community (informal discourse 13 per cent). When we total these figures we arrive at the following key totals:

1) self-organising discourse – 53 per cent;
2) formal discourse – 46 per cent;
3) informal discourse – 13 per cent.

This suggests hypothetically that this on-line community (post-structural therapists) as an organisation placed a slightly greater value on self-organising and building community over the six month period of discussions. The above represents *some* findings from a surface analysis of all discussion messages. Findings from an in-depth analysis of key discussions pertaining to conflict and the conversational engendering of desired social realities are still in progress and have not been discussed here. I am also currently working on a similar case study based on the on-line discussion texts of organisation behavior and development consultants.

Concluding Thoughts

Drawing from observations of the goings-on in virtual discourse communities and other sources this paper has introduced the basic seeds for an alternative way of envisioning organisation through the lens of on-line textual interchange. Like relational theory, the paper has sought to expand possibilities as opposed to describe things in virtual and non-virtual organisations 'the way they really are'. The virtual community is a recent development in popular culture, and little research has been done to date in examining its potential (Utz, 2000). In an organisation, as in the virtual community, particular discursive moves bring about supplemental moves, sometimes fostering mutually desired outcomes, sometimes fostering conflict or confusion. If organisations, like virtual communities, are discursive by nature, then some discursive moves bring about a greater flow of formal discourse, which translates to getting more of the everyday work done. And isn't that the desired end result of most consulting processes?

Language is the major factor in the construction of both preferred and undesired futures (see Woodsmall, 1988). The realisation of preferred realities and desired outcomes involve conversations for relatedness, possibility, opportunity, action, interpersonal-need assessment, and renewal. It is through such conversations that mutually desired outcomes are brought about, whether those be greater productivity, greater teamwork, greater levels of belonging in relationship and communities, greater levels of governmental response and electorate appreciation, or greater levels of buyer-seller activity translating to greater levels of business.

Within this approach visionary leadership becomes associated with the acts of initiating the conversational moves and relational acts of creating and sharing conversations which open up conceptual space (Tomm, 1992) with 'others' and relationally interweaving these conversations, bringing about new information and 'news of difference' (Bateson, 1979). Such practices and speak-set are akin to those found with whom Bushe (2001) describes as the 'new leaders' who are focused on solutions (what's working) and possibility rather than problem-solving, leaving the latter to subordinates. Such leading practices might be termed by therapists White (1990) and Tomm (1989) as 'externalising the problem and internalising personal agency'. News of difference, rather than being news of something different, is a perception of difference in the narrative of circumstances, gained when conversation enters into dialogue, 'in the moving, momentary, dialogic, living relationships that occur in the streams of life between us' (Shotter, n.d.), and an ingredient which engenders desired social and organisational change, via the navigation of complexity and possibility.

References

Ackoff, R. (1980), 'Games, Decisions and Organizations', in D.M. Jamieson, G. Chen, L.L. Schkade and C.H. Smith (eds), *The General Theory of Systems Applied to Management and Organization*, Seaside, CA: Intersystems Publications.

Akhmanova, O.S. (1980), 'On Psycholinguistics', in D.M. Jamieson, G. Chen, L.L. Schkade and C.H. Smith (eds), *The General Theory of Systems Applied to Management and Organization*, Seaside, CA: Intersystems Publications.

Anderson, H. (1997), *Conversation, Language, and Possibilities: A postmodern approach to therapy*, New York: Basic Books.

Anderson, H. with Goolishian, H.A. (1988), 'Human Systems as Linguistic Systems: Preliminary and evolving ideas about the implications for clinical theory', *Family Process*, Vol. 27, December, pp. 371–92.

Argyris, C. (1980), 'Understanding Organizational Change', in D.M. Jamieson, G. Chen, L.L. Schkade and C.H. Smith (eds), *The General Theory of Systems Applied to Management and Organization*, Seaside, CA: Intersystems Publications.

Austin, J.L. (1962), *How to Do Things with Words*, London: Oxford University Press.

Bakhtin, M. (1973), 'Problems of Dostoevsky's Poetics', trans. R.W. Rotsel, Ardis: Ann Arbor.

Bakhtin, M. (1986), *Speech Genres and Other Late Essays*, trans. V.W. McGee, Austin, TX: University of Texas Press.

Balka, E. (1991), 'Woman-talk Goes Online: The use of computer networks in the context of feminist social change', doctoral dissertation, Simon Fraser University.

Bandler, R. and Grinder, J. (1975), *The Structure of Magic: A book about language and therapy*, Palo Alto, CA: Science and Behavior Books.

Bandler, R. and Grinder, J. (1976), *The Structure of Magic II: A book about communication and change*, Palo Alto, CA: Science and Behavior Books, Inc.

Bateson, G. (1962), A Note on the Double Bind, *Family Process*, 154-161.

Bateson, G. (1972), *Steps to an Ecology of Mind*, New York: Ballantine.

Bateson, G. (1979), *Mind and Nature: A Necessary Unity*, New York: E.P. Dutton.

Baudrillard, J. (1988), *Semiotext(e)*, US: Automedia, Inc.

Beer, S. (1985), *Diagnosing the System for Organizations*, New York: John Wiley and Sons.

Berrien, F.K. (1980), 'Homeostasis in Groups', in D.M. Jamieson, G. Chen, L.L. Schkade and C.H. Smith (eds), *The General Theory of Systems Applied to Management and Organization*, Seaside, CA: Intersystems Publications.

Bertalanffy, L. (1980), 'General Systems Theory', in D.M. Jamieson, G. Chen, L.L. Schkade and C.H. Smith (eds), *The General Theory of Systems Applied to Management and Organization*, Seaside, CA: Intersystems Publications.

Bion, W.R. (1961), *Experience in Groups and Other Papers*, London: Tavistock.

Bohm, D., Factor, D. and Garrett, P. (1991), 'Dialogue: A Proposal', paper found at web page *Dialogue and more*, http://www.cgl.org/Dialogue.html.

Burr, V. (1996), *An Introduction to Social Constructionism*, London: Routledge.

Bushe, G. (1995), 'Advances in Appreciative Inquiry as an Organization Development Intervention', *Organization Development Journal*, Vol. 13, No. 3, pp. 14–22.

Bushe, G. (forthcoming), *Clear Leadership: How Outstanding Leaders Make Themselves Understood, Cut Through Organizational Mush, and Help Everyone Get Real at Work*.

Cooperrider, D.L. and Srivasta, S. (1987), 'Appreciative Inquiry in Organizational Life', in R. Woodnam and W. Pasmore (eds), *Research in Organizational Change and Development: Volume 1*, Greenwich, CT: JAI Press.

Csikszentmihalyi, M. (1991), *Flow: The Psychology of Optimal Experience*, New York: Harper Collins.

Denzin, N.K. (1998), 'In Search of the Inner Child: Co-dependency and gender in a cyberspace community', in G. Bendelow, and S.J. Williams (eds), *Emotions in Social Life*, London: Routledge.

Dilts, J., Grinder, J., Bandler, R., Bandler, L. and DeLozier, J. (1980), *Neuro-linguistic Programming Volume 1: The study of the structure of subjective experience*, Cupertino, California: Meta Publications.

Egan, G. (1988a), *Change-Agent Skills A: Assessing and designing excellence*, San Diego: University Associates, Inc.

Egan, G. (1988b), *Change-Agent Skills B: Managing innovation and change*, San Diego: University Associates, Inc.

Fiske, J. (1996), *Media Matters: Race and gender in US politics*, revised edn, Minneapolis: University of Minnesota Press.

Foucault, M. (1979), *Discipline and Punish: The birth of the prison*, Middlesex: Peregrine Books.

Foucault, M. (1995), *The Archaeology of Knowledge*, London: Routledge.

Frame, R.M., Hess, R.K. and Nelson, W.R. (1982), *The OD Source Book: A practitioner's guide*, Toronto: University Associates, Inc.

Funches, D. (1989), 'Three Gifts of the Organization Development Practitioner', in W. Sikes, A.B. Drexler and J. Gant (eds), *The Emerging Practice of Organization Development*, Alexandria/San Diego: NTL Institute for Applied Behavioral Science and University Associates, Inc.

Gergen, K.J. (1985), 'The Social Constructionist Movement in Modern Psychology', *American Psychologist*, Vol. 40, No. 3, pp. 266–75.

Gergen, K.J. (1989), 'Warranting Voice and the Elaboration of the Self', in J. Shotter and K. Gergen (eds), *Texts of Identity*, London: Sage.

Gergen, K.J. (1991), *The Saturated Self: Dilemmas of identity in contemporary life*, New York: Basic Books.

Hall, A.D. and Fagan, R.E. (1980), 'Definition of a System', in D.M. Jamieson, G. Chen, L.L. Schkade and C.H. Smith (eds), *The General Theory of Systems Applied to Management and Organization*, Seaside, CA: Intersystems Publications.

Honeycutt, L. (1994), 'Bakhtin, Chapter 2: Bakhtin and His World', http://www.public.iastate.edu/~honey/bakhtin/chap2a.html.

Hosking, D.M. and Bass, A. (1999), 'Social Construction as Process: Some new possibilities for research and development', *Concepts and Transformation: International Journal of Action Research and Organizational Renewal*, Vol. 4, No. 2, pp. 117–32.

Lanham, R. (1993), *The Electronic Word: Democracy, technology, and the arts*, Chicago: University of Chicago Press.

Lewin, K. (1948), *Resolving Social Conflicts: Selected papers on group dynamics*, New York: Harper and Row.

Lincoln, Y.S. and Guba, E.G. (1985), *Naturalistic Inquiry*, Newbury Park, CA: Sage Publications.

Miller, J.K. and Gergen, K.J. (1998), 'Life on the Line: The therapeutic potentials of computer-mediated conversation', *Journal of Marital and Family Therapy*, Vol. 24, No. 2, pp. 189–202.

Naisbitt, J. (1984), *Megatrends: Ten new directions transforming our lives*, New York: Warner Books.

O'Hanlon, W.H. (1994), 'The Third Wave', *Family Therapy Networker*, November/December, pp. 19–29.

Parker, I. (1989), 'Discourse and Power', in J. Shotter and K. Gergen (eds), *Texts of Identity*, London: Sage.

Potter, J., and Wetherell, M. (1987), *Discourse and Social Psychology: Beyond Attitudes and Behavior*, London: Sage Publications, Inc.

Sampson, Edward E. (1989), The Deconstruction of the Self, in J. Shotter and K. Gergen (eds), *Texts of Identity*, London: Sage.

Satir, V., Banmen, J., Gerber, J. and Gomori, M. (1991), *The Satir Model: Family therapy and beyond*, Palo Alto, CA: Science and Behavior Books.

Schein, E.H. (1965), *Organizational Psychology*, Englewood Cliffs, NJ: Prentice-Hall, Inc.

Senge, P. (1990), *The Fifth Discipline: The art and practice of the learning organization*, New York: Doubleday Currency.

Shotter, J. (1993), *The Cultural Politics of Everyday Life*, Milton Keynes: Open University Press.

Shotter, J. (n.d.), 'Living Moments in Dialogical Exchanges', in V. Hansen (ed.), *Dialogue og Refleksjon: A festschrift for tom andersen on the occasion of his 60th birthday*, Tromso, Norway: University of Tromso.

Spradley, J.P. (1979), *The Ethnographic Interview*, New York: Holt Rinehart and Winston.

Spradley, J.P. (1980), *Participant Observation*, New York: Harcourt Brace Jovanovich College Publishers.

Studer, R.G. (1980), 'Human Systems Design and the Management of Change', in D.M. Jamieson, G. Chen, L.L. Schkade and C.H. Smith (eds), *The General Theory of Systems Applied to Management and Organization*, Seaside, CA: Intersystems Publications.

Tomm, K. (1989), 'Externalizing the Problem and Internalizing Personal Agency', *Journal of Strategic and Systemic Therapies*, Vol. 8, Spring, pp. 54–9.

Tomm, K. (1992), 'Therapeutic Distinctions in an Ongoing Therapy', in S. McNamee and K.J. Gergen (eds), *Therapy as Social Construction*, Newbury Park, CA: Sage Publications.

Ury, R., Fisher, W. and Patton, B. (1991), *Getting to Yes: Negotiating agreement without giving in*, 2nd edn, New York: Viking Pen.

Utz, S. (2000), 'Social Information Processing in MUDs: The development of friendships in virtual worlds', http://www.behavior.net/JOB/v1n1/utz.html.

Vaill, P. (1989), 'Seven Process Frontiers for Organization Development', in W. Sikes, A.B. Drexler and J. Gant (eds), *The Emerging Practice of Organization Development*, Alexandria/San Diego: NTL Institute for Applied Behavioral Science and University Associates, Inc.

Watzlawick, P., Bavelas, J.B. and Jackson, D. (1967), *Pragmatics of Human Communication: A Study of Interactional Patterns, Pathologies, and Paradoxes*, New York: Norton.

Weinstein, J. (1997), *Social and Cultural Change: Social science for a dynamic world*, Toronto: Allyn and Bacon Publishers.

Weisbord, M. and Flower, J. (1978), *Organizational Diagnosis: A workbook of theory and practice*, New York: Addison-Wesley Publishing Company.

Weisbord, M. and Flower, J. (1987), *Productive Workplaces: Organizing and managing for dignity, meaning, and community*, San Francisco: Jossey-Bass.

Weisbord, M. and Flower, J. (1995), 'A Conversation with Marvin Weisbord, Future Search: A power tool for building healthier communities', *Healthcare Forum*, Vol. 38, No. 3.

Woodsmall, W. (1988), *Business Applications of Neurolinguistic Programming*, Arlington, Virginia, published by author, http://www.peoplepatterns.com http://www.inlpta.com/trainers/trainers.htm.

Index